D1745175

Making the Mark

Ohio University Research in International Studies

This series of publications on Africa, Latin America, Southeast Asia, and Global and Comparative Studies is designed to present significant research, translation, and opinion to area specialists and to a wide community of persons interested in world affairs. The series is distributed worldwide. For more information, consult the Ohio University Press website, ohioswallow.com.

Books in the Ohio University Research in International Studies series are published by Ohio University Press in association with the Center for International Studies. The views expressed in individual volumes are those of the authors and should not be considered to represent the policies or beliefs of the Center for International Studies, Ohio University Press, or Ohio University.

Executive Editor: Gillian Berchowitz

Making the Mark

GENDER, IDENTITY, AND GENITAL CUTTING

Miroslava Prazak

Ohio University Research in International Studies
Africa Series No. 93
Ohio University Press
Athens

© 2016 by the
Center for International Studies
Ohio University
All rights reserved

To obtain permission to quote, reprint, or otherwise reproduce or distribute material from
Ohio University Press publications, please contact our rights and permissions department
at (740) 593-1154 or (740) 593-4536 (fax).
www.ohioswallow.com

Printed in the United States of America
The books in the Ohio University Research in International Studies Series
are printed on acid-free paper ∞™

26 25 24 23 22 21 20 19 18 17 16   5 4 3 2 1

Library of Congress Cataloging-in-Publication Data

Names: Prazak, Miroslava, author.
Title: Making the mark : gender, identity, and genital cutting / Miroslava Prazak.
Other titles: Research in international studies. Africa series ; no. 93.
Description: Athens, Ohio : Ohio University Press, 2016. | Series: Ohio
  University research in international studies, Africa series ; no. 93
Identifiers: LCCN 2016024889| ISBN 9780896803091 (hc : alk. paper) | ISBN
  9780896803107 (pb : alk. paper) | ISBN 9780896804975 (pdf)
Subjects: LCSH: Female circumcision—Kenya. | Circumcision—Kenya. | Kuria
  (African people)–Rites and ceremonies. | Kuria (African people)—Social life and customs.
Classification: LCC GN484 .P73 2016 | DDC 392.1096762—dc23
LC record available at https://lccn.loc.gov/2016024889

For Robert, Megan, and Dylan

Contents

Illustrations

Figures

Map

Photographs

Omosaamba pausing at cattle gate amid revelers

Returning to an initiate's home

Male initiate (left rear) resting upon return home, guarded by other *abasaamba*

Homestead flying flags of initiation

Following page 112

Female initiate leaving circumcision ground

Escorts on hillside encountering living bushes

Musicians with *ekegoogo* and *ibiraandi*

Escorts in marketplace

Female initiate walking home with escorts

Father, grandmother, and relatives waiting to greet initiates as they return home

Omosaamba resting upon returning from cutting, counting up her money

Following page 169

Youths posing/threatening at *ekehonio*

Male *abasaamba* waiting to be fed at *ekehonio*

Serving food for the *omooramia*

Female initiates eating at *ekehonio*

Male a*basaamba* eating at *ekehonio*

Males singing praise poems at *ekehonio*

Mother and daughter during seclusion

Abasaamba being consoled at *ekehonio*

Male *abasaamba* at *ekehonio*

Anointing relatives prior to coming out of seclusion (*okoroka*)

Table

Acknowledgments

Almost thirty years ago a colleague in graduate school suggested that I do research with "his people." This led to the voyage of a lifetime—geographically, physically, culturally, and intellectually. In the intervening decades I have spent many years with Kuria people in southwestern Kenya, living my life alongside theirs, studying, learning, teaching, and enjoying. I started out there as *umuiseke*, and now I am *umukungu*, with grown children of my own. Over the many years I have enjoyed the generosity, kindness, understanding, and empathy of many individuals and families. Here I would like to acknowledge their importance in my life.

I begin with my father, Jiri, who, had he lived two centuries ago, would have been an intrepid explorer. He did not allow his birth in a small central European country to contain him. His genuine eagerness to explore places he knew only from a map in an atlas, and curiosity about ways of life other than his own, led him all over the globe. My mother, Katerina, accompanied him and, despite a longing for home, set up households on four continents. My sister, Alena, was my soul mate and constant companion, and to this day embodies family—the family that was the one constant of our wandering youth. Together we moved through life, and ultimately found ourselves in North America. Our journeys were not only through geographical space, but through ways of living.

My second family is from my life in the United States. John and Martha Conant hosted me, a Czech student coming from Pakistan at the beginning of my college career, and have remained a supporting, loving family in the decades that I have made my life here. My "second" siblings Alex, Tim, Chris, Johnny, Justus, Sophie, and now their families, continue to share many of the adventures, milestones, and everyday moments in which our lives unfold.

Just as my life has unfolded in different phases accompanied by significant change, the lives of the people I came to know in East

Africa have passed through dramatically different periods of social change. From early on in my stays in Bukuria, I was incorporated into a large and important family in the community central to my work, and through its kindness of spirit and willingness to associate with an outsider, I came to know Kuria life from the inside. I thank my Kuria parents, the late Irisabeti Wankio and Boniface Rioba, for treating me as one of their own, teaching me right from wrong and the skills of acceptance and tolerance. My Kenyan siblings, my brothers Nyamoraba, Bageni, and Machera and sisters Robi, Nyangige, Monika, Rose, and Maseke, have each in his or her own way made important marks on who I am. I have relied on all of them at various points and have been so very grateful for their being a part of my life. Their spouses, children, and extended families are my people. On the occasions my European parents, my sister, or my nephew JP visited Bukuria, they were accepted as family, linking our worlds in yet another way.

I have been friends with, spoken to, interviewed, and hung out with many, many other Abakuria. I acknowledge those whose participation was crucial in the research and the writing of this book on genital cutting. I begin with the people who opened their homesteads to me, giving me a central home during my *esaaro* research. They are the late Anna Gaati Chacha and family, including Mwita, Boke, Mariba, Maria, Daudi, Sarah, and Jenipher; Susan and Sawi Maroa and family, especially Mwita and Machera; the late Boniface Rioba Machera and my brothers, Nyamoraba, Bageni, and Machera, and their families; and the late Joseph Mahanga, his wife, Robi Christine, and their family.

In the course of my research I employed a number of people who helped arrange and carry out interviews, collect data, transcribe, and translate tapes. These include Tyson Mwita Chacha, Christine Gaati Kisito, Mwita Kisito, Winston Mwasi Mahanga, Christine Nyandawa, Janet Weisiko Sawi, and Maroa Thomas. The work was often difficult and tedious, and their skill, dedication, and perseverance are greatly appreciated. In the preparation of this book, I relied on the assistance of Joseph Mwita Kisito for fine-tuning the translations of poems and songs, Erica Frohnhoefer in cataloguing images, and Rachel Kelleher in drafting the glossary and bibliography. Others have contributed to various aspects of the final product out of the kindness of their hearts. They include David Mwita Chacha, who tirelessly checked facts, searched for meanings, and followed up on unresolved questions; Tim Voice and Robert Pini, who created the illustrations; Heather

Booth, who helped in analyzing and clarifying demographic data; and Nino Mendolia, who aided in formatting and solving computer issues. Their contributions have made this book possible.

Equally important have been the contributions of friends who shared stories, answered questions, and in many ways ensured that my understanding was accurate and thorough. For their kindness and generosity with their time and patience I thank John Mupusi Marwa, Janet Nyagei Chacha, Brantina Boke Chacha, Gooko Serina Mupusi, Mwita Makanga, "Nyamoraba" Wambura Rioba, Rose and Sammy Muniko, Peter Muhiri Chacha, Father Matiko, Susan and Sawi Maroa, Daudi Mwita Chacha, John and Gaati Magesi, Pastor Mishael and family, Moses Mwita Masiaga and family, especially his brothers Muniko and Fred, and Chacha Ntogoro. Paulette McNeal generously shared her collection of newspaper clippings. Having resolved not to pursue this topic in the spirit of morbid curiosity, I attended only those events to which I was invited, hosted by people I knew from other contexts as well. I thank the people, too numerous to name, who issued invitations for me to join them at various stages of the initiation rituals. They enabled me to be a participant observer in the full sense of the label.

In the fifteen years I have been working on this project I have depended on a number of people in the United States to see me through, to encourage my progress and to kindle the fire when my energy and enthusiasm flagged. My gratitude goes foremost to my family and my husband Robert Pini, deputy anthropologist, who shared much of my fieldwork experience and cared for our children Megan and Dylan as they got older while I traveled, taught, and wrote. His willingness to take on being both parents for extended periods of time, and to reach across the distance to encourage and sustain me while we were on different continents, is what really made the work, both research and writing, possible. He has read the entire manuscript in many forms and lived parts of it.

As the only anthropologist at Bennington College for most of the past two decades, I have relied on colleagues at other institutions for ongoing grounding in anthropology and in the events of life in East Africa. Most especially I thank Bill Kelly, who has gone from being a teacher and dissertation advisor during my graduate studies to being a lifelong mentor extraordinaire. I appreciate greatly the colleagueship of Katherine Snyder and Jennifer Coffman, two East Africa hands and women with lives parallel to mine. They have kept me grounded in the discipline and the everyday lives we lead in Kenya. Encouragement and camaraderie on a daily level came from my colleagues and students at Bennington College. Becky Godwin originally published excerpts from my field diaries in the *Bennington Magazine*, and encouraged me to write a book that people would enjoy reading. Several deans have moved me forward in granting field time and Bennington College Faculty Grant funding for research, most notably Bill Reichblum, Elissa Tenny, and Isabel Roche. I am also grateful to friends and colleagues who have read sections of the manuscript and offered feedback, advice, and encouragement. They include Brooke Allen, Noah Coburn, Jennifer Coffman, Becky Godwin, Susan Hoffman-Ogier, Joseph Mwita Kisito, Joseph Mahanga, Sammy Muniko, Carol Pal, Alena Prazak, and Noelle Rouxel-Cubberly. They have improved the manuscript tremendously, and any mistakes that remain are my own. Bringing my research into the classroom has sharpened my thinking on the complex topics entwined in the study of genital cutting, and many students have, through their curiosity and critique, kept my focus on this topic. I express gratitude to my advanced Cultural Localities seminar, especially to Victoria Harty and Brittany Curtis, for their feedback and input. Ohio University Press, Gillian Berchowitz, and its fine readers have raised issues and contributed suggestions that have improved the book significantly. Special thanks are also due Wassim Nehme and Laurae Coburn, whose friendship and support enable me to live to the fullest.

In closing, I express my thanks to the Office of the President in Kenya for numerous research permits over the years. Further, sincere appreciation and thanks go to Samwel N. Chacha and Mohoni Rioba, who held official positions in my research communities throughout the past decade and a half, who supported my work and generously offered their official approval and protection.

Parts of chapter 7 in this book appeared in another version as "Introducing Alternative Rites of Passage," in *Africa Today* 53 (4):19–40, 2007. I appreciate the journal's permission to use that material here.

Families in the Book

Genealogical Charts

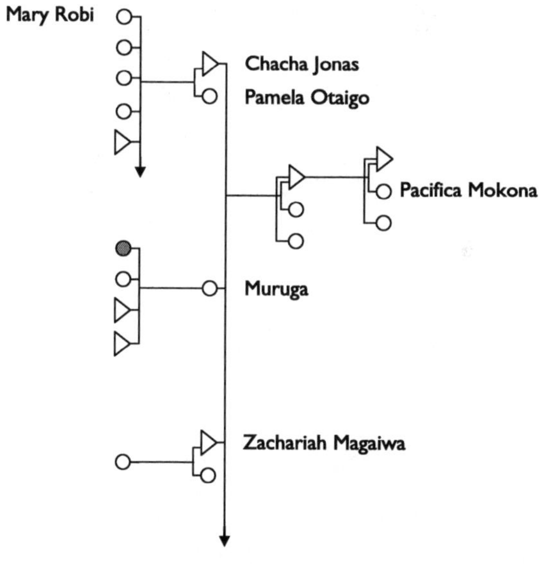

Figure 1A. People of Chacha Jonas

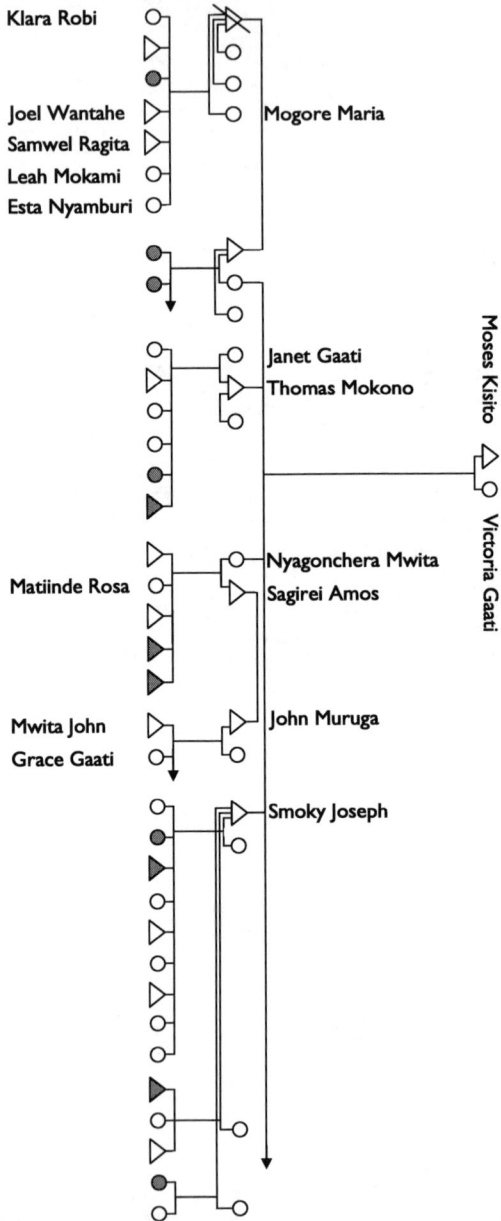

Figure 1B. People of Moses Kisito

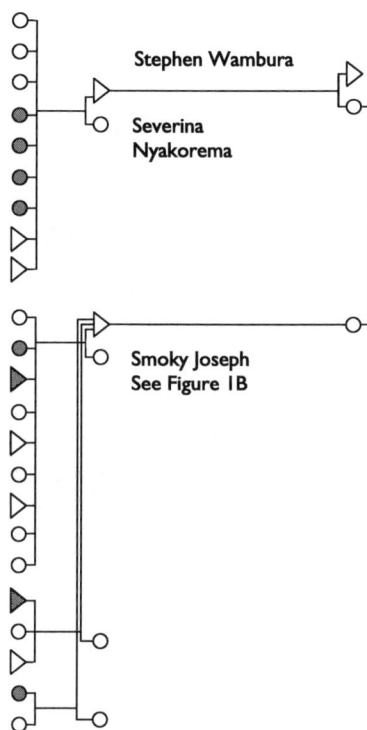

Figure 1C. People of Stephen Wambura

Key to Figures 1A–1C

△	male individual	○	female individual
▲	appear in the book	●	appear in the book
⚮	deceased	⊘	deceased
│	lines of descent	⌞___⌟	spousal relationship
		⌜‾‾‾⌝	sibling relationship

Named individuals appear in the book.
All names are pseudonyms.

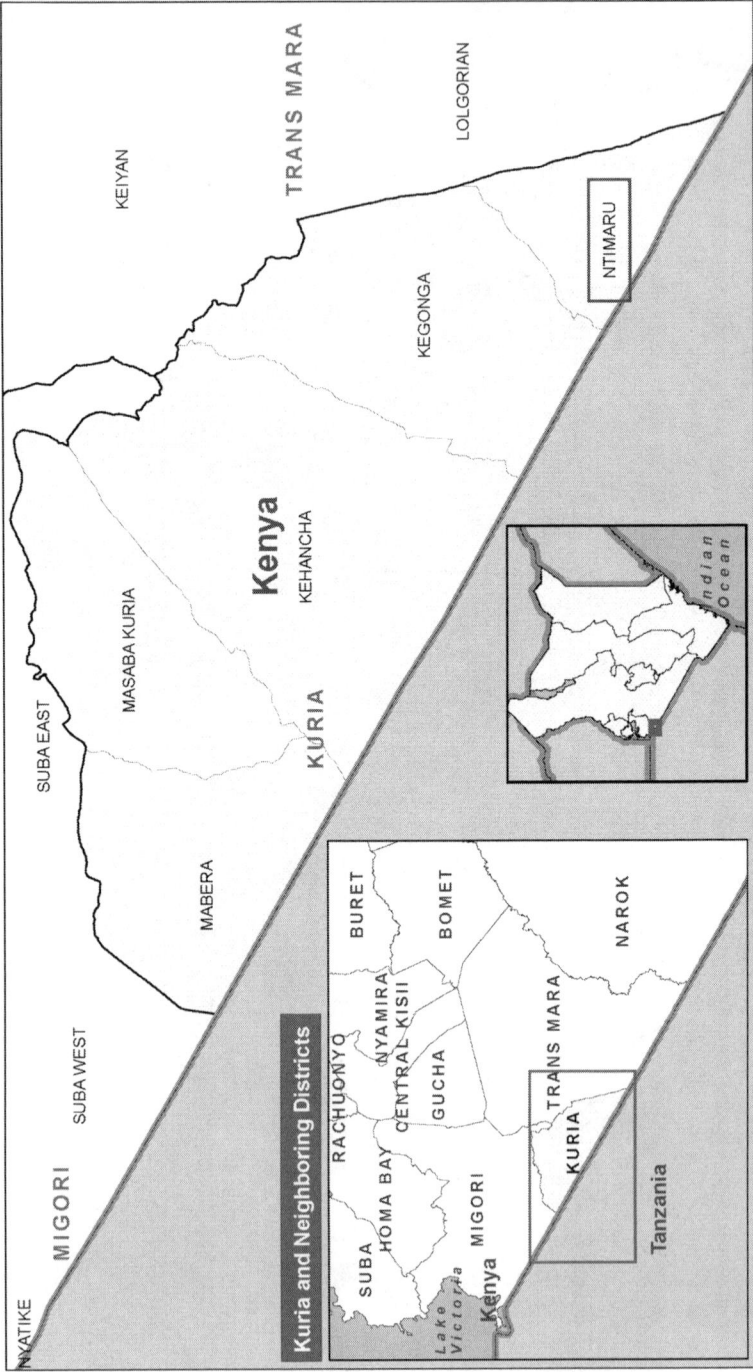

Kuria District. *Source:* Based on UN Office for the Coordination of Humanitarian Affairs, : "Kenya: Kuria District Clashes (as of 23 June 2009)," reliefweb.int.

Introduction

"Circumcision is our tradition. It is our culture. Since the time
of our ancient ancestors, the Kuria people have circumcised.
When we were born we found our people circumcising. Since
our ancestors did it, we must do it also."
—Klara Robi, female, nineteen-year-old Form IV graduate,
employed in family business.

My decision to write about genital cutting stems from a wish to share
the understandings I have gained in observing and participating in
initiation ritual cycles in Kuria communities of southwestern Kenya.
After years of experience and deepened relationships with practicing
members, I recognize that only through a holistic approach do these
practices make sense—not only to me, but also to practitioners. As
a spectator of genital cutting for the first time, I did not understand
this; I was not adequately prepared intellectually or emotionally for
what I witnessed. My responses were a mix of anxiousness and an
attempt at cultural relativism. In sum, context matters, and I needed
much more. So, I set out to learn the meanings—and significance—of
initiation rituals as described by practitioners.

Over time, I have come to acknowledge and appreciate how
members of the community move through an initiation cycle re-
plete with richly complex meanings. Even as I write this, I struggle
with how best to represent the many ideas and forms of genital
cutting as physical acts and deeply contextualized rituals; yet I hope
to do so in a way that may bring the material to various audiences
without apologizing for, defending, or condemning genital cutting.
Through this book, I hope to reach those who practice genital cutting as a part of their cultural heritage, and those who are curious

1

about traditions different from their own. I of course also hope to reach those who oppose genital cutting on principle, whether that perspective is based on ideals of what constitutes human rights, feminism, activism, or humanitarianism. My understanding may well remain partial, and although I am sometimes described as an authority on the topic, I prefer to consider myself a knowledgeable, critical observer.

My role as a knowledgeable, critical observer derives from having listened to many voices, collected many stories, and watched, discussed, and participated in rituals of initiation for more than a decade. While I do exercise authority in deciding which perspectives are represented in this book, I have endeavored to include a range of voices—a mosaic composed of the voices of representatives from five groups. Each voice is individual, but also representative of others who share that social identity, selected to offer the polyvocality essential in treating this sensitive topic. Throughout the process of writing this book, which has spanned the better part of a decade, my ideas have been shaped through interaction with others who engage in some way with this topic of genital cutting. Some are Kuria, some are not. Some are circumcised, some are not. Some are academics, some missionaries, some feminists. Most are concerned with doing the right thing.

My aim is to "reduce the puzzlement," to borrow the words of Clifford Geertz (1973, 16–17). I have had countless conversations with friends, colleagues, and students grappling with the issues of genital cutting, especially female genital cutting. I have presented and debated the topic through professional talks at learned conferences, lectures at universities, and all manner of discussions in meetings, in work and nonwork settings, and even on vacation with my family. Most important, I have more than two dozen years of experience within a particular Kenyan community in which circumcision is a foregone conclusion for males, and clitoridectomy is still almost universally practiced among females. Through these many interactions, I have arrived at a form I think appropriate for this book. That truth and reality are contingent on the person experiencing or observing has become a given in the decades following the postmodern critique. But clearly, understanding the complexities surrounding genital cutting can only stem from an account of the variety of perspectives that pertain to the practice.

The Voices

The first perspective is mine.[1] I present it throughout the book, and my participation, responses, and understandings gained though ethnographic research are written in the first person. But this book is not a journey of self-discovery, and genital cutting was almost never the main focus of the longitudinal study I conducted in rural Kenya. As Julie Livingston describes in her book on the cancer epidemic in Botswana, "I keep myself in the scene because my presence in the situations described undoubtedly shaped what happened, and to write myself out of the text in the language of dispassionate science or journalistic voyeurism would be misleading" (2012, 26). I am a woman and consequently have only been able to witness female genital operations. I mention this as a caution, because throughout the book I describe both male and female genital cutting, practices that are seen as equivalent by self-identifying Kuria themselves, and are described in identical language for both males and females. Thus I make no categorical distinction between circumcision and clitoridectomy/FGM/FGC (female genital mutilation/female genital cutting)—terminological distinctions favored by analysts and activists with the intention of underscoring the differences inherent in the operations when performed on males and females.[2]

In Kuria society, *esaaro* labels the series of rituals that includes genital cutting undergone by adolescents of both sexes. I follow this usage with the intention of respecting the indigenous construction of the practice and of not passing comment on the relative physical severity or implications of the operations themselves, or of the relative status of males and females in everyday realms within the society. The most apt translation, I believe, is provided by English-speaking Kuria who translate esaaro as "initiation," a term appropriate for describing the holistic practice and not solely the cutting aspect that so fascinates and horrifies Western observers. I will deconstruct the linguistic complexities and their associations with specific schools of thought—and brands of activism—when discussing the perspectives of international observers.

The second perspective is that of the initiates, the youths—both boys (*abamura*) and girls (*abaiseke*)—who have undergone the operation as part of their initiation into adult society. I have conducted dozens of interviews and participated in scores of conversations on the topic of genital operations, young people's personal experiences, the controversies surrounding them, and their ideas regarding the future of the tradition. Further, their ideas were captured through opinion polls I conducted in primary schools in 1988, 1993, 2003, and 2007. All Standard 8 pupils in the administrative locations inhabited by the Abairege[3] were asked to participate on each of these data collection points, and in 2007 this included 391 youths.[4]

The third perspective is that of circumcisers (*abasaari*), as embodied by the man and two women who performed the operations in Kenyan Bwirege during the years of my research. These perspectives are based on interviews, as well as participant observation. The main female circumciser refused to be interviewed, despite her participation in other aspects of my research (she was a respondent in my socioeconomic survey four times across three decades). Her younger sister, who became the "traditional" circumciser at the mission, engaged me in a discussion of the controversy, and opened up her thinking and her practice to my scrutiny. The male circumciser I interviewed performed operations both in the open and at his clinic. He discussed his work with me extensively. Sadly, he was killed in a raid on his cattle prior to the publication of this work.

The fourth perspective is that of the parents, the people who support or oppose the practice in theory, but who have nonetheless almost unanimously chosen to have their children circumcised. Their opinions and ideas were gathered through interviews, conversations, and participant observation, and represent a wide range of thinking, corresponding to the many challenging situations in which they have found themselves. Among them are men and women, mothers, fathers, and grandparents, as well as teachers, headmasters, medical workers, religious personnel, administrators, farmers, and tradespeople. Many of them are good friends, and most of them are people with whom I share the experience of parenting.

The fifth perspective is that of observers and critics, as well as local activists and leaders spearheading opposition to genital cutting practiced on girls. Non-Kuria perspectives are gathered from the academic record, Kenyan and international media, conversations, documentary films and informational videos, papers and talks, policy statements and statistical abstracts, as well as opinions expressed directly to me. Interviews and participant observation have been conducted with directors of local nongovernmental organizations (NGOs), missionaries, leaders of community-based organizations (CBOs), and government officials.

In all instances, the perspective of this text is a polyvocal one, and is characterized by numerous divergences and inconsistencies that reflect different individuals and their social positions. By maintaining the individuality of the voices, I aim to create "a mosaic—an image made up of unique and separate, even contradictory voices, concepts, and practices—an arrangement of individually shaped and colored elements that together make a meaning larger than that offered by any single piece, any solo voice" (Zingaro 2009, 13). The decision to include them in specific arenas has been mine as the author of this text.

The Field Experience

I witnessed the genital cutting of a prepubescent girl for the first time in December 1988. Despite having been in the field for eighteen months by the time initiations were held, I was unable to observe this particular set of rituals with impartiality. I was quite shaken, both by what I was witnessing and by my response, even though it was my third visit to the field. In the course of my research on the relationship between economic development and cultural change, I had appreciated my experiences, had come to like and respect many of the people in the community in which I worked, and was able to understand their way of life with increasing sophistication and subtlety.

As I watched the ritual procedure, a young girl—in my mind the size of a six-year-old—struggled to keep her legs together while women attending her pried them apart. Deftly, the circumciser removed the girl's clitoris, and shortly afterward, the group of girls cut in those few minutes stood up and walked away. I was stunned. Then, I saw the severed parts lying on the ground and two thoughts passed into my mind: I would be ashamed to be the only person present to faint, and this practice was totally awful. Thoroughly shaken, I was unable to remain detached or impartial, as the passing moments played out all around me: women trilling; a young girl, looking dazed, standing with her head bowed while women solicitously tied a *kanga* (cloth wrap) around her neck, praising her bravery all the while; a woman turning away from the cutting taking place, weeping quietly. And though I did not faint, my mind was flooded with images and ideas emanating from my own *mzungu*[5] upbringing. These imaginings had nothing to do with realities of Kuria life, nor with indigenous conceptions or constructions of the practice of genital cutting. As I squatted down, light-headed, I was suddenly distracted by the temper tantrum of a newly cut girl. Unlike her fellow initiates, this girl tore off the wrap previously tied around her by her women escorts, and proceeded to stomp around the circumcision ground. Able to regain my composure, I stood up and began the long walk home with the initiate my friend and I had escorted to the event. I wondered intensely as I walked, why the different responses? What did it mean? How would the stomping girl now be regarded by these women?

Later, removed from the immediacy of the genital cutting operations, I felt that my conversations with both women and men on the subject were unsuccessful and distorted by a lack of deep communication. My own response seemed so visceral, so uncontrolled, and so partial. I then realized that the questions I was asking emanated from my assumptions, from preconceived notions that reflected a very personal view on what was taking place. They clearly were not aligned with how others in the community regarded the events. A friend admonished me, saying "Nyangi,[6] you are asking the wrong questions" when I confessed my inability to comprehend what was happening around me. Though I continued to observe the ritual activities for the duration of the community's genital cutting season, I resolved not to write about any of it since I was apparently missing the point.

In witnessing initiations then, I gained a sense of how these events unfold, the level of communal excitement, and the ritual events that most closely surround genital cutting. I also experienced my own reaction to observing the rituals, and I reflected on these ceremonial circumstances and outcomes. I remained reluctant to write about genital cutting because my personal response was so overwhelming. At that point I was unable to even begin to understand what these events meant to the lives of Kuria people. Though I continued to speak with women, girls, men, and boys, I did not feel that I made much headway toward unraveling the complex cultural strands that are woven together to make this event one of the key moments in both an individual's life and the life of the community. Though I sought explanations, none were offered to me that seemed to add up to the momentous transformation this ritual causes in a young person's— especially a young girl's—life. "This is our tradition"—a response I received repeatedly when asking why people do this—hardly seemed to explain anything. No one offered or articulated any reasons more comprehensible to me than that.

A decade later I was offered another opportunity to engage with this topic. In the summer of 1998, I began to get word from various friends and informants in Kenya that initiations would be held that year. By the fall, a letter from a former assistant confirmed the news, announcing that the Abairege would be circumcising at the end of the year. He invited me to join his family in celebrating the "circumcision," of his oldest brother's firstborn (a daughter). His grandmother had asked him to write and invite me. This kind and generous woman was a key informant who treated me as a granddaughter, and taught me a tremendous amount about Kuria life, welcoming my participation in the daily life of her family. I was touched and became excited at the prospect. Not only would the rituals take place that I wanted to understand for so long, but I would also be an integral part of the celebrations for at least one of the families participating.

This personal invitation was followed by a second letter, from a Kuria academic.[7] His letter, too, was galvanizing. In describing the reasons why it was essential for me to attend the ceremonies, he entreated: "Kuria people of Kenya have maintained a distinct culture and traditions despite constant encounter with Western culture. However, there has been no proper way in which these have been preserved. As regards circumcision ceremonies they are being eroded by modernity but [have] maintained resilience over past years." The closing sentence convinced me to go: "The next circumcision ceremonies will take place in [three years]" (B. K. C., pers. comm.). I certainly did not want to wait any longer, as I finally felt ready to open my mind to this ritual in ways I could not a decade before. So I began to prepare to participate in the initiation season, which nowadays begins in late November when schools close for the end of the school year and concludes in the beginning of January.[8]

The initiation season I witnessed from beginning to end in 1998 is the core of the account offered in this narrative, and many of the descriptions of people and events stem from that time. But since then, and through multiple visits, I have spent a total of nearly three more years in the field and have witnessed two more genital cutting seasons. Those events, along with scores of conversations, interviews, discussions, and debates, inspire the content of this account, as they form the basis of my understanding of the changing meanings initiation holds for the various participants who play a role in the ceremonies. Since 1988, when I first witnessed genital cutting in initiation ceremonies, the controversy has continued to grow. Genital cutting—most often labeled in the West and increasingly in Kenya as female genital mutilation, or simply FGM—has become a hotly debated topic on the international scene, decried by feminists, policymakers, immigration officers, human rights watch groups, and health-care providers, to mention only some of the most prominent opponents. The World Health Organization (WHO) defines female genital mutilation as all procedures involving partial or total removal of the external female genitalia or other injury to the female genital organs for nonmedical reasons (Oloo, Wanjiru, and Newell-Jones 2011, 4). This debate, along with initiatives by various NGOs, has informed the understandings and practices around genital cutting in Kuria communities. As the "tradition" has become increasingly contested and reshaped by pressures from numerous directions, it seems appropriate to document these pivotal cultural moments.

In this ethnography, I describe initiation rituals of Kuria people as they were taking place around the turn of the millennium. I represent an outsider's growing understanding of *emic,* or insider, conceptions of genital operations and their roles within society, as a counterbalance or an addition to the ongoing furor over this custom in practicing and nonpracticing societies. This account documents the rituals and highlights the transformations taking place—in both indigenous conceptions and social practices—in an environment where genital cutting has become increasingly scrutinized. I aim to create a cultural record of an old practice that has been challenged for about a century, and that may eventually be stopped. But for now, it persists.

This ethnography describes genital cutting as a set of grounded practices, occurring within a particular sociotemporal location. Though the location might be seen as remote, this genital cutting ties rural Kuria society into a truly global discourse. This parallels the ways in which the socioeconomic and political lives of the people are carried out locally, yet shaped by the current and historical realities of their connection with the colonial and postcolonial world within which East Africa developed over the past century. Though genital cutting persists in Kuria society, the custom is not a primordial throwback but rather a practice responsive to individual and family concerns arising in response to sensitization campaigns and efforts to eradicate the practice. Genital cutting has not fallen into desuetude. It continues to be meaningful even though people realize the validities of the criticisms. Genital cutting still embodies and enacts useful, even powerful elements guiding everyday life. More than two camps (those who adhere to the practice and those who oppose it) exist in Kuria communities, and the direction people align with is shaped by local circumstances and alternatives that combine endogenous and exogenous elements for consideration. So, rather than being simply prescriptive, culture offers a range of options for defining acceptable and unacceptable courses of action. Cultural practices change as innovation and borrowing expand the acceptable options and eliminate or discard other variations that become outmoded or impracticable.

Politics of Writing

Studying genital cutting—in its multiple dimensions as a social, cultural, political, ritual, and individual-altering experience and institution—places the anthropologist at the nexus of intersecting discourses. An investigation of arguments and meanings that various parties articulate vis-à-vis this practice reveals a contrast between outsider and insider perspectives, and also a diversity of positions within each camp. In Kuria, as in other societies that practice genital cutting, the attitudes of individuals and groups reflect the variety of cultural contexts, responses to socioeconomic and political change, and the ideas people hold about identity as mediated by descent, gender, ethnicity, and, increasingly, class. These attitudes also reflect the influence of outsider positions on local practices. Drawing on participant observation in four initiation seasons in rural Kuria District of Kenya, and extensive correspondence via mail and e-mail over the decades, this account highlights the multiple realms where negotiation takes place, both for the participants and the observers; it also explores the anthropologist's relationship to respondents, to activism, and to a commitment to human rights.

Western interest in genital operations has come and gone in waves. The most recent wave rolled in during the mid-1990s, when the practice of genital cutting in Africa gained prominence in the eyes of the world through the efforts of medical practitioners, human rights proponents, and the general public. Western media became thoroughly engaged by the legal cases of African women seeking asylum in order to forestall deportation from France and the United States, doing so by appealing to Western abhorrence of female genital cutting.[9] In Western discourse, the altering of female genitalia is usually deemed barbaric and harmful to the women involved, and the term "female genital mutilation" (or the well-known acronym FGM) is routinely employed by the media and various influential Western observers and organizations. In the associated discussion of medical and psychosexual complications, FGM tends to be used indiscriminately to refer to many different forms of operations, though each carries different potential complications and outcomes. Moreover, the term FGM is rarely used in discussions that include the viewpoints of African women who have undergone any of a variety of genital cutting procedures, and in turn acculturate their daughters, nieces, and granddaughters to the practice in their communities. These discussions tend to lose the sociocultural context of genital cutting, and many Africans feel that the negative attention directed at their customs is both insensitive and intrusive. Even those who welcome change maintain that the best solutions would be proposed by Africans, not by Western critics.

Two seminal articles on the topic of genital cutting published in the 1990s (Parker 1995; Walley 1997) address questions similar to those I had as I participated in and observed initiation rituals. Both authors focused on how people of the West regard and talk about female circumcision practices. And both made it clear that, regardless of whether it was scientists, social scientists, members of the media, or members of the legal profession who were expressing their views, none of the discourse was objective or scientific in the way that is valued by our science-based worldview.

Having witnessed female genital cutting operations in northern Sudan, Melissa Parker was struck by the intense emotion that underlay her Western colleagues' and friends' interests and concerns about the practice. She concludes that unless greater attention is paid to understanding the source of the emotions and the ways in which they influence fieldwork and data analyses, our understandings of female genital cutting will remain partial (Parker 1995, 506), while researchers would run the risk of lending credence to fierce moral judgments and campaigns aimed at remaking other cultures in our own image. This runs counter to the avowed aims of anthropological academic research, which seeks to conduct investigations from a scientific, neutral, or relativistic stance. Dominant Western views regarding female genital cutting appear uncomplicated: Female genital cutting, regardless of the particulars of a surgery or the context in which it occurs, is viewed as abhorrent, and is described with an array of derogatory and insulting adjectives applied to the women who carry out genital cutting and the societies that allow it.[10] Many of those who condemn genital cutting see their attitudes as unequivocally right and good, even enlightened. Few opponents of genital cutting appreciate the importance of thinking about the issues of genital cutting in terms other than physical mutilation and the presumed consequent denial of sexual pleasure.

Clinical evidence has revealed a number of complications associated with specific female genital surgeries, including problems often evidenced immediately or soon after the operations, such as shock, hemorrhage, injury to adjacent organs, difficulties with retention of urine and menses, and infections. In addition are long-term problems, such as scarring and keloid formation, recurrent urinary infections, vulvar cysts and abscesses, pelvic inflammatory disease, formations of fistulas, and potential hazards in childbearing. All of these are grounds for serious concern, but the frequency with which they occur is far from certain. Data collected in clinical settings do not convey information about the proportion of females who experience gynecological problems from genital cutting. Focused epidemiological research could provide a detailed understanding of the overall effects of female genital cutting for female morbidity and mortality, but it has not been carried out. In the absence of wide-ranging data collection, clinical accounts too often focus on anecdotal sources or the severe cases that do involve hospitalization. The anti-FGM responses to such cases are often filled with anger and frustration over the "needless" damage to health, yet generally fail to appreciate the rationale for the practice, and sometimes even convey racism and paternalism (Parker 1995, 514–16).

Sentiments run high in all directions. For example, at the 2006 annual meeting of the African Studies Association, a woman identified herself simply as African and proceeded to passionately denounce the hypocrisy of Western critics of genital cutting in vilifying African practices while ignoring parallel activities that take place routinely in the United States.[11] She implored the audience to recognize that women the world over alter their bodies to become more attractive as sexual partners, citing surgeries performed in the United States and Europe to augment or to reduce women's breasts. Such surgeries, she argued, also have lasting repercussions for women's health, including possibly affecting their abilities to nurse their infant offspring. To her, these seemed as senseless as genital cutting in Africa appears to many Western observers.

Beginning in the 1970s, key anthropological publications studying the social and cultural aspects of female genital cutting were often written by women academics informed and influenced by social movements in their home countries, and this, of course, affected the questions they asked, as well as their findings. These findings include that genital cutting denies women the right to a full and satisfying sexual life (Hosken 1981); that genital cutting is a reflection of the asymmetrical power relations between men and women (Hayes 1975); and that genital cutting is primarily a socially important procedure concerned mainly with establishing clan membership and adult status (Lyons 1981). The work of Janice Boddy in northern Sudan describes genital cutting as an assertive and symbolic act, controlled by women, which emphasizes "the essence of femininity: morally appropriate fertility, the potential to reproduce the lineage or to found a lineage section" (Boddy 1982, 696). Though many elements of Boddy's formulation hold true for Kuria practices as well, the type of operations the two societies practice are physically and surgically different.

Christine Walley's critique of the FGM literature centers on the two seemingly polar viewpoints commonly expressed in western countries toward female genital operations—moral opprobrium and relativistic tolerance (1997, 406). Questioning whether these perspectives are sufficient to construct an adequate feminist and humanist political response to the issue of female genital operations, she argues that, to some extent, Westerners hold responsibility for the terms of the debates over female genital operations that have been adopted widely in Kenya and other African countries. She cautions that Western interests stem not only from feminist or humanist concerns, but also from the desire to sensationalize, titillate, and call attention to differences between "us" and "them" in ways that reaffirm notions of Western cultural superiority (409). Accounts of female genital cutting disseminated through Western media feed into powerful and value-laden understandings of the differences between Africans and Euro-Americans, presuming a radical difference between the first and third worlds, between "modern" Euro-Americans and "traditional" others. Further, the very concepts of "culture" and "tradition" are constructed in problematic ways. As Walley argues, "Rather than focusing on 'culture' as historically changeable and broadly encompassing beliefs and practices characteristic of a social group, the discourse on genital operations understands culture as ahistorical 'customs' and 'traditions.' Such 'traditions' are simultaneously depicted as the meaningless hangovers of the premodern era and as the defining characteristic of the Third World" (421). The allegedly coercive and oppressive nature of African cultures and societies is emphasized, and, from dominant Western perspectives, collective culture is judged to be less relevant than rights premised on the individual.

Examples supporting Walley's position abound in Kenyan media. Increasingly, accounts of genital cutting emphasize the distinction between traditional (rural) and modern (urban), using the same language and concepts as Western media. For example, a feature article in Kenya's popular newspaper the *Daily Nation* from the late 1980s discusses the time for boys to graduate into "manhood" in the following terms: "In the olden days, boys became men by undergoing traditions circumsicion [*sic*]. They were expected to demonstrate courage through withstanding the severe pain inflicted on them by the traditional surgeon. Times have changed however and the ritual is now rather outmoded due to the physical risks involved. Besides the risk of Aids [*sic*], the candidate stands the possibility of losing his manhood" (Sipakati 1988, 14).

More recently, in the *Daily Nation*, Beth Mugo, a member of parliament and an assistant minister of education, wrote an editorial titled "FGM is Barbaric and Retrogressive." She condemned forced circumcision of schoolgirls in the northern parts of the country, reminding politicians representing those areas that they had voted for the Children Act of 2001 and thus had a duty to protect children (Mugo 2005). As the language of condemnation shows, the outsider/insider dichotomy of perspectives is without a doubt too facile in a world where information and opinions flow easily even between geographically distant locations. To understand initiation practices, an outsider needs the insiders' understanding and perspective. Most particularly, outside of practicing societies, discourse on female genital operations tends to ignore the other aspects of the ritual complex of which it is an element, including the fact that in societies where females undergo genital cutting, males do as well. In many of those cultures, the two are constructed as equivalent rituals, both seen as achieving a similar cultural end: adult membership in the society and its structures.

Male and Female Genital Operations

In Kuria society, genital cutting is seen as a requisite step toward adulthood that prepares both genders (there are only two among Kuria) for marriage. Kuria people are well aware of the international condemnation over the genital cutting of girls. Male genital cutting is not seen as problematic by most Western societies and is usually left out of the discussions on genital cutting practices in Africa, indicating that it is not genital cutting *per se* that infringes human rights (we don't hear of "male genital mutilation"). This is the case whether it is the American practice of using medical practitioners to cut away the foreskin of infant boys' penises in routine postnatal surgery, or the religious practice in Jewish or Muslim communities where specialists cut the foreskins of infant males as a rite of inclusion.

Male and female genital cutting are rarely related in Western analysis, largely because male circumcision is regarded as more superficial than the operations performed on females and consequently less dangerous, while also conferring health benefits. Some opponents of circumcision argue that genital cutting should be understood largely in terms of male control of female sexuality, and therefore, male and female genital cutting are not comparable (Caldwell, Oroubuloye, and Caldwell 1997, 1188). Further, genital cutting in sub-Saharan Africa is embedded in a ritual context where scarification and other bodily alterations may also be undertaken to prepare the candidate for initiation. Genital cutting does not occur as an isolated phenomenon. For Kuria youths through the 1950s and 60s, genital cutting was preceded by the cutting and stretching of ear lobes and the filing of incisors.

Circumcision of Kuria males involves the cutting and removal of the foreskin of the penis. Female genital cutting in Kuria involves clitoridectomy, defined by WHO's classification system as involving partial or total removal of the clitoris and/or the prepuce: Type I (Oloo, Wanjiru, and Newell-Jones 2011, 6). In Kuria communities, as the human immunodeficiency virus (HIV) epidemic expanded in the 1990s and 2000s, health concerns led to changes in genital cutting practices, especially in various forms of medicalization. Genital cutting was increasingly performed in hospitals and clinics. Throughout the 1980s and early 1990s, young men who underwent circumcision in clinics and hospitals were met with derision and exclusion from the events of the seclusion period. Then, as the stigma against clinical circumcision dissipated somewhat, a local church mission set up a genital cutting clinic for girls in the center of the community. In the initiation seasons of 1998 and 2001, that clinic successfully attracted a small number of girls until it was shuttered following opposition from traditional circumcisers and an international group called Catholics Against Circumcision campaigning on the Internet, and reevaluation by activists and policymakers, national and international. Thus, after the 2001 season, medicalized operations were no longer available locally to girls. Medicalization was hotly debated. Feminists, human rights advocates, and others saw that making the operations safer for the youth would simply perpetuate the practice. For them, the objective was to eradicate genital cutting, especially that of females, not simply lower the risks by changing the venue. At that point, the interest of the international NGOs concerned with the eradication of female genital cutting became focused on alternative rites of passage.

Emphasizing that genital cutting of girls was wrong, Christian, medical, and media discussions portrayed FGM as a sign of being backward, out of step with development and progress (see, e.g., CCIH 2004). The risk of the exchange of blood in traditional ceremonies was considered to be a potential locus for the transmission of the acquired immune deficiency syndrome (AIDS) virus. These elements began to shake the unquestioning conviction with which everyone had previously undergone the rituals and gave support—especially to young girls—to take a stand in opposition to the practice. In, say, the year 2000, no one in Bwirege would admit to not being circumcised or to not having had his or her offspring circumcised for fear that it would be done by force. By 2014, however, there were families known to have children who would remain uncircumcised.[12]

In ways often perceived as contradictory to discourse against FGM, the media and activists began the discussion of male genital cutting in Africa in earnest in 2006, in the context of recognizing circumcision's potential role in slowing down the transmission of HIV in countries with high prevalence rates.[13] Because Kuria widely believe that HIV (and venereal disease more generally) is spread by women, the actual connection between genital cutting and HIV remains obscure.[14]

Though Kuria people view and describe the practice of male and female circumcision as equivalent and use the same word (esaaro) to describe both, they are well aware that this view is not shared by others. Scholars and activists have made concerted efforts to differentiate the two practices, creating several lines of argument. The first focuses on the extent of the cutting, and the position is that for females, cutting is usually much more extensive than for males. This is not currently the case in Bukuria, where cutting is more extensive for males than for females. The second focuses on what is removed, and the implications that has for future well-being. For males, only skin is removed; for females, the clitoris or a piece thereof is removed. The consequences are not equivalent. For observers, does regarding the practices as equivalent offer better insights than regarding them as incomparable? For policymakers and activists, what position helps build the momentum to end FGC? And though a few scholars argue that male and female genital cutting should receive equal treatment and opposition (see, e.g., Caldwell, Oroubuloye, and Caldwell 1997; Darby and Svoboda 2007), most academics take the position that the two are fundamentally different, and that focus should be placed on female genital cutting (Ahmadu 2000; Hernlund and Shell-Duncan 2007; Shweder 2013).

Opposition to Genital Cutting

Female genital cutting attracted missionaries' attention early in the history of colonialism in Kenya, and led to the passage of resolutions as early as 1918 (Murray 1974, 101). Medical men, missionaries, and administrative officers were aware of the custom in many parts of the colony, but they each had different interests with regard to it. Administrative officers' ethnographic interests led them to collect material and publish articles on the custom as early as 1904: "Their interest was detached and academic, and genital cutting had not yet arisen as an issue of contention between the missionaries and the Africans" (101 and footnote 4). Some of the earliest controversy, in 1911, was not actually about the physical operation, but about the rites surrounding it, especially the dancing. At heart were basic issues of individuals' social acceptance in their community, of missionary versus "tribal" authority, and of parents' rights over their offspring enrolled in a mission institution (103). In one form or another, these issues have remained at the core of controversy.

In the words of Jomo Kenyatta,[15] "the custom of clitoridectomy of girls . . . has been strongly attacked by a number of influential European agencies—missionary, sentimental pro-African, Government, educational and medical authorities" (1965, 125). Kenyatta describes the 1929 attempts by the Church of Scotland Mission to break down the custom among Gikuyu—attempts that led to the issuance of an order demanding that all followers and those who wanted their children to attend schools pledge not to adhere to or support this custom, and not let their children undergo the initiation rite. This order led to a great controversy between the missionaries and the Gikuyu, and to the establishment of schools free from missionary influence, both in educational and religious matters.

The following year, the question of whether the custom should be outlawed was raised in the House of Commons in England. A committee appointed to investigate concluded that the best way to tackle it was through education, not by force of an enactment, leaving the people concerned free to choose what custom was best suited to their condition (Kenyatta 1965, 126). Kenyatta's voice was one of the few African voices heard within the controversy at the policy-, strategy-, and decision-making level (Murray 1974, 285ff). In 1931, at a conference on African children held in Geneva under the auspices of the Save the Children Fund, several European delegates urged that the time was ripe for the "barbarous custom" to be stopped, and, that like all other "heathen" customs, it should be abolished at once by law. It was seen as the duty of the conference, for the sake of the African children, to call on the governments under which customs of this nature were practiced to pass laws making it a criminal offence for anyone to practice clitoridectomy (Kenyatta 1965, 126-27).

The "female circumcision controversy" of 1928–31 was not the only era during which genital cutting was banned in various parts of the colony (Thomas 2003, 82). In fact, many of the issues at the forefront of the debates at the beginning of the twentieth century are also at the forefront of debates at the beginning of the twenty-first century.[16] In the 1920s, a key issue was the struggle for influence between the administration and the missionaries. Each had its own agenda and priorities. For the missionaries, the problem was how to control the relationship between parents (the heathens) and their children (the converts). The administrators grappled with whether to pass laws or achieve change through education. Further, clitoridectomy became a potent realm of state intervention in the 1930s, because various Africans and Europeans viewed it as a basis for broader political concerns. While Africans understood it as sustaining two pillars of political order—gendered personhood and generational authority—Europeans claimed that it threatened "tribal" and imperial health, perpetuated the subjugation of African women, and confounded colonial rule (Thomas 1998, 137).

Another important moment in the circumcision controversy took place in 1956. Thomas (2003, 81) demonstrates that Meru women and girls responded energetically in support of circumcision following the Meru African District Council ban that year, reflecting the continued importance of female initiation for remaking girls into women and transforming adult women into figures of authority within the community (Thomas 1996, 346). As she documents, the practice increased in Meru after the ban, and girls went to the bush to circumcise each other (347).

The Kenyan government began its involvement in the controversy in 1982, following the deaths of fourteen girls as a result of genital cutting. President Moi issued a statement condemning the practice and ordered that murder charges be brought against practitioners who carried out genital cuttings that resulted in death. This order was followed by another, forbidding medical personnel to carry out the operation without the specific permission of the office of the Director of Medical Services. In 1989, he again called for an end to the practice, and, six months later, an official ban was announced (Rahman and Toubia 2000, 177). A motion to make female circumcision illegal in Kenya was defeated in parliament in 1996 (Ntarangwi 2005; Rahman and Toubia 2000, 176), but the practice was made illegal by governmental decree in 1999 (Oboler 2001, 312). The National Plan of Action for the Elimination of Female Genital Mutilation in Kenya emphasized education and outreach over criminal prosecution (Ministry of Health 1999; Rahman and Toubia 2000, 177). Yet, two years later, Parliament recognized that education alone was not enough and included prosecution under the Children Act of 2001 prohibiting anyone from carrying out FGM on a female under eighteen years of age (United Nations 2002; Mwaura 2004). The passage of a law once again proved ineffective in stopping the practice as the gap between law and the social system still needed to be bridged. For that to happen, as Mwaura contends, the communities in which female genital cutting was practiced needed to be involved in implementing the law.

Throughout the 1990s, opponents of FGM launched numerous campaigns in Kenya to end the practice. The opposition had been gathering steam since the early 1990s. Kenyan government, international development agencies, the United Nations, international and national women's organizations, and professional associations all developed policies condemning the practice of FGM. This condemnation was articulated most forcefully at the International Conference on Population and Development (Cairo, 1994) and the Fourth World Conference on Women (Beijing, 1995), where FGM was labeled a harmful traditional practice affecting women and targeted for elimination (Kenya Ministry of Health 1999, 7). But significant awareness, interest, and commitment to fight FGM in all its forms did not translate into tangible or effective projects at the community level.

By the end of the 1990s, several international development agencies were increasing support and vocalizing their stand on "this sensitive issue," according to the authors of the National Plan of Action for the Elimination of Female Genital Mutilation in Kenya (Ministry of Health, 1999, 7). They argued that "with these types of movements, continued and future FGM programs in Kenya can succeed using financial and technical support and an approach that empowers the local communities, especially the affected Kenyan women and girls, to take a stand against FGM" (7). Kenya's campaign against FGM was centered in the adoption/ratification of various plans of action viewing FGM as a violation of human rights against women and girls and a threat to women's reproductive health (9–11). The action plan spelled out objectives to reduce the proportion of girls and women who undergo any type of FGM; to increase the proportion of communities supporting the elimination of FGM through positive changes in attitudes, beliefs, behaviors, and practices; to increase the number of health-care facilities that provide care, counseling, and support to girls and women with physical and psychological problems associated with FGM; and to increase the technical and advocacy capacity of organizations and communities involved in FGM elimination programs (12). This plan was to be implemented in collaboration with partners.

At the end of 2001, Kenya passed the Children Act which made FGM illegal for girls under the age of eighteen. This included potential penalties under Kenyan law for anyone subjecting a child to FGM, including one year's imprisonment and a fine of up to KShs. 50,000. Few cases of successful legal action against perpetrators of FGM have been reported, and the law has come under widespread criticism for being ineffective and poorly implemented, and for failing to curb FGM (Oloo, Wanjiru, and Newell-Jones 2011, 9).

In the first decade of the new millennium, many nongovernmental and community-based organizations actively participated in the effort to eliminate FGM. For example, No Peace without Justice—an

NGO campaigning for the advancement of human rights, democracy, the rule of law, and international justice—reported in early 2003 that five NGOs had formed a joint network, an anti-FGM front in Rift Valley, to "crusad[e] against female genital mutilation ... to boost the war against the rite in the region" (*Standard* 2003). The network included World Vision, Shelter Yetu, Centre for Human Rights and Democracy, and Maendeleo Ya Wanawake, and their efforts were to be coordinated by Nairobi-based National Focal Point (Ibid.). The NGOs' language largely reflected their orientation rather than the voices of the people whose communities were targeted for this war. In some practicing communities in various parts of Kenya, NGO activities strove to offer alternatives to FGM. Eradication strategies included information and education campaigns, initially focused on making known the health risks entailed in genital operations, and on sensitizing key members—leaders, elders, and teachers—in practicing communities. Next, alternative rituals were introduced in a number of communities. Some NGOs focused on changing legislation. Building on the momentum of the 1999 National Plan of Action and 2001 Children Act, many domestic and international organizations launched a plethora of initiatives, which are given more context in chapter 7.

Kuria and Bukuria

Kuria people live in the rolling hills of southwestern Kenya and northwestern Tanzania. They make their living as small-scale farmers, cattle keepers, and petty entrepreneurs, remote from the centers of power and development in both nation-states in which they live. The name Abakuria refers to a Bantu-language-speaking people living east of Lake Victoria, largely between the Migori and Mara rivers. The term Kuria does not describe a traditional political group with clearly defined territorial or group boundaries, but rather a people who have a common cultural and linguistic identity. Cultural and linguistic features shared between Kuria and other groups indicate a past rich with interactions over centuries of migrations. These shared features can make drawing sharp distinctions between Kuria and non-Kuria difficult. Colonially induced cessation of movement left Kuria with Luo and Maasai neighbors to the west and east respectively, Gusii and Luo to the north, and Ikoma, Ngoreme, Naata, Isenye, Igishu, Chizaki

(Ruel 1959, 2), and Zanaki (Bischofberger 1972) to the south. Perhaps this history of intermingling is responsible for the prominence of a cultural repertoire offering grounds for establishing/proving cultural identity.

After independence, Kuria were a minority ethnic group in South Nyanza, a district dominated by Luo people. Then Kuria lands became a new, separate district following the 1992 election when Kuria people gave their political support to the dominant party at the time. Kuria leaders saw this as a major accomplishment and gain. Following the 2007 election, the district was split in two, gaining Kuria people further administrative structure with accompanying funds—a fairly remarkable feat for a population of about two hundred thousand people.[17] The potential gain of influence in parliamentary politics was curtailed in the new constitution of 2010, which subsumed both the districts of Kuria East and Kuria West districts into constituencies of Migori County. The two districts then contained four clans (*ibiaro*), which were the administrative locations of the postcolonial era. This political reorganization administratively separated Kuria from the Luo-speaking majority in South Nyanza and Migori districts, and brought in resources as well as employment opportunities within the several levels of the newly created administrative structure.[18] But lack of qualified candidates, particularly experienced ones, to fill many of these positions ensured that they were filled by non-Kuria workers. The presence of professionals from other parts of Kenya, as well as growing interest on the part of NGOs (particularly those concerned with "the girl child," with the eradication of FGM, and/ or with HIV/AIDS) reflect Kuria's growing ties to the national and international scene.

Kuria life is rich in traditions and has historically centered on a ritual cycle that individuals and the community undergo. They speak of themselves as "doers of ritual" (*abakora nyangi*), and compare themselves according to this criterion with other peoples having or not having a similar ritual complex (Ruel 1965, 298). The ritual cycle is a central institution that regulates the rhythm of individual as well as communal life and is crucial to Abakuria self-identification as a people. Genital cutting is one ritual, a part of esaaro, which constitutes the transition from childhood to adulthood, marking the changed status of an individual and his or her family with concomitant changes in roles, responsibilities, control, and power. Genital cutting marks the identity of an individual as a member of the community and defines a person in relation to extended family, lineage, descent group, and ethnic group. As much as genital cutting unites people, it also divides them. It identifies those who belong to the group and those who do not, and by extension, those who control the ritual event and its outcomes and those who do not.

In the cycle of Kuria individual and social life, the highest position within the society—elderhood—is open to all by virtue of reaching the requisite age and reproductive history. The council of elders convened by the chief's *baraza* serves as the body of decision making most approachable by ordinary citizens of the community. A second council, *inchaama*, is the secret conclave responsible for ensuring the ritual well-being of the community. Membership in the conclave and knowledge of its meeting places are known only by its members. Their communication with the general public consists usually of swiftly moving rumors, and the presence of the inchaama is felt rather than witnessed. To declare the start of initiation season, the elders of the secret council must study a number of physical and metaphysical signs to determine whether a particular year is propitious for a round of initiation. If it is determined to be so, hundreds of adolescent boys and girls undergo a series of culturally prescribed rituals, including genital cutting. The rituals are carried out separately by each clan (*ikiaro*)—the maximal unit of the descent structure—and adjacent clans generally avoid carrying out rites of passage during the same years. The interval between initiations also varies among the clans. In Bwirege, initiation takes place about every three years. Years ending in seven are usually passed over, since the number is considered extremely unfavorable.

Tradition and Innovation in Kuria Genital Cutting

Kuria youths say that an uncircumcised child is "despised."[19] Initiates look forward to gaining respect more than any other aspect of the ritual event. They become adult members of the society (albeit still low-ranking at that point) and they can look down on the uncircumcised. Initiates know that by undergoing the ritual, they earn their spot on the lowest rung of the ladder of the ritual cycle, which is the backbone of the status hierarchy in this rural area. Age and gender continue to be primary criteria of social hierarchy, although stratification in postcolonial Kuria society stems from additional criteria, such as education, employment, and wealth. Both gender and age are combined to secure an individual's appropriate place in a social system still organized on the basis of age-grades and generation classes. Immediately upon being circumcised, the individual gains the status of *omosaamba* (initiate). After ending seclusion the female initiate becomes *umuiseke*, a young woman eligible for marriage. The male initiate becomes *umumura*, a young man who can be held responsible for protecting the family herd or providing future opportunities for the family by devoting himself to his studies, thus building his skills for gaining access to potential employment and the much esteemed and needed off-farm income.

In customary practice, ritual mechanisms create both an egalitarian ethos among members of an age-set and a way to identify leaders within it. It is an oft-repeated truth that if a youth cries during the operation, he or she will be taken less seriously thereafter than a youth who was stoic. At a *baraza* or any other convocation, his or her word carries less weight as a result of not having shown bravery at that crucial time. Otherwise, all the members of an age-set (but divided according to gender) are seen as equal, an egalitarianism underscored by the fact that they pass from then on through the major stages of life and the ritual cycle together. During the time of seclusion, leaders emerge from the localized bands in which the *abasaamba* wander about the countryside, seeking diversion while they are restricted from productive work. And upon becoming heads of households, some prosper more than others, but the ritual recognition of fundamental equality remains. Young women become members of their husband's circumcision set at marriage, and their status within the set is equal to that of all others.

There are, however, other initiates who, by their structural position, are leaders at another level. These are the *amanaanai*, the first eight persons to be circumcised during any circumcision season. The amanaanai represent each of the eight named generation classes (*amakora*) of Kuria society. In this manner, the society is divided into moieties, the Abasaae and the Abachuma. Each moiety has four named generations. Men are coeval across the moieties, but stratified within them on the basis of age and birth order. Each generation class is said to give birth to the one following it, and to be born of the one preceding it. Kuria follow kinship norms of respect and joking associated with adjoining and alternating generations respectively. The generation class system is cyclical.

Drawing on my experiences beginning with the 1998 initiation season and continuing through the new millennium, this book highlights some of the various arenas of deliberation: between parents and their children; between initiates and circumcisers; between individuals as members of descent groups; between the traditional ritual authority of the *inchaama* (secret council) and the contemporary political authority of local administration; between the weight of tradition and the power of churches and missions; between the executive role of the police and the power of witchcraft; and, increasingly, between being modern and being backward.

Significantly, the 1998 season marked the beginning of a period of heightened innovation in initiation practice. Changes unfolded in a way that challenged communal norms and expectations. For the first time, medicalized genital cutting for girls became available. Many months before the initiation season got under way, Kenyan president Daniel arap Moi had dramatically increased his public opposition to female genital cutting. Many Kuria believed this was due to the pressure he faced from international donors, while others claimed that he came from a noncircumcising ethnic group and, therefore, opposition came easily to him.[20] In response, national media—radio, newspapers, and television—amplified the anti–female genital cutting message daily across the country, sensationalizing the danger of HIV transmission through the assumed sharing of genital cutting implements. The president had opened public discussion on the topic of HIV/AIDS in 1997, after years of increasing infection and death nationwide.

In Bukuria, such fears did not stop circumcision, where each female initiate had for years already provided her own personal blade for cutting. But they made alternative forms of the practice acceptable. Most notably, people heeded the message of potential transmission of HIV/AIDS via traditional procedures. Local circumcisers were trained in government clinics on sterile procedures, and the option of being circumcised in a clinic rather than in the mainstream initiation process became available to girls in the local community. This option had been available to boys previously, but initiates who had been circumcised in clinics had been looked down upon prior to this season, treated by the community as if they had cried during the operation.

Undergoing genital surgery in a clinic became a vector for identity formation in an unaccustomed way. Parents who opted to forgo a traditional procedure associated their decision to do so with the preaching of the leaders—starting with the president of the nation and continuing through the self-defined "progressive" elements within the community: the government officials, church leaders, the educated, and the employed. The medicalization of the operation allowed the better-off members of the community to separate themselves from a practice that had been at the core of status ascription, thus redefining the criteria by which status could be attained. In a certain sense, what had been a more or less ascribed status became an achieved one; those who could afford it took their children to the clinics. The impetus for the change came from outside the community; however, when the procedure became available, those who could afford it chose to do so. They thereby separated themselves and their families from the shared experience of the community while still adhering to the basic core value of the rite of passage. The potential consequence was undermining or eroding the *communitas* achieved through rites of passage.[21]

Each new initiation season brought further changes. During my fieldwork in 2003, a local NGO had been formed in the hope of getting access to some of the funds coming into Kenya to eradicate female genital mutilation. Because the amount of money available was on an order unimaginable for many in the community, people were eager to get onto the bandwagon. And though the ikiaro where circumcisions took place the previous year followed the usual procedures, there was a great deal of activity on the ground to eliminate the female element of the practice. People wore shirts printed by the NGO with the slogan "Female circumcision is taboo!" and groups of community leaders attended seminars on alternative rites of passage.

Those involved in the NGO initiative were primarily concerned with the end result of interest to the outside funders, namely the elimination of FGM, a term that gained common currency among Kuria speakers themselves. Unfortunately, little discussion occurred regarding the impact this innovation might have on the status of the girls, particularly if the practice continued to be carried out on boys and closely associated with belonging, identity, status, and thus, of course, upward mobility.

The Current Direction

To what extent can observers look for similarities in practices across societies and use those to spark understanding, promote policies, and lead change? For anthropologists as well as activists, it is important to recognize the dangers of lumping together diverse forms of a practice, diverse geographic locations, meanings, and the politics in which such practices are embedded. All observers need to beware of constituting a generic "they" who conduct such practices and a generic "we" who do not. Instead, we must begin with a particular place at a particular point in time to describe specific encounters with specific people as a means to explore the myriad issues surrounding genital cutting, and then we must phrase the kinds of questions that might help elucidate these practices. These questions should reflect the meanings and understandings held by practitioners and should also take into account the gendered politics of family organization, ethnic identity, colonial and postcolonial states, and the assumptions people make about the relationship between women and culture (Walley 1997, 429).

So what direction might one take to overcome the shortcomings of anthropological accounts of genital cutting? Firstly, anthropological accounts need to provide historically based, nonessentialized documentation. People who experience and reproduce genital cutting need to be allowed to express their understandings. Secondly, analyses need to focus on recognizing diversity rather than assuming homogeneity of practices or interests. Thirdly, conceptions of tradition and innovation with regard to the contested practices need to be examined. As Kratz (1993) maintains, tradition is part of a set of notions that brings together representations of time, history, and identity within particular political contexts. In her work on Okiek ceremonies, she raises questions about the intersection of local and academic concepts: "The people with whom we do research often have concepts that parallel and intersect those used in scholarly analyses...and we need to engage them" (61).

The first step in the process Kratz advocates is paying detailed attention to the situated discourse, actions, intentions, and effects of particular people in order to focus on the ways in which "tradition" is both an outcome of daily life and a means through which it is understood. Then, it is necessary to consider several scales of action and analyze domains that interpenetrate in the cultural dynamics of tradition. And finally, varied insider perspectives on traditions need to be captured, since no one social group or individual has a monopoly over the particular forms and meanings of tradition. They are changeable and sometimes contested. Continuity implies neither uniformity nor rigidity, as research in Kuria District over the past fifteen years amply demonstrates.

My analysis of Kuria initiations goes a step beyond the investigations of tradition outlined by Kratz. Drawing on work by Hobsbawm and Ranger (1983, 1–3), I contend that current re-creation of initiation rituals in Bukuria has much in common with the invention of tradition their analysis traces. Kuria insistence that genital cutting is a tradition allows practitioners to structure at least some parts of social life taking place within the context of ongoing change and innovation of the modern world where they control few aspects of their existence. In this setting, tradition—with its set of practices governed by overtly or tacitly accepted rules inculcating certain values and norms of behavior by repetition—automatically implies continuity with the past even as it responds to challenges of novel situations, pressures, and constraints.

Plan of the Book

This is an ethnographic study that attempts to discover and characterize ideas and values—but also structures, meanings, emotions, and lived experiences—that reflect patterns of behavior occurring in a given social context. Despite the transformations genital cutting practices have undergone over the past century and the ongoing efforts and pressure to eliminate female genital cutting, initiation rituals remain compelling, with a 96 percent prevalence rate for female genital cutting and 100 percent rate for male circumcision. The high adherence to genital cutting underscores its significance within practicing communities and how the opponents of FGM have not been able to redefine it in terms that resonate within the context—cultural, social, and economic—where the rituals actually occur.

Throughout this book, each chapter contains an ethnographic account of participant observation from one of the ritual seasons covered (1998, 2001, or 2004). Each chapter combines individual narratives with the theoretical discussion necessary to analyze and understand the larger picture. The narratives are taken from interviews, paraphrased, and edited for clarity, voice, and continuity. Sometimes, where possible, quoted statements appear amid extensive paraphrasing. Interviews were carried out in Igikuria or in English and were transcribed, translated, and, in all cases, edited for readability.

Capturing various dialectical dynamics—between local and exogenous, traditional and modern, backward and progressive or enlightened, collective and individual, duties and rights—necessitates concepts and constructions that inform the discovery of the many layers of initiation practices. Kuria society and culture, in addition to concepts of initiation and genital cutting, provide the basic underpinning of the emic milieu. The aim of this book is to create a record of a long-established practice, and to share the description of initiation rituals of Kuria people and of the transformations taking place during the two decades spanning the change of the millennia.

In this introduction, I have discussed how I came to be concerned with the topic of genital cutting, the initial fieldwork context in which I witnessed initiation rituals in the late 1980s, and a return to that milieu in the 1990s. My intention is to capture the emic conceptions of genital operations and their roles, and this can only be carried out by contextualizing the changes arising out of national and international concerns that have defined the discourse and that aim to eradicate the practice. I have offered a brief history of the efforts to eradicate genital cutting in order to access the perspective of the agents of change. And though I see that Kuria perceptions and understandings are indeed shaped in the context of the discourse unfurling around their practices, I resist the pull to privilege the discourse of academics and activists over the voices of the practitioners. In order to achieve some balance, I strive throughout to present multiple voices addressing specific issues.

Chapter 1 documents some of the social context of initiation. Focusing on the power of witchcraft to bring the initiation season to a halt, I examine how rumors serve to identify and mark anxiety and discomfort within the community as well as some of the underlying issues that gave the late 1990s a character of uncertainty that permeated all aspects of Kenyan rural life. Witchcraft, thus, allows an investigation of the tension between, on the one hand, historical structures that order life through descent-based social, economic, and political organization and, on the other hand, destabilizing socioeconomic and political changes that result from a nation-state on the path of free market development. In this chapter, I look at responses to socioeconomic change and the ideas people hold about identity as mediated by descent, gender, ethnicity, and class.

The initiation experience for males is the subject of chapter 2. Beginning with the opening of the initiation season, the process of initiation is revealed, both as it was shaped in the 1990s and as it took place in the 1970s. In both cases, the discourse is centered on the experience of individuals. I explore the ritual cycle and generation class membership as important loci for marking identity. In chapter 3, I discuss the initiation experience of females, focusing on three periods: 1998, 1992, and 1931. Using this diachronic perspective allows for an investigation of tradition and innovation in Kuria initiations, as well as a focus on gender and age as identity markers.

Chapter 4 focuses on the controversy over female genital cutting and medicalization of the practice. The ethnography follows initiation at the mission, carried out by a trained nurse. Interviews with a clergyman and circumcisers, among others, reflect on what this innovation means for Kuria society and culture. Because Kuria people consider the ritual context and celebrations to be a central part of initiation, chapter 5 offers an in-depth look at the liminal stage the initiates undergo, the importance of relatives in comforting, consoling, and sponsoring feasts, and the reinforcement of connections between kin and affines. In coming out of seclusion, the initiates step back into the social world, and the circumcision set they belong to becomes a lifelong marker of their identity.

Chapter 6 introduces some of the many voices taking part in the genital cutting controversy. The final chapter begins in 2004, and focuses on the newly introduced alternative rite of passage for girls. It begins with a look at the efforts to eradicate genital cutting since the introduction of the Children Act, and briefly summarizes the state of current practices for the people of Bwirege and Kuria more generally. Further, I focus on the specific perspectives and positions of the three main parties concerned with genital cutting practices within the community: the elders, the youths, and the parents. The book ends with an epilogue that presents a view of the latest initiation season (2014), showing the ongoing concerns over the practice and partiality of media coverage.

1

Trouble with Witchcraft

The initiation season began in November 1998 in an unremarkable way. As the school year drew to a close, rumors cropped up in the marketplaces and in homesteads sprinkled across the rolling hills that this was the year for holding initiation ceremonies. Elders discussed the implications at every chance—over cups of tea, sharing pots of home-style beer, or simply while perched on a log at a kiosk watching a bicycle being repaired. Women vendors chatted about this in their market stalls between customers or with shoppers stopping by to assess their vegetables. Youths coming of age ran around the neighborhoods in high spirits and invited relatives and friends to come participate in their festivities. Mothers prepared for feasting by drying cereals in the sun, grinding flour at the *posho* mills, and sprouting finger millet for *obosara*, the much-loved beverage of celebrations. Fathers appraised their livestock with slaughter on their minds. Three years had elapsed since the last initiations were held and potential candidates were many. Free on school vacation and in high spirits, adolescent boys with bells tied around their calves stirred up commotion wherever they went, decked out in the assorted regalia of initiation. And though kept by custom out of public spaces, adolescent girls would be a part of the celebration, too, and enjoy increased attention in their homesteads.

Having received an invitation to attend the initiations and permission from my dean to miss two weeks of classes, I set off to join the festivities. The trip from Bennington, Vermont, to Nyankare,[1] Kuria District, took me from Wednesday to Saturday morning. Reaching Nairobi on Friday, I made contact with many of my urban Kuria acquaintances, hoping for a ride to Bukuria, a distance of some 400 kilometers as the road goes. I was unlucky. Everyone had either left already to participate in the initiations or had their vehicles full. Spurred to action, and fearful of missing too much, I boarded an overnight bus. I squeezed into the last row amidst packages, bags, and too many people on too few seats. I sat, jetlagged but awake, as fellow passengers dozed around me. The moon outside was full, and the night so bright that the zebras grazing along the road on the dusty plains of the Rift Valley were clearly visible. As the bus crawled up the western escarpment in the wee hours of Saturday, we were attacked by bandits. They had piled logs on the tarmac, barricading the road.

December is a dangerous time to travel from the city into the countryside. Returning to their natal homes for the month of school vacations and holidays, many people carry gifts and goods in preparation for Christmas. Most highway robberies take place during this time of the year, and overnight buses are obvious targets. A million thoughts went through my mind in the next minute, as passengers woke up shouting, and the driver lurched the bus off the road. "What will happen to my children? I left them for this experience, and I will die on a stupid bus in the middle of nowhere, for nothing" was prominent among them, as well as "What are the chances of my being passed over, the one mzungu at the very back of a bus filled with Kenyans?"

We were lucky. Thanks to the driver's vigilance and presence of mind, the worst we sustained were a few bruises and jolted bones. The driver aimed the bus directly at the bandits, who scrambled to escape getting run over. Then he gunned the engine and somehow managed to haul the bus over the piled obstacles. For the next hour or so the bus was animated with relieved chatter. Passengers replayed the scene, taking special delight at the retreating bandits' faces when their plan backfired. As people drifted off to sleep again, I stayed bolt upright, busily planning how I would alight and save myself if such a thing happened again. We reached Migori, our terminus, after daybreak. I was starting to feel sick with fatigue, not having laid down to sleep since Tuesday night in Bennington. I incoherently but effusively thanked the driver and stumbled from the bus.

I got a ride on the first morning run of a *matatu*² going to Nyankare. I didn't recognize any of the drivers, conductors, or passengers—not surprising after an absence of four years, but certainly not an auspicious beginning. The women squeezed in next to me were Luo traders, heading to Nyankare for market day. In the past, people from Nyankare had always traveled to Migori for its market day, not vice versa. I focused inward, savoring my return to a place that had been very meaningful to my life for the past fifteen years. It looked much the same—the rolling hills, the alternating clusters of thick, short trees and bushes, and grasslands—and as we got farther from the paved road, cultivated fields took up ever more of the land. I noted extensive new construction as we drove through areas that had, in the past, consisted of isolated shops. Strips of buildings lined the road and held all types of commercial interests, including restaurants (known as *hoteli*), hardware shops, retail stores, grain purchase stores, clinics, and posho mills.

The matatu stopped at Kehancha, the district capital. Four years earlier, this rural center had encompassed mainly maize fields and low, one-story wattle-and-daub structures. The capital now sported several multistory buildings (most still under construction), a bank, a gas station, and a busy matatu stage. Hawkers plied their assorted wares up to our vehicle's windows. My fellow passengers examined the cheap Chinese plastic goods with interest, though they didn't buy anything other than cornets of groundnuts, artfully wrapped in pages from children's school exercise books. As we were pulling out of town, we encountered a group coming home from the circumcision ground. It made for an impressive and awe-inspiring sight. An initiate was being escorted by thirty or so adults, many of them draped in branches, shouting, whistling, waving weapons, and surrounding the vehicle, menacing in gesture and word. The Luo traders shrank in their seats.[3] I was not frightened, having experienced this numerous times before. I was actually, despite my fatigue, exhilarated to see the force of initiation celebrations unleashed. The pulsing music of the *ekegoogo*, the resounding gourd rattles, and the shrillness of human voices and whistles all formed an exuberant backdrop to the powder-streaked faces of the initiates, their liminal status indicated by the sheets tied around their necks, draped like wide aprons and stained with blood from their genitals. Members of the entourage flexed their muscles and, in keeping with their duty to protect their charges from both physical and supernatural threats, brandished machetes, *rungu*, cooking spoons, and other potential as well as real weapons. Some, disguised by foliage to resemble walking bushes, charged in unison, chasing invisible malevolent forces, the spirits of aggression. Protection and jubilation intermingled in a cacophony of sounds. This was what I had come for.

We came across five or six similar groups walking on the road in Bukira[4] and were brought to a standstill each time. Even though I was tightly squeezed inside a vehicle, I felt the surge of dizzy, contagious exhilaration of the crowds. Sounds, sights, and smells saturated my senses. I felt ready to understand this. I felt far different from my previous exposure to initiation ceremonies.

Of Kuria clans, Abairege live the farthest away from the tarmac road. They call themselves *abatuuri ba isaahi,* meaning "settlers of the bush." In their northward quest for pastures and land for cultivation at the beginning of the twentieth century, they had penetrated deep into Maasai country to their north and east. The leopard is their totem, and Abairege fancy themselves brave, fierce, and staunch supporters of tradition. As the dusty red murram road approached the boundary between the administrative locations of Nyabasi and Bwirege, I noticed evenly spaced utility poles alongside the road, signifying a new kind of development. I was stunned that no one had thought to inform me about this, and contemplated the enormous change in living and working conditions it signaled.[5] Distracted by changes to the otherwise extremely familiar countryside, I felt the remaining stretch of the trip pass very quickly. In no time, we were disembarking from the matatu at Nyankare market. I heaved my tightly packed carry-on, containing all my necessities for the next two months, including a camera, tape recorders, gifts for friends, clothing, and bedding, onto my shoulder and crossed the market to the house of a good friend.

"She doesn't live here anymore," I was told. "They built a new home near the police post." So short a time had elapsed since I confirmed my travel plans that I had notified few people of my return. Only my former assistant knew, but his home was four miles from the market—too far to walk in my fatigued state. I shuffled back into the market square and was approached by a young man who greeted me respectfully and kindly. Samwel Ragita, the son of another good friend, and the spitting image of his late father, told me his mother was home. He invited me to go there with him. Gladly I acquiesced, and during our short walk, I thought about how odd it was to see him grown up, and how happy I was to see him lift my bag without even asking and carry it for me. The four years since I had last been in Nyankare had brought many changes to my life, no doubt etched in my face, but Samwel, at thirteen, was physically transformed. I was glad he was so much his father's son in appearance, or I would not have recognized him. As we left the hubbub of the market behind, I told him briefly about the processions we had encountered along the way. "So how are the circumcisions going over here?" I asked eagerly. He looked at me, seeming puzzled, and responded, "They have been canceled."

"How can that be?" The shock of his statement sent ripples of disbelief into me.

"There is too much witchcraft," Samwel replied matter-of-factly.

"Settlers of the Bush"

From the earliest colonial records, it is evident that migrations of Kuria people were ongoing at the time of the establishment of colonial rule. Writing about 1907 and 1908, the District Commissioner for South Nyanza District notes that "there is a marked increase of huts all along the German border from Mohuru on the Lake [Victoria] to Uregi [Bwirege]. This is most noticeable in Uregi where in March there were only six huts. In August I found 25 and on my safari last month [March 1908] when I collected hut tax there the number had risen to 94" (Kenya National Archives, DC/KSI/1).[6] By 1911, the settlement at Bwirege had increased to nearly 200 huts (Kenya National Archives, DC/KSI/3/3). The people's primary identification, then as now, was with the clan (ikiaro). The designation of Abairege as the settlers of the bush (abatuuri ba isaahi) by other Kuria is meant as a pejorative, but Abairege take pride in the designation, stressing those elements they perceive as prideworthy—independence, ruggedness, and a pioneering spirit, as well as their status as the ones who challenge the boundaries of Maasai.[7] Because their area has, in the past century, been seen as remote, it has been the last affected by contact with outsiders and external institutions, including organized religion, formal education, and the market economy. Whereas other Kuria see Abairege as backward, other Kenyans level that same charge against Kuria in general. Despite the epithets, Abairege and Kuria of other ibiaro are well aware of changes in their lives on many fronts—economic, political, and social, as well as cultural. Though Kuria people were not recognized as a unitary ethnic group, or "tribe" in the colonial parlance, until the late 1950s, a shared history is referred to and cherished by many residents in the area. The importance of the overarching Kuria identity is growing, as is a sense of national identity, of being Kenyan. But since more than half of Kuria live in Tanzania, national identity has been slow to take full hold. Instead, underlying these emerging identities is an important, localized designation reflecting clan and lineage membership—that of the ikiaro, recognized as the maximal unit of affiliation prior to the late colonial era. Its enduring importance warrants examination and delineation.

Major demographic, social, economic, and political transformations on the national level in the past thirty years have not bypassed Kuria District.[8] Many people living in this rural area aspire to be progressive and rue what they see as backwardness (Prazak 1999). Electricity in the district was limited to sporadic service in the capital until 2012, when even Bwirege became linked to the power grid. A growing number of people have solar panels at their homes, used in the past decade to recharge batteries for mobile phones and, in a few cases, to power television sets. Since 2005, the isolation of the area has been broken by mobile phone technology, and Nyankare market now hosts a phone booster tower, connecting the area with the rest of the globe. Another, just on the other side of the international border, allows people to communicate easily with kin south of the border in Tanzania.

The only paved road in Bukuria, a mere 20 kilometers, runs south of Migori to the Tanzanian border. The murram roads, on which the bulk of humans and cargo are transported, are pitted, potholed, poorly maintained, eroded, and overused. During the rainy seasons, their clay base makes them dangerous or impassable. Large lorries come into the district to remove maize surpluses accumulated and stored in the capacious warehouses of the Cereals Board, which buys up the harvests of Kuria and the adjacent Transmara districts. Lorries also export the tobacco harvest of smallholder farmers supplying British American Tobacco, Mastermind, Stancom, and Alliance companies, which compete for the best leaf to sell on the international and national markets for cigarette making. The only running water is in rivers and streams, and these have become increasingly polluted by runoff from tobacco nurseries, in which seeds are germinated and nurtured prior to transplanting. Girls and women fetch water from these sources, sometimes multiple times a day, to meet the needs of their homesteads.

Kuria widely regard educational attainment as the principal way to get ahead economically, as well as to gain access to horizons broader than the rural countryside. Nonetheless, educational attainment for Kuria men and women is lower than the national average and, perhaps consequently, employment levels are lower as well. Since very few people are able to survive by subsistence farming alone, most resort to multiple strategies to make a living (Bryceson 2002).

Though employment options have been more accessible to men than to women, women are also intricately tied into the global economic system through cash-crop production (coffee, tobacco, maize), agricultural labor offered for sale, and petty trade.

In the last few decades, a number of important changes occurred in Bukuria. In the late 1980s, a large-scale in-migration of families placed a new burden on the resource base of these rural communities. The families had been squatting for the previous fifty years in the adjoining Rift Valley areas and were dislocated in the name of majimboism (Klopp 2001).[9] This influx of peoples, whose livelihood was based on large herds of cattle, reinforced the most conservative elements within Bwirege society (Prazak 2000, 25). This is true, too, of neighboring Abanyabasi, who also squatted in adjoining Maasai areas.

That the initiation season was canceled because of witchcraft seemed impossible. It did not square with the image Abairege and Kuria generally have of themselves as the intrepid challengers of obstacles that stand in their way, an image reinforced nationally by the significant role they took historically and play currently in the police, army, and security industry, including private forces.

But that was the state of affairs when I arrived in the community on December 2. I had received my invitation back in October, and excitedly stayed up nights, preparing for the opportunity to fill this hole in my experience and knowledge. There and then, in the dusty marketplace, my heart sank to the pit of my stomach. After such a long journey, my purpose had suddenly vanished. This was too unexpected to contemplate. Despite the warm welcome of Samwel's mother, Mogore Maria, and the excited whispering and nudging of her younger children, I felt dizzy and nauseated, hardly believing my bad fortune. It took me into the next day to get over the shock. I went from tears of disappointment, fatigue, and frustration, through a lot of rationalizing, to the beginnings of formulating a new plan and reason for being there. I decided that since I was already there and couldn't go back home, I was ideally located for the study of witchcraft.

The Challenge of Studying Witchcraft

Studying witchcraft is an intractable endeavor. Raised in a secular humanist tradition, I have little background to help me come to grips with the ideas and reported realities of witchcraft.[10] Like Ashforth, I am not predisposed to find higher or hidden meaning or purpose in the workings of the world (Ashforth 2000, 249). Yet witchcraft is nonetheless a meaningful category of thought and action to Kuria and many other peoples of the world.

Scholarship on this topic has a very long history in anthropology. E. E. Evans-Pritchard proposed that if one assumes unseen forces exist in the world and nothing happens to people by accident, then beliefs and practices concerning witchcraft (as well as magic and oracles) are rational (1937). Beliefs and practices resembling Azande witchcraft in southern Sudan, where Evans-Pritchard studied, are found in many societies, and a great deal of work has been done to identify patterns and underlying meanings of witchcraft accusations (see, e.g., Stewart and Strathern 2004; Fisiy and Geschiere 1996; Green 1997, 2003).

How do we understand witchcraft in the context of a circumcision celebration in Nyankare village in Kenya? Currently, a commonplace position of academics is that witchcraft is an idiom through which other realities, such as misfortunes, social stress, strain, unemployment, and capitalist globalization, to mention a few, are expressed (Ashforth 2000, 245). A study in postcolonial Africa in recent decades has recognized that local discourses on witchcraft and sorcery have always centered on power and inequality, on the tension between individual ambition and communitarian control. Fisiy and Geschiere (1996, 194) argue that these conceptions are invoked more often and more openly to interpret new inequalities. In the case of Cameroon, they argue that witchcraft discourses offer the idiom of choice for trying to understand and control modern changes. In some cases, witchcraft discourses pose obstacles to change, while in other contexts, they intertwine easily with new developments, with the form "modernity" takes. Sanders (1999) makes a similar point for rural north-central Tanzania. He shows that older notions of Ihanzu witchcraft—which are and always have been linked to material wealth and its accumulation and destruction—have been redefined and redeployed in more contemporary settings, and that "African witchcraft can be properly understood only as an historically conditioned phenomenon that is itself eminently modern" (127–28). Further, he proposes that though African witches represent an attempt to demystify modernity and its perverse inequities, currencies, and pieties, and its threat to the viability of known social worlds, witchcraft also critiques local forms of "tradition" by pointing up the moral and economic difficulties associated with a conceptually closed, finite-good economy. As Adam Ashforth discusses in his work in South Africa, people living in a paradigm of witchcraft seek meaning for misfortune in the actions of ill-disposed people nearby (2000, 253). And if nothing else, as one of a variety of interpretive schemes available through numerous agents, including doctors, traditional healers, missionaries, and ministers, witchcraft offers one way of deciphering signs of invisible power that shape the texture of everyday life.

Witchcraft ideas in contemporary Africa have become a prominent way of conceptualizing, coping with, and criticizing the very "modernity" that was supposed to have done away with them (Stewart and Strathern 2004, 5). James Smith (2008) elaborates the case for witchcraft as a tool to interpret new inequalities arising in Taita social life in Kenya. Smith's detailed exegesis argues that witchcraft beliefs demonstrate how people conceptualize social boundaries (where threats to order and the good life emanate from), and how to shore up those boundaries against malicious forces (91). While teasing out Taita understandings of witchcraft, Smith highlights the ambivalent and relative nature of power and the perceived importance of creating and maintaining spatial and temporal boundaries in a reality where domains are also selectively permeable. He finds that witchcraft represents the dark antithesis of everything that Taita felt modernity should be. Different forms of witchcraft reference and represent different social dangers. In Smith's assessment, witchcraft is a synonym for breached boundaries (93). Further, witchcraft draws attention away from structural issues by blaming evil individuals whose actions can be believed to affect structures (115). Ideas about witchcraft are intimately connected to more general notions about morality, sociality, and humanity (Green 2003, 124). Witches are people who are excessively greedy and antisocial, to the point where they quite literally embody the inversion of normal human attributes. The core antisocial quality of witches is their inability to eat with people (125).

The Kenyan Context

Seeing witchcraft through this lens makes one wonder what Kuria were so anxious about as they prepared for initiation season. The community was on edge. In Kenya, the 1990s were a difficult period of enormous political and economic uncertainty. A relatively stable democracy since independence in 1963, Kenya's political changes, including the organization of a multiparty political system and accelerating incorporation of the economic spheres into the neoliberal global economic order, were leading to greater tolerance of dissent (Booth 2004, 16). By 1997, President Moi and his party no longer held the unquestioned support that had characterized the sociopolitical and economic character of the 1980s. On the economic front, Moi repeatedly failed to implement the structural adjustment programs that were imposed and reimposed on the country by the International Monetary Fund (IMF), which resulted in the cancellation of monetary aid and loans from multilateral and bilateral agencies supported by North American and European governments. Newspaper and radio reports showcasing Moi's attempts to blame "western imperialism" for the country's increasingly severe economic crisis contributed to an atmosphere of tension, confusion, fear, and uncertainty. Moreover, open discussion of the rapidly growing HIV epidemic fanned tensions, as did the hugely unequal distribution of income and land, especially evident in rural areas (14).

Economic prosperity declined sharply as a consequence of complex, interacting influences. These included rapid population growth, punitive measures imposed by multinational donors, declining revenues from tourism and agricultural production, the Structural Adjustment Program, the effects of incorporation into the global economic system as a peripheral state, corruption, and mismanagement (House-Midamba 1996, 291; NCPD, CBS, and MI 1999, 2; Turner 2002, 982). Decades of economic decline culminated in 2000 when Kenya's economy reached its lowest GDP growth level in history (about 0.2 percent), reflecting the deterioration in well-being that most of the Kenyan population was experiencing. One correlate of chronically weakening economic performance was the inability to create jobs at a rate that matched the growing labor force (CBS, MOH, and ORCM 2004, 2).

Moreover, the institutions and practices that had shaped Kenyan political life for at least a generation became unhinged during the 1990s. Political dissent broadened while government coffers dwindled, disabling the fulfillment of policy and future development visions. As Smith notes, "The state appeared hopelessly segmented, each nominal part seemingly pitted against the other, as the promise of the developmental state became the object of national ridicule" (2008, 179). With the state apparatus in retreat, foreign aid began to be channeled through a panoply of national and international NGOs, which became a new locus in the struggle for politics and patronage. Civilian members of the population could appropriate government roles by accessing and controlling money from NGOs for programs in the community. Through this process, localized social conflicts, such as those that pertained to the domestic sphere (gendered and generational conflicts with a long history), acquired public prominence, at the same time as the terms of public political debate (progress, development, transparency) permeated domestic group discourses and relationships.

These macro-level changes created significant new influences for individuals to negotiate on a daily basis. As neoliberal economics and globalization penetrated localities, people saw new channels to meet their household needs, while economic deregulation threatened the ability of local communities to retain established ways. The concerns and hopes embodied in foreign donors were accompanied by the spread of language that became ubiquitous by the end of the twentieth century and redefined the terms in which people thought about their realities. One of these notions was that culture had potential utility and was "good" when it could be deployed and rationalized to benefit the public (Smith 2008, 89). In addition, dispositions and states of mind were held to be the main factors that could influence whether things were moving forward, moving backward, or going nowhere.

The Power of Witchcraft

In December 1998, interterritorial witchcraft (*okogenderana*, literally "to act against") was on everyone's lips. Even though the initiation season had been called off some weeks earlier, a pronounced tension reigned in the community. Virtually all conversations, however casual, included the latest bit of news about the unusual, unsettling things going on. For me, the next week was devoted to conversations, interviews, meetings, and discussions on the topic of witchcraft, particularly as related to initiation. In two weeks, an assistant and I collected dozens of versions of accounts about why the initiation season had been called off. The stories and rumors whirled. Some versions seemed to be dismissed, only to reappear at another time and with further embellishment or evidence. The tellers drew gasps of astonishment, fear, or doubt, but the listeners dutifully passed on the stories, adding fuel to the fears of supernatural attacks being carried out by covert agents.

Early the next morning, a great ruckus emanating from the marketplace reached Mogore Maria's house. An intensifying buzz, sounding like a crowd at a sports event, was punctuated by periodic crescendos. We were simultaneously curious and concerned. Samwel went running off to see what the excitement was about. As we drank porridge, passersby supplied commentary on the action in the market. A mysterious animal that people couldn't identify had been spotted on top of one of the trees. It was not a cat, nor a monkey, but had a long tail and five fingers, just like a monkey. Eerily, it cried like a baby.

The tension was palpable as people speculated about what it could possibly be doing on top of a tree in the busy marketplace. They reasoned that it had been sent by Abanyabasi to bite someone. Or it had been sent by Abanyabasi to find out whether circumcisions were taking place in Bwirege. Either way, general sentiment marked it as a portent of evil. A crowd a hundred strong gathered around the tree where it was hiding, and people were laying out strategies for how to thwart the danger the animal presented. The discussion took several hours. Around noon, a young man came forward, suggesting that if he were given KShs. 200, he would climb an adjacent tree and bring the suspicious animal down.[11] People pooled money and soon the amount was collected. The young man pocketed the money and, true to his word, climbed the tree. After a few attempts to capture it, he brought the animal down to the unmerciful multitude, who stoned it to death. The carcass of the bushbaby was unceremoniously thrown into a ditch and the crowd broke up.

For the next week, I continued to listen to and engage people in conversations about witchcraft and other initiation seasons. I began to discern that the stories circulating through Bwirege as explanations for the cancellation of the initiation season addressed different points of tension.

Rumors

The first type of rumor was of the general "bad omen" nature, as epitomized by the following story I first heard from a young market woman. She described an incident that was alleged to have taken place where the Bwirege secret conclave held its clandestine meetings. As the members of the inchaama arrived at their usual meeting place, they discovered a passing hyena. All recognized the sighting of a hyena as a bad omen. This was further compounded by their finding that the *egeteembe* tree, used by the conclave members to read portents regarding the initiation season, had dried up on the right side. The right side symbolizes the males, and that occurrence was seen as indicating that many boys would die, beginning with the eight youths who open a period of circumcision. If that were to happen, initiation ceremonies could not proceed. This was probably the most often repeated tale I encountered.

Another widely repeated story was of a young girl who, dismayed that the initiation season had been called off, decided to circumcise herself. Youths told this story with awe for her audacity and determination. But she failed to complete the job and someone had to be called to finish it. All recognized she had seriously transgressed social rules, and thus the representatives of the inchaama were said to be visiting that home and gathering evidence. As no one would name her, I could not verify or follow the tale. I thought the story unlikely and categorized it as a contemporary legend. In a time fraught with incredible rumors, parsing stories for embedded facts can be astonishingly difficult. This story appeared not to be of witchcraft, but was clearly of transgression of normative behavior, and seemed to pertain to a genre of tales that stress the initiates' expectation of participating in the ritual. However, many years later, a similar story came to light once more, this time in a BBC News radio program (2006), which reported that a girl who had started to circumcise herself had died in the attempt. In scholarly literature, the threat of self-circumcision appeared in a paper describing the defiance with which Meru women and girls met colonial prohibition of genital cutting in the 1950s (Thomas, 1996).

Other rumors revolved around Muniko Zachary, a renowned circumciser from Bwirege in Tanzania. He had been operating on boys for the past forty-plus years, but lately had been ailing for some time, and his eyesight was failing. Rumor had it that he had been bewitched. While a circumciser with bad eyesight is reason enough for an initiate to be concerned, community members worried that even greater misfortune could pass on to the boys he would circumcise. Still, this explanation left room for the inchaama to reverse their decision to cancel initiations. For instance, a cleansing ceremony (*ogosonsoora*) could be carried out and the initiation season could proceed.

In a different version of the story, his recent sickness had made him partially blind. He wanted to seek medical help in Dar es Salaam, and thus requested the council of elders to release him from his initiation duty. Because of his long and dedicated service, he was told he could retire the following year. But in preparation, he was to identify his successor, and for this last year, be in charge of all the operations. The other man who had also been circumcising was unhappy with this decision, as it robbed him of a source of income. He is said to have bewitched Muniko Zachary, causing his illnesses and blindness. But because this younger man had himself been circumcised by Muniko Zachary, Muniko Zachary cursed the man for causing the loss of his vision, saying, "I am the one who circumcised you and you have seen it fit to do this to me. May everybody you circumcise die in your hands!" With these words, he compelled the younger man not to participate in the circumcision ceremonies. This version of the story came to me via a middle-aged man from Tanzania. A very similar version was circulating in Kuria-inhabited locations in the Rift Valley.

A more elaborate version was recorded from Victoria Gaati, the chief's wife in Nyankare. In her account, the circumciser was cursed by the father of one of the boys he had operated on, following a fight between the two men over where the circumcision of the latter's son had taken place. The father had been circumcised in the very first set Muniko Zachary operated on, and in his anger said something to the effect that since he belonged to the first set of boys who had been circumcised by Muniko Zachary, he was thus advising him to let the operation he did to his son be the last or else something dire would happen. Come this year's ceremonies, Muniko Zachary refused to participate unless the boy's father renounced his statement, after which a cleansing ceremony would need to occur.

Seeing that things were getting out of hand, the inchaama met and requested that the age-mates of the boy's father confront their colleague and ask him to retract his earlier threat, so that the circumcision ceremonies could go on as planned. That Muniko Zachary had been ill was a consequence of what the boy's father had said. According to Victoria Gaati, who was recounting the story, the cleansing ceremony could then take place and thus the initiation season could proceed as expected.

Yet another type of rumors circulating involved the internal dynamic of Bwirege's generation classes (amakora). About a century earlier, when the cycle was at a similar configuration, a serious famine devastated the area. The young men of that time had to leave their communities to find food. They were gone too long, and by the time they came back, the elders had starved to death. So in order to ensure that youths about to be circumcised would survive the operation, it was necessary for a series of rituals to be performed to appease the spirits of the elders who had died of starvation while their sons had gone off. Though this story is consistent with historical events of the past century, it did not circulate widely, and it was not possible for my assistant and me to ascertain whether people were taking steps to remedy past transgressions in order to bring about the current initiation season.

Generation Classes as Identity Markers

An important ingredient in determining the status of one individual vis-à-vis another is the cycle of amakora—a core institution that regulates the systematic pattern of relationships and provides the guidelines for appropriate interpersonal behavior (Ruel 1962, 17). Membership in the amakora is ascribed at birth, and a man's children are automatically members of the successive class; his grandchildren will then belong to the next class, and the great-grandchildren to the fourth one. Then, the cycle repeats. The formal relationship between the classes is fixed. All Kuria belong to one of two complementary cycles that each have four generation classes.

In the Monyasaai cycle, Abasaai give birth to the Abanyambureti, who give birth to Abagamunyere, who are followed by the Abamaina, who in turn give birth to the Abasaai. In the Monyachuuma cycle, the Abamairabe give birth to Abagini, the Abagini give birth to Aban-yangi, the Abanyangi give birth to Abachuuma, and the Abachuuma to Abamairabe. Membership in each cycle is patrilineal, and norms of coevality apply to each class in sequence.

A child remains a member of the class he or she was born into throughout life, and follows the rules of respect in regard to members of other classes. The rules are simple and apply to both cycles. Members of adjacent classes have a relationship of respect and reserve with each other, whereas members of the same and alternate classes enjoy a relationship of familiarity. The emphasis on a modal two-generational pattern of behavior norms is consistent with the basic two-generational form of the homestead. The relationships between actual lineal kin are at the center of the classificatory system of relationships established by the generation classes. But through the classes, the two broad types of relationships (those of respect and of restraint) are extended further to cover all members of the ikiaro, together with those of other ibiaro.

In kinship matters, class relationships are expressed in marriage rules. A member of one generation can only marry within his own generation class or within the next alternating group. He cannot marry the next younger group because those are his "children" and he cannot marry from the next senior group because those are his "parents." But "class norms and general patterning of relationships dovetail with and are subsumed by all kinship relations" (Ruel 1962, 28). On ritual occasions, generation classes delineate clearly defined social groups and dictate who may play a certain role, what shares of meat may be taken by whom, who may mix together, who should be kept apart, and so govern interactions according to the basic rules of respect and familiarity. Class membership orders behavior in a specific context of events and participants. It does not itself initiate what takes place (28–29). At the circumcision ground, the oldest amakora are the first to be operated on. In the past, members of the same generations were cut using the same knife, and members of the oldest generation walk first in the line of initiates.

Generation class membership is the most important in contexts of everyday interaction within the community, where the class system acts again as a general charter for social behavior and norms of respect. Underlying all greetings, social gatherings, chance encounters, beer parties, guest/host relationships, and feasting, the norms of respect operate between the different classes to establish generational groupings. Thus, for example, only members of the same class will share food from the same bowl. The more informal the situation, the less rigidly these codes are adhered to and behavior becomes more relaxed. Generation classes tend to be associated with certain age-groups of the community. In the past, the rough equivalence of the classes with the age-structure of the community was determined by a sequence of ceremonies performed by the classes in succession. Most of these ceremonies were no longer practiced in the 1950s and none took place in the ikiaro in the 1980s (Ruel 1959, 131–33). Still, Kuria use the names of the classes in referring to people of a particular generation or time. Thus, people refer to the movement of the Abahirichacha (a descent group) north into Kenya as having taken place in the time of Abasaai, who were accompanied by their children, Abanyamburiti.

The association between generation classes and age-groups of the community is seldom clear-cut and simple, and results from membership in a generation class being assigned on a genealogical basis. Thus two brothers, sons of the same man but by different wives, belong to the same class, even though the age difference between them may be thirty years. They will thus move through the life stages and age-statuses at different points in time, even though they are of the same generation class.

As I was listening to rumors of witchcraft and supernatural happenings, the troubles of the circumciser and debts owed to ancestors, the recurrence of blame and accusation being directed at the people of Nyabasi, the neighboring ikiaro, it became clear that the sociopolitical units of Kuria society figured largely in the unease expressed through rumors of witchcraft, pointing to arenas where local boundaries need to be revitalized.

More Rumors

The most frightening stories were the ones that focused explicitly on okogenderana—witchcraft carried out between clans (ibiaro). Three of the four Kuria clans in Kenya had decided to hold initiations that year. Abakira had already begun. But Abanyabasi and Abairege had both called off their initiation ceremonies. These two neighboring clans have a long history of hostility toward each other. For the past several decades they had been raiding each other's cattle, and it had become unusual for both groups to circumcise in the same year. The okogenderana power of the witchcraft on each side was a matter of substantial concern. Numerous accounts circulated of trespassers coming from Nyabasi, stealing hair, fingernails, and other small body parts through which to exact witchcraft on their unsuspecting rivals.[12] People told frightening tales of children being kidnapped, killed, and dismembered; adults being waylaid, beaten, and robbed; individuals unwittingly recruited to do evil.[13]As I later found out, many of these incidents were registered with the police and the civil administration, so the rumors were often based on some level of fact.

I heard the first account from Mogore Maria, my host. An independent businesswoman, a widow, and an elected local official, she

firmly blamed witchcraft for creating a climate where it was necessary to cancel initiation ceremonies. The day after my arrival, she
assured me that two or even three witches from Nyabasi had already
been apprehended in Bwirege, after a buried bag of magic had been
discovered. One of the witches, a woman, was caught in a market community in the southeast part of the location as she carried a basket in
which she was hiding a sheep's leg. In Nyankare, the main market of
the location, two men were caught, having been observed behaving
in a suspicious manner. They claimed they had come to buy cattle,
but instead left behind bundles containing fingernails and other body
parts. All three of these people/witches were severely beaten, and it
was said the woman lost an eye.

In another case, people believed to be from Nyabasi went to a farm
in Bwirege where they found a young girl, not yet old enough for
initiation. She was looking after her parents' maize, which had been
attacked by monkeys in the preceding days. The people from Nyabasi
shaved her head, scraped some skin from the front and back of her
head, and cut off her fingernails. They left her in the fields and walked
off. The girl immediately ran home and told her parents what had
happened. This, like some of the other stories, was repeated to me by
diverse people in various areas of the location. Because the parents of
the girl were named, it was easy to see that this particular story was
widely believed.

Stories of this sort of witchcraft (okogenderana) between Abairege
and Abanyabasi abounded. Two sisters, Nyagonchera Mwita and
Janet Gaati, wanted to circumcise their youngest sons, who were
insisting on accompanying each other through the process. But the
sisters had heard and repeated to me a story of a young boy (a potential initiate) who had been bewitched into running into Nyabasi,
to the secret conclave of that clan, where the elders killed him and
cut off his private parts. When the elected official for whom the boy
had been working followed the runaway to find out what happened
to him, the councilor was stabbed. Both sisters are schoolteachers,
traveled and well-educated, and their fear of witchcraft was palpable.
The other story they recounted I had previously heard. It was of the
two Nyabasi men, both married to Abairege women. The men had
traveled to Bwirege to buy cattle but were set upon by the mob at the
cattle auction and beaten badly. Some of their hair was shaved and
their fingernails cut to create anti-Nyabasi magic. Since the men were
sons-in-law to Bwirege, and were in fact quite well known, the sisters

found this story shocking, as it illustrated the escalated emotional pitch and fear building in the community.

One day, as I sat on a narrow wooden bench in front of a dry goods shop in the market, I listened to a conversation between two old men perched on small stools watching the goings-on in the market center. A sixty-year-old employed watchman, the younger of the two, recounted the story of a married woman from Bwirege who had gone to Nyabasi to visit her boyfriend. The boyfriend gave her a black sheep. Members of the secret conclave in Nyabasi decided that they would strike at Bwirege through this adulterous couple. When the woman got back to Bwirege, she went to her sister's place and asked her sister's uncircumcised son to assist her in slaughtering the sheep. He agreed, and when the meat was cooked, he ate it and went back to his home. Two days later, the boy was helping his parents transport maize home from the fields using a donkey. The parents were carrying sacks of maize on their heads, and were left behind. On the third trip, almost halfway home, the boy suddenly unbuttoned his shirt and dropped it on the road. He then began unloading the maize from the donkey and when done, took off, leaving the donkey and everything on the road.

He allegedly went to a place in Nyabasi, where he met some boys his age looking after a herd of cattle. The boys asked him where he was from and he promptly told them he was from Bwirege and just out for a stroll. He helped them drive their cattle to the river to drink, and in the evening they invited him to their home. Their father made some inquiries about the boy, and satisfied that the boy was indeed from Bwirege, he left the boys at his home and went to inform and consult with the council of elders. He told the elders that everything had turned out as planned and expected. After supper, the other boys went to bed and the visiting boy asked to be shown where he was to sleep. He was led to where the council of elders was meeting and was killed. His genitals, nose, and right ear were chopped off, and his eyes and intestines gouged out. His badly mutilated body was found some days later in a river in a border area with Bwirege.

The storyteller went on to describe how the secret conclave of Bwirege dispatched members to the scene where the body was found to ascertain that the body was actually that of the missing boy. This done, the elders decided that the body of the missing boy should not be brought back to Bwirege. The woman who brought the black sheep had since separated from her husband and been taken to the council of elders in Bwirege, Tanzania, to be punished. She was asked to pay two cows as a fine or be killed.

The day after I heard this detailed story in the market, I stopped by the home of John Muruga, who was relaxing in the shade cast by the conical thatched roof of one of the three circular wattle and daub traditional houses that made up his homestead. We talked about the stories going around. He had heard them all, but was confident that initiation would nonetheless be carried out in Bwirege this year. He claimed not only that it would happen but also that it would begin on December 14. He was planning to circumcise his two oldest children, son Mwita John and daughter Grace Gaati. While I was talking with John, his brother Sagirei stopped by, along with a friend named Kehongo Elias. Sagirei and Kehongo had become close friends when they studied together overseas in the 1960s. Then, their provenance from different clans (ibiaro) did not matter. But now, with one an elder from Bwirege, the other from Nyabasi, Kehongo marveled at how apprehensive he felt driving into Bwirege to visit his friend, something he had done routinely for decades.

Quite a heated discussion followed. Kehongo insisted, "What is happening now is thuggery." The Nyabasi woman who was beaten was mentally challenged as well as poor. She was visiting her daughter in Tanzania, who gave her mother some roasted meat for the long walk back home. She didn't have money for the ferry at Nyamongo to cross the Mara River and so ended up having to walk through Bwirege. Though initially walking with others who eventually hived off upon reaching their destinations, she reached the marketplace in the southeastern part of the location alone. There she was noticed eating dried meat (a sheep's leg).[14] People beat her and she lost an eye. A Good Samaritan took her to a clinic. Her husband was told she was dead, but was afraid to come get her body from Bwirege. He got the administration to come get her and they found her alive. She was taken to Ombo Hospital in Migori.

Sagirei proposed that this was the first time in his memory that initiations had brought about such serious misunderstanding between Nyabasi and Bwirege. "This is thuggery," Kehongo Elias repeated. "This has nothing to do with witchcraft." As proof for his stance, he brought up the case of the two Nyabasi men married to Abairege women. They were well known in Bwirege, but they were beaten, their hair and nails cut. They were robbed of KShs. 15,000 and 8,000, respectively.[15] Both Sagirei and Kehongo agreed that this was not likely to be the work of the secret conclave, which does not operate in such a flamboyant way. To support their conclusion, they spoke of the incident in which the bushbaby was killed in the market. If the real concern had been witchcraft, it would have been killed quietly and been taken to the inchaama, instead of the spectacle that took place.

Later that day I visited Stephen Wambura and his wife Severina Nyakorema, two schoolteachers. They were planning to initiate their three oldest daughters that season, and had been working to amass a large amount of food for the celebrations. They felt thwarted by the elders calling the whole process into question. But they believed initiations would happen, perhaps after Tanzanian schools closed. They had heard about the boy who was killed and then thrown into the river in Nyabasi, at the border with Bwirege. In the days that had passed, the story had taken on additional details. Allegedly, his throat was cut, and his external organs were chopped off and circumcised by the Abanyabasi. This action was intended to signify that Bwirege's initiates were going to lose a lot of blood and would be washed away, just like the blood in the water. Abanyabasi expected that Abairege, upon hearing that one of their own had been killed, would go get his body. But Abairege did not, and the body, after being positively identified, was buried there. Abairege claimed that since the boy was maimed and killed by Abanyabasi, and his blood washed into the water source used by their people, Nyabasi initiates would be the ones to die on being circumcised.

I have presented the rumors in quite some detail because this was the predominant discourse taking place in Bwirege during the time initiations were called off, and as people tried to understand why the *abagaaka* had abruptly terminated the season, the uncertainties of various individuals became clear in the specifics of the rumor. The rumors drew attention to the perceived frailties of the group by those who repeated particular stories (Smith 2008, 182).

Descent as Identity Marker

Principles of descent are of paramount importance in organizing Kuria social life. Descent relations achieve depth over time, based on the parent-child links that connect generations by blood. In Kuria society, people are connected patrilineally, with the most significant link being father-son. A group formed by links through males over five or more generations constitutes a lineage, which includes people who can specify the father-son links that connect them to a common ancestor. This happens at each genealogical depth—those who share a paternal grandfather are distinct from those who have different grandfathers. This belonging is mobilized situationally.

The identity, behavior, and status of each individual are determined first by the family group or *umugi*, the primary social unit comprised of a man, his wife or wives, and their children, as well as the wives and children of their sons. The umugi is based on the male homestead owner (*umuene umugi*). A child's place in the family lineage is confirmed by circumcision, the first step an individual takes in the ritual cycle. Many East African peoples were and, to some extent, continue to be socially organized in this manner, classified as "segmentary lineage societies." Historically, these societies lacked institutionalized rulers and centralized government, yet had the ability to act in unison regarding specific issues. Lineage was the main political association, and individuals had no political or legal status except through lineage membership.[16] They had relatives outside the lineage, but their own political and legal status derived from the lineage to which they belonged. Because people were born into them, lineages endured over time in societies where no other form of organization lasted, and the system of lineages became the foundation of social life, but that doesn't mean they were immovable and inflexible. People used lineage and clan membership to pursue their interests. Lineages were described as corporate in that they controlled property, such as lands or herds, as a unit. Though the colonial era eliminated communal ownership among Kuria, lineage membership continues to carry benefits.

When members of a descent group believe that they are in some way connected but cannot specify the precise genealogical links, they compose what anthropologists call a clan. Bwirege is such a unit. Usually, a clan is made up of lineages whose members believe they are related to one another through links that go back to mythical times but cannot be traced exactly. So whereas lineage members can specify the precise genealogical links back to their common ancestor, clan members cannot. The clan is thus larger than any lineage, and more diffuse in terms of both membership and the hold it has over individuals. It is also territorially based.

Early cultural history of East Africa described by Davidson identifies dispersal and migration as the basic characteristic of the spread of indigenous populations in precolonial times (1969, 47). For Abairege, as for other migrants, connection with descent groups provided a source of identity and security, and regulated social relationships with other migrants settling on nearby ridges or lands. Accordingly, members of the same lineages would move to be near each other for mutual assistance and defense, and over time the descent groups became territorially based. So a particular ridge became the land of the Abahirichacha, and members of that descent group would receive land for use from the lineage elders. On the ground, lineage affiliation served as the charter for social relationship, identifying those whom one could marry or rely on for help, as well as those who were outsiders and thus enemies.

Ruel describes traditional Kuria society as composed of four levels of descent groups at the time of the late colonial period. Ikiaro, translated as province or clan, was the most inclusive, followed by *egesaku* (descent section), *irigiha* (clan segment), and *eeka* (lineage). According to Ruel, these units of sociopolitical organization had lost all their relevance by the 1950s, except for the levels most (ikiaro) and least (eeka) inclusive (1959, 56). The characteristics of the segmentary lineage system he describes probably functioned exclusively until the 1920s, when colonial administration reached Bukuria and introduced territorially defined political units, controlled through the colonial administrative structure. As the precolonial lineage structures lost clear definition over time, administrators and anthropologists observing Kuia people and writing about them deemphasized the importance and primacy of the descent system, and focused instead on the forms of colonial administration as the salient pillars of political and social organization in Bukuria during colonial and early postcolonial eras: chiefs and administrative locations. Yet, what becomes clear by focusing on the ritual life of Kuria people today in the performance of circumcision is how descent continues to define identity, social relationships, and the shape of current events. Where the colonial observers saw lineages as principally elements of political organization, their significance persists because they are units governing social life that, in particular circumstances, take on political significance, even in the context of introduced governmental institutions.[17]

Ruel characterizes an ikiaro as having changing descent composition resulting from the dispersal and reformation of groups within it (1959, 28). As the most inclusive level of the descent system, the ikiaro was defined primarily as territory belonging to specific people with an assumed relationship to a common mythical ancestor rather than any traceable lineage. The people who occupied a common province showed solidarity in shared means of settling disputes, compensation for homicide, and mechanisms for collective labor. The territorial base was the vicinity in which people lived. The occupants shared a sense of common identity and distinctiveness from other groups of the same level. Each ikiaro had its own totem, and its distinct ceremonies, though traditions were shared with other ibiaro. Abairege have the leopard as their totem, as do Abagumbe and Abanyamongo. All ibiaro perform initiations, but each at their own time, following their own sequence and form. Each ikiaro had (and has) its own ritual center and its own inchaama.

According to Ruel, the *ibisaku* were the most clearly "political" of all descent units because the common ancestor was hypothesized rather than known, and obligations associated with membership had the least to do with kinship duties.[18] Fighting between ibisaku was common, as were rivalry and hostility. Starting in colonial times, the allocation of political office was often influenced by descent section solidarities. Moreover, colonial archives from 1931 mention rivalry between the two ibisaku groups in Bwirege, the Abakehenche and the Abarisenye. Political jockeying continues today. Conflict between these two descent sections during the 1998–99 circumcision season and again in 2001–02 highlights the social and political functioning of intermediate levels of segmentary organization, contrary to their believed irrelevance fifty years ago.

In the past, groups based on descent—ibisaku and *amagiha*—had two primary functions: (1) cooperation in war, defining those who could be called on for support in case of conflict; and (2) cooperation in work groups performing tasks necessary for survival. Pax Britannica was meant to put an end to fighting, but cattle raiding persists even today. Raiding provides a source of bridewealth and is still regarded by some members of the society as a legitimate occupation of youths. Accordingly, people know the ibisaku and the amagiha they belong to because the traditional functions persist. But they often misuse descent group terminology because the groups have become so large, and because the term ikiaro is identified with modern political boundaries more than with traditional descent structure. So the grouping Abahirichacha, a subsegment of the Abakehenche, is regarded by some as an egesaku; by others, an irigiha. In general discourse, people refer to their memberships by their descent group names, not by categorical referents.[19]

Descent sections of the Kuria   Descent sections of the Abairege

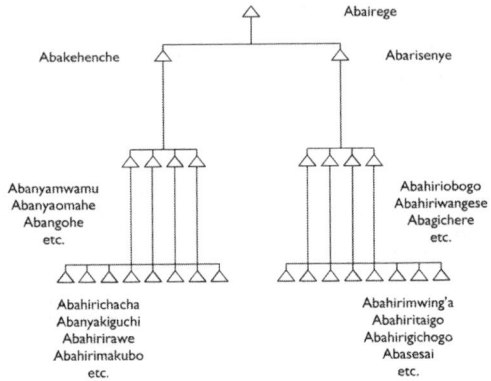

Figure 2. Kuria descent structure

Even though people continue to identify with and shape social behavior around their ikiaro, the traditional social evolution of communities from eeka to irigiha to egesaku to ikiaro is no longer possible because the ibiaro became territorialized with fixed boundaries in the early decades of the twentieth century, as administrative locations were delimited by the colonial government to correspond closely to the territories of the ibiaro. Consequently, the descent structure cannot operate as a segmentary lineage system because there is no longer free and open land available for active segmentation to continue. The ibiaro are fixed and there is no movement within the hierarchy. So, though the designations Abakehenche and Abarisenye no longer fit into a traditionally functioning descent section model using the terminology ikiaro-egesaku-irigiha-eeka, all Abairege affiliate with either the Abakehenche (seen as the larger/senior segment) or the Abarisenye (seen as the smaller/junior segment).

Although today the ibiaro are territorially based rather than descent based, they still constitute the maximal unit to which an individual belongs within Kuria social reckoning. Furthermore, private ownership of land, widely encouraged in the colony under the Swynnerton Plan (1954), created a situation where territory associated with specific descent groups is no longer strictly in the hands of the elders of that descent group. So if the Abarisenye and Abakehenche were to split into two ibiaro, the social and territorial units would no longer be coterminous, since people of each branch live intermingled in the communities of Bwirege. According to my household survey data, this shift in landholding and settlement patterns has taken place increasingly in recently settled communities.

The ikiaro remains the main focus of Kuria identification. Among Kuria, people speak of themselves as members of an ikiaro (e.g., Abairege, Abanyabasi, and so forth), rather than as Abakuria. The relationships between ibiaro are generally hostile, unless (totemic) alliance is shared. Outsiders from other ibiaro are enemies and always potentially dangerous, thus girls and parents alike fear the threat of a pregnant, uncircumcised girl exiled to a neighboring ikiaro. People from other ibiaro are distrusted, and when traveling by road through Bukuria, passengers fear getting stranded by a vehicle breakdown in any of the other ibiaro. This is especially the case at times of heightened ritual activity, such as initiations, when it is believed that misfortune, in the form of death to the initiates, is threatened by contact with members of other ibiaro.

More than a dozen Kuria ibiaro exist. Most are in Tanzania, four are in Kenya, but only one has its territory completely in Kenya. The three divided by an open international boundary, including Bwirege, have thriving social and economic cross-border exchange, and people can escape from the laws of home by shifting into the other country. So when the laws against female genital cutting were being enforced in Tanzania in 1998, Abairege parents brought their girls to be cut in Kenya. Similarly, if the Umwirege circumciser in Tanzania was operating close to the boundary, Kenyan Abairege did not hesitate to cross into Tanzania to have their candidates undergo initiation.

Some observers of the initiation cancellations were talking about a rift that was increasingly threatening the existence of the secret conclave as a unitary decision-making entity in Bwirege. Though the perceived division had been there for a while and not affected the discharge of duty to the people in the past, it became increasingly clear that the two descent sections comprising Bwirege—Abakehenche and Abarisenye—were conducting their affairs independently.[20]

Abakehenche are regarded as the "bigger house" and Abarisenye as the "smaller" house. According to custom, Abarisenye are not allowed to conduct any affairs without first consulting Abakehenche. Abakehenche are seen to be on the "right side" where such activities as initiation ceremonies are concerned, and are expected to begin, while Abarisenye are expected to follow. But Abarisenye had been

dominant in decision making for this initiation season, prompting
the current crisis. So Abakehenche were counseling that initiations
be postponed, while Abarisenye wanted to proceed. To make matters
even more extraordinary, a third descent group was beginning to
act as a corporate entity. Abaseese, with lineages in both Burisenye
and in Bokehenche, were beginning to assert independent authority,
challenging both the ibisaku widely recognized as legitimate sociopolitical groups of Abairege.[21] This crisis of traditional authority was
taking place on both sides of the international boundary, in Kenya
and in Tanzania. The district commissioner in Kenya was rumored
to have ordered chiefs from Bwirege to ensure that the inchaama in
Bwirege was not divided, thereby ensuring that the tension between
groups did not translate into structural fissioning.

The Uncertainty Continues

Despite the widespread concern about witchcraft that sprang up
in late November and early December, people carried on with their
preparations for initiations, though quietly. The public pageantry associated with the rituals came to a complete stop. Locally, outbreaks
of cattle rustling fanned fears of crime.[22] As this type of theft became
the focus of public discourse, it became another topic that put people
on edge. So did the measures to address it. An *iritongo* meeting was
held near the market to discuss cattle theft. Nyankare was said to be
harboring cattle thieves, and the people of the community were asked
to disclose the thieves' names. This was done systematically, with all
community members present at the meeting filing past the secretary
and telling her either the name of a cattle thief, or that they didn't
know one. The *sungusungu*, a posse of men, was then empowered to
hunt the accused down and beat them until they returned the stolen
cattle.[23] The people at the meeting were told that the iritongo would
meet every week until all the thieves had been found and punished.
Two days after the iritongo meeting, a posse of about twenty-five
men went charging past our homestead, heading toward the Tanzanian border, arguing and calling out, spreading news of what was
happening as they passed. And indeed, women cried out on numerous
nights as homes were visited by vigilante justice. The anxiety over
witchcraft was augmented by this additional type of fear, that of accusations and vigilante justice.

Circumcisions, nonetheless, remained the primary topic of private conversations, as did the many accounts of witchcraft acts occurring in various places in the location. On December 9, Abanyabasi began circumcising. In Bwirege, at the official Jamhuri Day celebrations on December 12 at the district officer's camp, the crowd slowly assembled to hear speeches by government officials commemorating the establishment of Kenya as a republic. People seemed resigned to the cancellation of initiations in Bwirege. The rumor of the day was that circumcision would not take place, as this was the day that the first eight—the amanaanai representative of the amakora—were to have been circumcised as a precursor to the community-wide event, but were not. And the reopening of schools was drawing closer, so the time for healing would possibly be inadequate. People speculated that the old circumciser had gone blind, or the youth to be circumcised had refused to be operated on because of his blindness. The rumor seemed confirmed when Mogore Maria, in her role as elected councilor for this area, urged people not to kill their cattle, because in a few weeks' time they would need to pay school fees.

After her, a wealthy Kuria businessman who usually lived and conducted his activities in Mombasa gave a scathing speech, berating the elders for having called off the initiation season. "We have brought our children from all over Kenya to become abaiseke and abamura within our communities, to become Kuria," he said.[24] He went on to say that the inchaama were joking with people, they'd postponed the operation three times. The people who had brought their children back there for it would have to go back with them uncircumcised. Were the inchaama defeated, leaving everyone to do it in any way they liked? Taking the children to the hospital? If they were circumcised at that time they would only have two weeks to heal. In the past, abasaamba had had six months to recover. Why should the young ones now only have two weeks? "But if the abagaaka don't allow them to be circumcised according to our tradition, we'll take them to be circumcised in clinics or hospitals wherever we live." He articulated most clearly what others were not willing to state openly: the elders had lost their power to order the affairs of the localities in which they had been regarded as the ultimate culturally designated authorities. Many people clearly agreed with his assessment. They were furious at the possibility that circumcisions might not take place. Everyone had prepared food, brewed beer, and come from long distances to be here when their children were initiated, and all that seemed to have been in vain.

Talk of initiation ended with the district officer, a young man from northeastern Kenya. He spoke of esaaro bitterly and disparagingly. "I called a meeting of the iritongo and no councilors came. The leaders only talk, they don't do anything. And people talk about witches and being bewitched." Though he had been in the district only two months, he was already seeking a transfer, because he felt he could not work with the people. "In many parts [of the country] they have stopped the primitive methods. But here it is still going on in that way." What his perspective overlooked, in his equating of the witchcraft beliefs with only superstition, ignorance, and backwardness, was that Kuria he administered were trying to retain their sense of Kuria cultural uniqueness, hence their adherence to tradition as they sought to bolster claims to be given their own administrative district. The role and position of elders in Kuria society, among other things, was being challenged and renegotiated. The elders had not been the leaders in the struggle for the district earlier in the decade. That had been spearheaded by the generation of men who were the sons of the elders, whose children were to be circumcised during this season. So on one level, the struggle embodied in the witchcraft events and rumors was an internal dynamic of a clan (ikiaro) needing to revitalize local boundaries, develop a self-identity, and encourage a self-sustaining future based on local language and values. On another level, the struggle was between various segments of descent groups, vying for seniority and increased power to determine their own agendas with regard to the dynamics of the ikiaro. Within the ikiaro, members of competing ibisaku and amagiha were negotiating their own structural positions. As the public dispersed from the meeting ground, people speculated that some would probably go and have their children circumcised in clinics.

Rumors of witchcraft had succeeded in bringing preparations for an initiation season to a halt. The threats posed by outsiders, whether human or animal, were scrutinized for hidden meanings and indications that supernatural forces would negatively affect the outcome of the initiations and lead to deaths among the initiates. Despite their wide repetition, the rumored incidents remained opaque. But clearly, people of Bwirege were anxious, and locating the cause of uncertainty required teasing out a number of forces, local, national, and international. Locally, uncertainties about group definition raised fears of territorial realignment, consequent expulsion, and homelessness. Further, descent segments of various depths were staking claims for positions of power and authority within the local context. On the national level, insecurities brought on by the economic and political weakness of the state manifested in a widespread reliance on concepts of evil as a propagated supernatural force in order to rationalize the declining control of the state in areas meant to promote public good. And as the state tried to negotiate its position with international donor organizations, it focused on the eradication of female genital cutting as the cause that would highlight the clear trajectory it was committed to, moving the nation from traditionalism to modernity.

2

Boys Lead

Two days after the Jamhuri Day celebrations, I was walking home from the wedding of a research assistant from a previous field season, Helen Motongori. She had confided in me her fears in linking her life to a man who would take her far away to Dar es Salaam. The 5-kilometer hike offered plenty of opportunity to reflect on that and the events of the past few days. Tired from participating closely in the myriad elements of a marriage celebration, I was happy to reach the marketplace as the sun sank and the tropical darkness almost immediately swallowed up places and people. I was even happier to find Joel Wantahe waiting to escort me home, given that Nyankare market is the domain of drunks and thugs during the dark hours of the day. As we threaded along narrow paths invisible without moonlight, Joel Wantahe gave me a bit of good news—the initiation season had been declared on again, and the first eight candidates (amanaanai) were to be circumcised the next morning.

The amanaanai represent the eight generation classes (amakora) in Kuria society. Always the first to be operated on, these boys are a bellwether for the initiation season. If their operations go well, the elders of the secret council declare the season to be open. We continued home and found everyone excited and chattering about the imminent celebrations. As the news spread, we could hear people filling the market. Around 7:30 in the evening, we heard the candidate from the neighborhood take off with his group of escorts, chanting, singing, and shouting. They were off to Tanzania, to a place near Kiribo. In the market, people were jubilant—singing and dancing, blowing whistles, screeching, trilling, and carrying on. We could hear them all evening as we prepared and ate dinner, and late into the night.

But not everything felt right. People were wondering whether only the Abarisenye (the junior house) were circumcising or if the Abakehenche (the senior house) were joining them, too. Rumor had it that the amanaanai were from the junior segment, which was surprising since the usual protocol would be for the senior house to go first. The initiation season continued to be fraught with tension. Everyone was hoping that none of the amanaanai would die or have to be taken for treatment—that would surely result in the initiations being called off. With the season opening, numerous considerations weighed on people's minds.

Preparing for an initiation season requires many resources, from material goods to labor. Sufficient food has to be available for entertaining, which includes large quantities of obosara for celebrants, as well as *amaroa* for the elder males. Animals for slaughtering have to be identified and purchased. The initiates need sheets and kanga to wear during seclusion, as well as utensils to use during that time. For coming out of seclusion after recovery, they need soap, body oils, and new clothes. Everyone needs cash to reward the bravery of neighborhood and kin group initiates, and to welcome them into the new phase of their lives. Money needs to be paid to the circumciser. Some money should be set aside in case the initiate needs medical attention. Musicians need to be paid, and entertainment usually involves providing sodas, and laying in stores of salt, cooking fat, rice, tea, sugar, and other purchased foods.

Another pressing constraint is time. Initiation is carried out during December school vacation. Virtually all of the several thousand candidates are primary school pupils, so their recovery needs to be completed before schools resume in early January. The two-week delay in the beginning of the initiation season this year had narrowed the time available to the initiates for recovery. What a difference a day makes, I thought, as I lay in bed reflecting on circumcision and witchcraft.

Opening the Initiation Season

The next morning everyone who didn't go to the actual genital cutting site was anxiously waiting for the initiates (abasaamba) to come home, completing the several-hours-long walk from Kiribo to Nyankare.[1] Large groups of escorts and greeters repeatedly ran up the path that wound in front of our homestead toward Tanzania, about a mile away. Heavily armed and colorfully costumed, these groups threaten—actually and symbolically—anyone they encounter, providing a show of force to keep physical and metaphysical dangers away from the vulnerable initiates. Many people had smeared their bodies with red clay, painted designs on their faces, or donned fearsome masks. A number of the men were bedecked with Maasai headgear made of ostrich feathers and shaped like a large horseshoe, imposingly framing their heads. Some sported the red, clay-encased braids often seen on Maasai warriors. Musicians accompanied many entourages, urging them on with their rhythmic and explosive sound. The wind seemed to carry the high-pitched fiddling of the ekegoogo ahead of an entourage, announcing its advance and retreating with gaiety as the group moved on with their booming *ibiraandi* gourd rattles. Others carried blaring boom boxes, playing traditional Kuria initiation music, perhaps recorded during the previous season. Some wore flowers, branches, or shrubs gathered into sheaves of colorful disguise. Noise reverberated in all directions: whistles, rattles, iron sheets banging, sounding like strings of firecrackers popping. People sang and chanted the unique songs of the season.

At 9 a.m., a newly made initiate (omosaamba), one of the amanaanai, returned up the path, crowded in by hordes of escorts, spectators, and greeters—great jubilation reigned in the neighborhood. People in the market sang and danced. This initiate, the firstborn son of a prominent headmaster and businessman, entered into the marketplace surrounded by approximately seventy-five men and women who led him around the marketplace several times, then took him to his parents' home at the market. His father, fully costumed and jubilant, greeted him at the entry to the initiate's mother's house. The initiate's mother, also costumed and sporting a headdress of brilliant polychrome mylar, proudly welcomed her son and his escorts. This event set the initiate on the threshold of adulthood and his parents onto the path to elderhood.

Throughout the day, the remaining amanaanai arrived home and were thereafter secluded in their homesteads to recover from their ordeal. By custom, they are confined to the homestead, where they walk around gingerly, keeping the sheet they wear away from their genitals to avoid friction. As the skin heals, they lose the tentativeness of movement of the early stages of recovery.

After weeks of uncertainty and doubt, the parents of other potential candidates hurried to prepare for their own celebrations, for the initiation of their boys and girls, which had seemed rather unlikely. And just as parents had been resigning themselves to wait three more years for the next initiation period, they realized now that their children's initiation was imminent. Adolescent boys ran about inviting people to escort them to their tests of courage, to come celebrate at their homes, or simply to let their kin know that they were about to take the first step toward respect. Everywhere, people made a lot of noise as excitement mounted for the initiation season, and they hurried about making the necessary preparations. The next day genital cutting would open to all boys. The subsequent day would be the start for girls.[2] In the market, people sang and danced, dashing from place to place swept up in the frenzy. Several very drunk men waved weapons, scaring those they encountered with the possibility of real violence. Already a story was circulating in the community of a male omosaamba who was attacked during the night on his way home from the operation.

Throughout the night, candidates and their escorts once again headed past our homestead, making lots of noise on their way to Tanzania. By leaving during the night they hoped to secure the opportunity to be operated on the next day. Many people wanted to have their children initiated, and because it was already mid-December, they were concerned they might miss the opportunity. Once a candidate leaves the homestead, he or she cannot return home without having had the operation performed. Escorted by their sponsors and entourage, the candidates do not eat or drink as they await the operation. Candidates must stay at the genital cutting site until they are operated on. In the marketplace and in their homes, people gossiped that the *omosaari* (circumciser) was operating by the light of a lantern.[3]

On the third day of initiations, some of the boys who had been circumcised in the first two days were already out and about, strolling in the neighborhood and bearing witness—by their dress, their aimless loitering, and their cocky and aggressive attitudes—to the growing number of youth in the liminal stage of *obosaamba*, the seclusion period. By custom, the youths to be initiated the following day are also costumed, and distinguish themselves from those who have already undergone the operation by their ease of movement and manner of self-presentation, as well as the bells they wear around their calves that mark their every movement.

During initiation season, the entire community is enthralled by the activities. The spectrum of daily life revolves around the performance of rituals and their accompanying celebrations. Paths are filled with people and initiates. From the early hours of the morning until the middle of the day, groups of fifteen to twenty people, and at times

even more than a hundred, flooded up the path in front of our homestead on their way to the day's cutting site, then dancing, singing, and
celebrating their way back toward their own homes. On roads, paths,
and in the market square, women paraded with mylar headdresses
and men dressed in drag, flouting normal social order, gyrating and
shouting. Men wearing Maasai-style lion headgear proclaimed their
identity as warriors, pranced, and threatened bystanders, enlivening
the market scene.

Boys invite people in person to witness their genital cutting,
whereas girls or their parents invite by letters sent out, or invitations issued orally on their behalf by their parents. Girls aren't free
to wander around like boys. The preinitiation finery of boys includes
bells for the calves, shields, feather headdresses, shiny rows of safety
pins hanging off the hem of their shorts, and short swords or daggers.
As an alternative to the everyday attire of usually quite ragged shorts
and T-shirts, this represents an impressive and imaginative display of
accoutrements. Girls usually go to their operations wearing school
uniforms. It is during seclusion that they wear clothes usually not
worn by females, such as hats.

In their invitation poems, boys praise the person they have come
to invite to the operation and say things to give themselves courage at the prospect of the operation. As *abariisia* (uncircumcised boys,
literally "herders") they are not esteemed or respected, so they dream
of becoming *abamura* (circumcised young men) and being worthy
of greater respect. As abariisia, their primary duties are to take the
cattle out for grazing, watch and protect them from wild animals, and
keep them from ruining people's crops. As abamura, their tasks are
to protect the animals from thieves, to protect the community, and
to undertake cattle raiding to increase their domestic herds and to
acquire cattle for paying bridewealth when it comes time to marry.
They must also continue with their education.

Issuing an Invitation

Mwita John came to the homestead early one morning to invite his
father's older brother to witness his operation. He was dressed in initiation finery, including shorts decorated by dangling rows of safety pins,
a feather headdress, bells circling his calves, a shield, and a short sword.
He was accompanied by a similarly bedecked friend, and the shrieks and

bells accompanying their arrival were in sharp contrast to Mwita's usually quiet, self-effacing demeanor. He sang his invitation poem, eliciting
trills and exclamations of approval from his uncle's family, who appreciated the wording of his poem as well as the splendor of his attire. In a
staccato rhythm, his voice rising and falling, he recited:*

> *Come out and escort me to the circumciser*
> *So that he can circumcise me*
> *And make me man enough*
> *To fit among warriors, and earn respect*
> *So that I am not despised like I am an orphan.*
> *I respect you a lot*
> *Because your presence is domineering*
> *Like the impact created by the 1998 Nairobi bomb blast*
> *That scared Kenyan president Moi and Tanzania's Mkapa*
> *Because it caused heavy destruction*
> *Including flattening multistory buildings.*
>
> *Our warriors,*
> *I equate your bravery to that of Zacchaeus*
> *Who designs missiles that are fearsome and destructive,*
> *Even frightening [president] Moi and Mkapa.*

Some youths compose the poems they recite personally, though
relying on formulas from the past; others repeat the poems they have
been taught by their relatives. Occasionally, the poems include very
contemporary concepts; for example, "My mother is a missile." Some
make reference to current events like the poem above, referring to the
bombing of the American embassies in Nairobi and Dar es Salaam on
August 7, 1998. The tone of hyperbole, bravado, and braggadocio the
poems take is meant to exalt the power and bravery of the candidate
and the people he is descended from.

Upon delivering the messages, Mwita John and his friend ran off
amidst jangling bells and intimidating and fearless shouts.

The Business of Escorting

Before dawn the next morning, Mwita John's aunt (his father's
brother's wife) Nyagonchera Mwita and I set off to greet him when

he exited the site of his operation. Because we could not know where the operation would take place even the evening before, rumor was all-important in determining which direction to go. The Abairege believe that a set operation spot would prove to be too easy a target for witchcraft and other mischief to find and harm the initiates.[5] So people say to each other, "Today the omosaari will be at Gwitembe," or one place or another, and those who have candidates start in that direction when they leave their homestead.

On this particular day, since we were going to greet boys who had been operated on (women are not allowed to witness the cutting of boys), we were confused from the beginning. Where had they gone? We set off towards the north, the rumor being that the omosaari was in Kenyamangari, a Kuria squatter settlement in the adjoining Rift Valley Province, where his second wife lived. Along the way we met with a number of groups of greeters, all trying to meet their abasaamba and escort them home. Everyone was traveling in that direction on the authority of roadside gossip. We moved at a semi-trot, our pace intensifying as the sun rose. We met one group of abasaamba and several groups of greeters. We had covered about 4 kilometers when we ran into the omosaari on the road. He looked like a pleasant, elderly man, someone's grandfather, with an unmistakable air of authority. Clearly no more circumcisions would take place in Kenyamangari, so we reversed direction. We heard that the other place boys were being circumcised was at the Tanzania border, in the opposite direction from where we were going.

As we turned around and trotted back, we learned that Nyagonchera Mwita's eldest brother's two sons had been circumcised in Kenyamangari and were now walking home on a path parallel to one we had taken. For a married woman, primary allegiance rests with the family into which she is married, so in a situation of competing loyalties, her husband's kin take precedence over her natal family. Following allegiances, we continued south. Once we were almost all the way back to where we had started, we again caught sight of the omosaari—this time on the back of a motorcycle being driven in the direction of Tanzania. So we followed the motorcycle's track. We trotted through the lowlands along the international border, the swampy ground covered in tough thatch grass that cuts shins and feet. From an overlook we saw nobody in the whole expanse except crested cranes quietly feeding from the wetland. Going past some outlying homesteads, we were directed by kids to go further south. Feeling nervous about straying into Tanzania without carrying my passport, I was relieved when some minutes later we heard the sound of jubilation nearby. Nyagonchera's nephew was returning from his operation.

Though there were only two abasaamba coming in this direction, many people were escorting them amidst noisy celebration of the boys' accomplishments—dancing, singing, and praising the boys for their bravery in facing the knife—while using threatening gestures to ward off evil spirits and potential malevolence. For the actual cutting, the omosaari uses whatever tool each candidate provides. Understandably, each boy devotes quite a bit of attention beforehand to sharpening the short sword, knife, or machete to be used on him. The omosaari's assistant collected the payment of KShs. 210 each before the cutting began. The newly initiated abasaamba, sixteen and seventeen years of age, were both bleeding profusely, the fronts of their sheets streaked in fresh red blood. Despite the stop-and-go nature of the processions from the operation to the initiates' homes, the group was moving at a fast pace as the sun had fully risen and it was beginning to get quite hot, circumstances in which bleeding could increase. The friend was escorted home first, and then the entourage turned toward the homestead in which Mwita John lived.[6]

Reaching the homestead, the group became even louder and wilder, all the energy now focused on welcoming the boy home and keeping danger away by the level of noise. Women of the home, as well as female relatives helping out for the day, began ladling obosara out of buckets, passing the refreshing, cool drink to the escorts. At 10:00 a.m., Mwita John stood at the arched gateway (*ikihita*) waiting to enter the cattle enclosure (*oboori*). This most ritually and symbolically important entrance to the homestead, through which cattle pass when driven daily to pasture, is one through which esteemed visitors enter and all ritually significant transitions pass. As people loudly praised him, danced, and sang in a frenzy, Mwita John smiled at the people celebrating. He then ducked down and waddled through the gate and into the house in which his recovery process would begin. Not allowed to sleep on beds, initiates spend the period of seclusion sleeping either on hides or on mattresses on the ground. An extensive round of prohibitions accompanies the behavior of initiates throughout seclusion, and sleeping on the ground is one of the requirements of the period.

As Mwita John went on to rest after the morning's exertions, it was the turn of his fifteen-year-old sister, Grace Gaati, to set off with her escorts. That day girls were being operated on in the market center of the adjoining location, a two-hour walk in each direction. Some discussion ensued over whether it might not be wiser to have Grace Gaati cut at the mission, an innovation of that season and a major change to custom. Reaching the market, we met the entourage escorting Nyagonchera Mwita's brother's two daughters and the daughter of an elementary school headmistress. The three were coming down from the mission, along with a crowd of at least a hundred people dizzy with excitement, accompanied by several musicians playing ekegoogo, *iritiingo*, and ibiraandi, as well as by the omnipresent boom boxes. The girls, though just initiated minutes earlier, seemed okay, walking with surprisingly light steps, even moving to the rhythm of the music.[7] Some of the observers commented that the circumciser at the mission seemed not to be cutting much off. Meanwhile, Grace Gaati's escorts turned off from the market onto the unpaved road leading toward the southeast. She and her group of escorts did not return to the homestead until after dark. A grueling test for the young candidates, they walked about 20 kilometers, without eating all day, and since they returned so late, no feast was held at her father's homestead that night. Without electricity, the community is extremely dark when the moon is hidden or small, and people are loathe to be out in the evenings and at night.

The events of the day were recounted everywhere. This group, as well as others I had met earlier in the day, was full of news about the huge number of people seeking the traditional omosaari, with estimates of up to four hundred girls having been operated on that day.[8] The high demand and the crush of people led to fighting at the initiation ground as escorts jockeyed for position for their candidates, trying to ensure they would succeed in their quest to turn their *omosaagane* into an omosaamba, on her way to becoming an *umuiseke*. Apparently the escorts were fighting with the omosaari as well, verbally abusing her for being too slow. Impatient with her changing gloves between operations, they forced her to shed the gloves altogether, hastening the process. The occasion sounded more like a brawl than a joyous, transcendent, and transforming experience. A number of people commented that this kind of brawling atmosphere had not been there in the past, and had come about since the mid-1990s. Previously there were certain specific homes that were always used, ones that the *abagaaka binchama* (elders of the secret conclave) preferred. Candidates would line up in order of arrival, and would get operated on in that order. Only the candidate and his or her assistants would enter the cattle enclosure, while the rest of the escorts would wait outside. Then there was no disorder. As the circumciser proceeded, he would call candidates into the cattle enclosure in groups. Within each group, candidates would line up according to their generation class (*irikora*). But this time, such orderliness was impossible given the vast numbers of candidates coming at the same time due to the shortened initiation period. Instead, candidates were only arranged when more than one came from the same home, and then they were operated on in birth order (oldest first) and lined up to walk home in birth order as well.

Feasting on Circumcision Day

Palpable excitement stirred in the natal home of Nyagonchera Mwita. Her oldest brother, Smoky Joseph, had had four children operated on that day. We had missed escorting his two sons, who had been cut in Kenyamangari before dawn by Joshua Maskio, but had met up with his two daughters and their jubilant escort coming from their operations at the mission. All of Smoky's siblings were in the procession, and as we neared the homestead, Smoky himself came out dressed in a kanga (a wrap usually worn by women) and headdress of ostrich feathers, wielding a bullwhip of braided leather. He was accompanied by his mother, the grandmother of the initiates, brandishing a cooking spoon in her hand and blowing shrilly on a whistle in her mouth. On this big day for Smoky at least one child from each of his three wives, had taken the step to elevate their status.

The crowd drew up to the ikihita and everyone danced. The entrance to the cattle enclosure had two gates next to each other, signifying that there were already three generations of circumcised adults living in the homestead. Smoky's parents were still alive, so the third generation needed to have its own gate to enter through. What a big day it was for the girls, I thought. In the last hour, they had had their external genitalia cut off without anesthesia and had hiked home during an interminable procession of stop-and-go movement not unlike a museum shuffle, finally reaching the threshold of rest only to have the accompanying crowd insist that they dance. The crowd was jubilant, dancing and singing, loudly proclaiming the girls' bravery, the superiority of the lineage they come from, and what a credit they were to it. The women who had held their heads during their operations were collecting money from the crowd as individuals danced up and sang praises to their protégés.

Inside a hut, both the boys who had been circumcised earlier in the morning were asleep on the floor, lying on foam mattresses atop cattle hides. Their paternal uncle, who had served as their assistant, watched over them. They had bled profusely, and the younger had fainted upon reaching the cattle gate. A doctor had been called to help them.[9] They were resting, with a crisis apparently averted, at least for now. Subsequently, the younger boy's excessive bleeding and collapse were attributed to his grandmother Victoria Gaati having forgotten to give libation to the apical ancestor of their eeka. When the boy (who is named after this great-grandfather) reached the ikihita, he leaned on it and told his assistant he would collapse. Then his uncle caught him, and lowered him to the ground. I was told by one of Smoky's cousins (mother's brother's son) that another namesake of that eponymous ancestor from a different branch of the family experienced exactly the same thing after his circumcision.

Smoky Joseph's sons remained in their hut as the homestead filled with people. There were men carrying their drinking straws and women carrying flour, all waiting for the slaughtering to commence, the prelude to a good feast. The feast followed the traditional patterns of Kuria meat distribution. An ox, or two in the case of the very wealthy, is killed, then divided up according to the prescribed appropriate distribution, in which each part has a rightful recipient. For example, the flat muscle off the chest (*esagarami*) is divided into two: the right side for the boys who take the animals to graze (abariisia), and the left side for the initiated males (abamura). The tenderloin (*ichinsangiri*) is for the old men (abagaaka), and the meat of the top vertebra just before the head (*iguutwa*) is for the uninitiated girls (*abasaagane*). The inner organs, collectively known as *etoti*, along with the head, go to the homestead head. Whereas individuals can go home with cuts designated for them, other pieces are there for the entertainment of guests and for consumption there and then.

Some meat was put on the fire to roast, while other cuts were thrown into a large pot and put to boil. A dipping sauce of upper-intestinal juice (*amara*) was made for the roasted meat, and tied-off segments of upper intestines, contents included, put into the boiling pot to add flavor to the broth. As cooking finished, people sat separated by gender and circumcision set (*esaiga*).[10] The groups shared baskets or plates of *ubukima,* the staple food similar to polenta and made of combined millet, finger millet, and cassava flour or simply of maize. They pinched off hunks of the boiled cereal paste, dipped it into a shared bowl of meat sauce, and shared the meat.

After food, serious drinking began. The older men went into a mud-walled, grass-thatched hut with a large pot of beer buried in the center of the dirt floor. Made of fermenting maize to which hot water was periodically added, the brew bubbled and exuded a strong yeasty odor. Men sat around the *ekegaancha* on the low, four-legged stools (*ibituumbe,* singular *igituumbe*) that they had brought along with their drinking straws (flexible reeds up to 6 feet in length), arranged in order of seniority according to their circumcision sets. Most of the men remained in the hut until all the beer was drunk.

Circumcising the Abagimuri (1971)

As a female, I am not allowed to watch male circumcision. My knowledge of what happens on the circumcision ground is not based on participant observation, but rather on interviews. I sought out my friend Stephen Wambura to tell me about his experience. The following description is based on an interview with him, a close friend in his mid-forties, who is an educator, businessman, and the father of nine children, the oldest six of whom had already been initiated. His account is based on his own experience, as well as on the circumcisions of brothers, nephews, and the children of friends and relatives. He belongs to the Gimuri set, circumcised in 1971. It is noteworthy that generally, other abamura are the males most likely to go to the actual circumcision ground. The elders (abagaaka) and the junior elders (*abasaacha*) generally do not go to the actual circumcision. According to Stephen, the young initiated males (abamura) are in control. They are young, muscular, able to walk long distances and run. The older men might not be able to do that. They are the ones who welcome the young men when they return. So they wait at home. Once they learn that their candidate has been circumcised, they begin drinking.

Stephen Wambura's Story

The night before circumcision is a night of celebration.[11] Neighbors
and relatives gather to give the candidate courage. They don't allow
the boy to sleep, they dance, they make a lot of noise—chanting to
encourage the boy, to make him become bold and courageous. As
he gains confidence, the boy will go to the houses of his relatives,
inviting them to accompany him the next day when he will be
circumcised. If the omosaari lives far from the candidate's home, they
will start out before midnight. The candidate sets off along with a
crowd of people responsible for protecting him, clearing the way for
him so that he is safe from any attack. This is done with a great deal
of enthusiasm and noise. If the destination is far away, they will run,
trying to reach there early, by 5:00 or 6:00 a.m., as operations usually
begin soon after dawn. Other boys coming from different homes all
converge at the home where the operation will take place. The cutting
is done within the cattle enclosure (oboori), not outside.

Some elders interview the candidates to learn which is from
the oldest generation class (irikora). Umugamunyeri would be
first, followed by Omomaina, and so on. The circumciser's assistant
arranges the candidates by irikora as they arrive. Later arrivals are also
grouped by irikora. The boys stand in a line, shoulder to shoulder,
very close to each other, carrying their spears to show their boldness,
their determination to be circumcised and become young men. They
also carry swords, either stuck into their shields or held in their right
hands as they wait for the operation to begin. They recite poems of
initiation (obosaamba), praising their ancestors and other people with
outstanding characteristics, doers of outsized deeds, warriors; those
who have done great things. They praise not only the relatives but
also notables from outside the Kuria community.[12] Meanwhile, the
candidates wait. Because there are many armed people in the ekebaga
and everyone is vying for a better position in the crowd, the elders
(abagaaka binchaama) use medicine[13] to neutralize any bad thing that
could happen there and to ensure the circumciser and candidates
are not hurt by any weapons. The medicine also prevents fights from
taking place at the circumcision ground. In the past, a candidate
could only have one person accompany him into the oboori, and the
chaos that has now become part of the event was avoided.

When the omosaari arrives, he confirms that each of the boys
is actually prepared, which means that he has somebody to assist

him, he has money to pay the circumciser, and he has his own knife to be used on him. Though in the past the omosaari used one knife on everybody, this is no longer done because of the danger of HIV/AIDS. The boys stand side by side, so close that their shoulders are touching. They are dressed in warrior gear: ostrich feathers, Maasai headgear, bells tied around their legs. Those are an important part of the costume; when a boy runs, the jingling music gives him motivation. They make him feel proud, prepared, and warrior-like. The only clothing the candidates wear is a sheet.

As the omosaari reaches the candidate, the boy surrenders the sword he is holding in his right hand. The omosaari tests it for sharpness. He is carrying his own knife, which he can use if the sword is not sharp enough. He finds out if the omosaamba has an assistant, called *umuimiirri* ("the one who stands by you"). The umuimiirri is usually a relative, like a brother, paternal uncle, or a cousin (father's brother's son). He cannot be the father. The umuimiirri can also be a close friend, if there is no relative available. The omosaari also has an assistant who collects money from the candidate's assistant. Once the money has changed hands, the event can proceed.

The assistant twists the sheet to the back, so the boy is exposed. Then the circumciser looks at the boy standing in front of him to see if he is bold enough, and takes the sword from him. The boy remains standing. The omosaari grasps the sharp knife firmly with his right hand, holds the foreskin with the left, stretches it and cuts. That stretch gives him room to cut, so he does not cut the penis itself. With one cut he removes the outer layer, with the second cut the inner layer. That now leaves the boy free. The operation is finished, and the omosaari looks to the next person. Each operation takes roughly two or three minutes. The circumciser works without a stop between the boys in a line, a number that varies depending on the pressure exerted by demand.

Everyone is watching the candidate's deportment during the operation. He is supposed to be bold enough to gaze at a particular spot without winking or blinking, or allowing any expression to cross his face. If any expression of pain, surprise, fear, unease and so forth crosses his face, it is said that he has cried. Crying is an abomination. It is not allowed. If one cries, that person will be a laughingstock. So the boys have to gaze at a particular point and keep focused until they are told they can move by their assistants when the operation is over. Then they are taken aside, assisted to remove the bells, remove their shoes, and led to a spot where they can be seated. They squat, waiting to be told by the omosaari's assistant that they can leave . During this time, the entire oboori is filled with chanting and dancing and hollering by the people watching. The noise is to make sure the initiates don't get scared and to help them sublimate any shock into the collective buoyancy and strength.

At this time, the boy's assistant has much work to do. He has to assist the candidate in handling the penis carefully so that he does not bleed profusely. The assistant trains the initiate on how to handle himself, to manipulate the skin. A vein has been cut, and that is where the initiates are bleeding from. The assistant helps the initiate to hold the vein, using one hand, usually the left. And the right hand is used to hold the sheet (*shuka*) away from the wound. The main task of the assistant from the time the initiate is circumcised to the time they reach home is to make sure that he can sit without disturbing or destabilizing the penis.

Once a boy has been cut, someone trills so that those waiting outside the circumcision ground (usually female escorts) know their candidate is done. If those escorts don't recognize the trill, they learn he's been cut as he leaves the *ekebaga*. At that time a fast runner, usually the boy's brother or relative, races to the boy's natal home to alert kin that the circumcision has been done and that the candidate behaved bravely or cried.

On the walk home, many people come to greet the newly circumcised, to praise him, and to encourage him. They dance, making him feel great, making him realize he has done something very special, something to be proud of. That helps him ignore the pain as he walks home. Of course he cannot really completely ignore it, but seeing people dance, and knowing they are dancing because he has been bold and brave, makes him feel that he has undergone a great exercise and done it well. Had he cried, nobody would have come to praise him. They would have seen him a coward, not deserving to be given any money or praise. He would just be taken home quietly and nobody would bring an ekegoogo or iritiingo or any other instrument to play music for him. Abasaamba are supposed to be bold warriors ready to face the challenges of life. When they come out of seclusion, they should be ready to protect the community from whatever attacks their enemies may launch.

As the initiate walks home, people come up, praise him, and dance for joy in front of him, handing money to his assistant.

Previously, the abasaamba had several safety pins attached to their sheets and on their headgear, so people could pin money on the initiates. The pins, in theory, were meant to fasten that gap which remains after the sheet is tied, so that the boys remain decent. Despite the stop-and-go pace at which the walk home proceeds, returning home feels like it takes a much shorter time than going to the circumciser.[14] The dancing, charging, shouting, and howling of the entourage around the candidate serves as a distraction to the extent that sometimes the newly circumcised are even able to dance along with the escorts.

"Going to the circumcision, you are worrying about how you will do.... You don't have the experience, you don't know what will happen to you, if you will cry, you don't know if you will be bold enough to stare at one place until the circumciser has finished with you. But once you have done it, and shown people exactly what they can expect of you, then you look even bolder.... The pain is immediate. Afterwards you feel that there is something trickling from you. You know that it is blood, but you don't feel so much pain as when you are cut. That's the most painful thing."

On reaching the homestead, people dance at the cattle enclosure, just in front of the ritual entrance gate (ikihita). The candidate recites a poem to the vociferous approval of the entourage, then is welcomed into the boma and assisted through the narrow, low gate and into his mother's house. In the *eheero*, the visitor's room, a cowskin is placed on the ground. These days a mattress may have been placed on the skin. His assistant and close kin watch and wait until the initiate has stopped bleeding, and then allow him to cover himself with a blanket for warmth. After a while a meal is cooked for him. The family doesn't wait for the animal to be slaughtered to give the initiate some beef and ubukima. Then the initiate waits for a major meal to follow as the ritual shifts into the feasting stage with extended family and friends, some of whom escorted the boy to his operation. The initiate often eats the major meal in his new hut, which is significant because it marks the start of his separation from the mother. The initiate is now on his way to becoming an umumura, an adult. He is on the pathway to becoming independent. For that first big meal, the assistant and relatives will assist him to his own hut. There the boy is expected to sleep on the floor for five days—the same number of days his mother got to rest when she gave birth to him.[15]

Ritual Cycle as Identity Marker

Kuria ritual is closely tied with social life and with the central values of the culture. Their self-identification as performers of ritual (abakora nyangi) is a key element to their identity as a people, establishing their ethnic separateness from their neighbors, as well as a basis of belonging within community and society. Both rites of circumstance and rites of passage are performed as individual and communal rites. Rites of circumstance, sometimes called rites of affliction (Turner 1967, 9), are performed on occasions of misfortune, illness, or untoward happenings, and are intended to assuage, appease, restore, or cleanse. Their general purpose is to right what was wrong, to render propitious what was unpropitious (Ruel 1965, 298). Rites of circumstance may have been performed during the witchcraft-induced hiatus in the early part of that season, and these might include blessings, sacrifice, cleansing, and restoring. Though I did not witness any, several people mentioned that steps were being taken to remedy some of the problems signaled within the rumors, for example, the amakora issues. In Kuria areas, rites of circumstance are performed in the secret sacred place of the ikiaro by the abagaaka binchaama.

The emphasis in Kuria ritual lies on rites of passage: a sequence of ceremonies that mark an individual's progress through life in establishing a family and founding a descent line. Initiation (esaaro) is the first, and today, the most important of these ceremonies, making accessible adult status and the right to bear or beget a child. Fifty years ago and more, initiation was followed by the complex of marriage ceremonies, by the first pregnancy rite, and finally, after many years when a man's family was fully established (usually when he and his wife were grandparents), by the rite of ritual elderhood (*isubo*). These individual rites had their counterpart in communal rites of passage performed for each generation class (irikora) within the clan. The two most important transition points were the time when the men of a generation class set up their own homesteads and, later, when they made way for their sons. Because celebrations are expensive, and because there are other criteria for establishing identity and status (including educational and occupational attainment, wealth, and prestige), few people undergo the full cycle in contemporary society. Other considerations, such as religious affiliation, put pressure on individuals to forsake practices that may be frowned upon due to their pagan association deriving from pre-Christian society. For example, through the isubo ceremony, elders are said to gain powers of witchcraft, which is one of the reasons they are feared and treated with a great deal of respect. But this is not an attribute that is desirable for Christian seniors, and most do not ever seek to attain the ultimate status within society.

In the 1950s, Kuria individual rites of passage were seen to have three notable features (Ruel 1965, 299–300):

1.) They concerned men and women equally in that the two sexes either shared in the same ceremony or parallel ceremonies were performed for them;

2.) Each of the ceremonies was associated with a transition in age and its linked kinship status: childhood to adulthood (with its implications of marriage and begetting children), marriage and incipient parenthood, and finally the achievement of full elderhood or family headship; and

3.) Rites of passage involved and reflected on the status of other lineal and collateral kin, even though they had primary reference to one person or a married couple.

The due sequence of ceremonies was strictly maintained on the individual, family, and community level. Thus ceremonies were performed according to seniority within the father-centered family, first by seniority of houses (the mother-centered units within the homestead), and second by seniority within each mother-centered family. The theme of strengthening or continuity was highlighted through the performance of ceremonies by a child of the same sex as the candidate, who accompanied the main protagonist and carried out the same formal actions as the older participant. The child supported the person for whom the ritual was performed and connected generations as a younger follower. The child is a ritual supporter (*omooramia*). The values of due order and sequence were central to Kuria ritual in the past, and continue to be in the present. The aspect of continuity embodied in the participation of omooramia in ritual events persists, and today ritual supporters accompany initiates through the various steps of the initiation ceremonies.

The most important value and the assumed aim of every person in Kuria society is to establish a family and to leave descendants. The ideal of ordered growth mentioned above is implicit in both Kuria supernatural concepts and in their ritual practices. Straightness (*oboronge*) is the quality preeminently sought through the performance of rites of passage, and is epitomized in the ordered growth of a child to social maturity and an ordered progression through the ritual cycle. As Ruel observes, "The fabric of kinship relations is woven and its strands held in place perhaps more directly by the sequence of rites of passage than by the physiological fact of procreation itself" (1965, 300). Establishing a family is done gradually and in phases. The term adult (*omonto omokoro*) or a socially mature person is used relatively to describe the reaching or achievement of any of a number of phases of development: puberty, initiation, marriage, parenthood, and finally, elderhood (302). The ritual cycle applies to individuals and families and serves to animate the very core of the social and cultural order of Kuria people.

While the initiation rituals were held in abeyance by the plethora of witchcraft activity described in chapter 1, rumors and accusations made clear the importance of descent and territory as elements in marking ethnic as well as clan identity of Kuria people. Whether as a result of successful rituals of propitiation by the elders of the secret conclave, or the growing power of a new rising class of elders, initiation season was reinstated following the national Jamhuri holiday and the circumcision of boys began.

In this chapter, I have examined the lifelong cycle of rituals to which circumcision marks the entry. The initiates become "performers of ritual," embracing the core values of Kuria culture, including the principle of orderly growth through a series of named social stages corresponding to gender and age. Circumcision thus serves as a key element of marking an individual's identity as a member of a lineage, a community, and Kuria society. It also establishes the individual's duties and privileges within the social group, including the acceptance of the values of the kinship system, one's placement within the descent structure of lineages, and the basic quality of the relationship one has with other members of the social group, especially with regard to differences of gender and age. These will be taken up in the next chapter, as will be a broader academic discussion of parallels and differences between male and female genital cutting. The main thrust of chapter 3 is to extend the argument that cultural practices are not merely prescriptive, but negotiated.

Male initiates beginning walk home from circumcision ground

Males walking back from circumcision

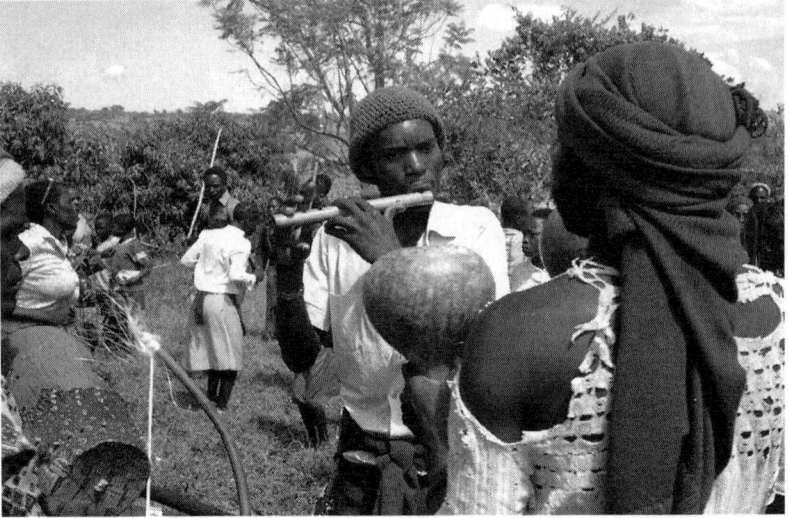

Musicians in front of homestead: flute, *ibirandi, ekegoogo*

Omosaamba pausing at cattle gate amid revelers

Returning to an initiate's home

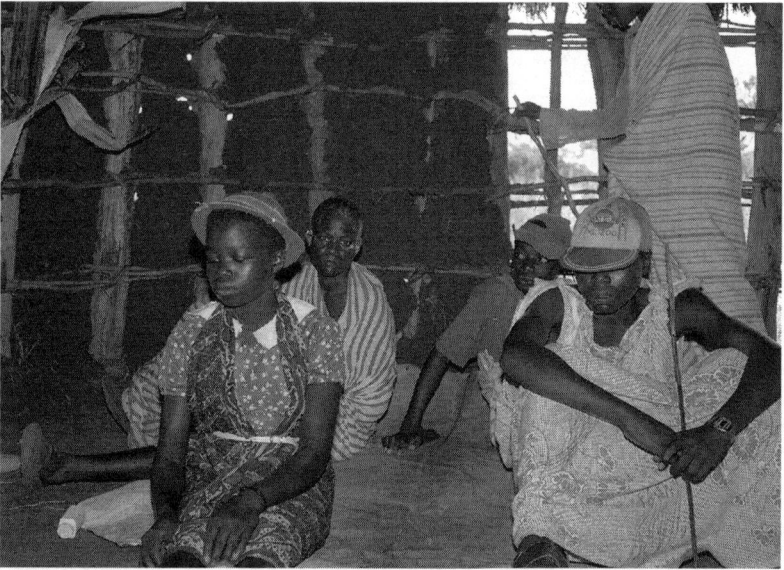

Male initiate (left rear) resting upon return home, guarded by the other
abasaamba

Homestead flying flags of initiation

3

Girls Follow

In late afternoon, a two-hour hike brought me to Chacha Jonas's homestead at the boundary between Bwirege and Nyabasi clans, nestled just below the apex of the ridge that points finger-like north into Maasai territory. A small river makes its course in the valley below, officially marking the boundary between the two clans. Colobus monkeys leap from tree to tree along the river, and homesteads dot the ridge. The valley and adjoining ridges often serve as the deadly battleground for interclan rivalries fought with spears, bows, and poisoned arrows. Rows of evergreen hedges or sisal plants clearly demarcate boundaries between homesteads, forming long lines from high on the ridge down to the river below. In Kuria topography, landholdings are vertically oriented from the river below to the ridge above. When fathers subdivide holdings, they preserve access to the river for each son to water his cattle and to supply the water needs of his family's homestead(s).

The age and status of family members determine their specific share in the subdivision of land and placement in homestead layout, imprinting the significance of age-based hierarchies onto the routines of daily life. A homestead is a manifestation of social order, of the relationships between its members, and between the homestead and other homesteads.

Chacha Jonas's cluster of homestead buildings sits well up on the ridge to the right of his younger brother Zachariah Magaiwa's cluster of buildings. Contrary to custom, the third brother's home is lower on the slope. Chacha Jonas's father was an only child, so his land is larger than the holdings of most of his peers. But he was a polygamist, with four sons by his first wife and one son by the second. For the first wife's sons, there isn't adequate frontage to divide up the ridgetop into sufficiently sized plots. Each son will only inherit one and a half acres of land. So the two oldest brothers have built their homes out of permanent materials closest to the top of the ridge, while the third son has placed his semipermanent home partway down the slope. The fourth brother is young, unmarried, and lives in a hut in the circle of traditional wattle-and-daub structures that are his mother's family home (*inyumba*) where her young daughters also live.[1] Making and firing enough bricks to build two permanent houses has left the very top of the property gouged out where the soil was removed, and thus far neither brother has made any move to reclaim it.

While in the United States, I had received an invitation to attend the celebrations of the initiation of Chacha Jonas's firstborn daughter, relayed by his brother Zachariah, my former research assistant. Chacha Jonas is an Umunginobo (circumcised in 1974) and during this initiation season he was ready to join his age-mates in moving up the status hierarchy of the community. His firstborn son had died in infancy, so Chacha had fallen slightly behind in his progression through the age-based hierarchy. An educated man, an ex-teacher, and an elected public official in his early forties, he is keenly interested in Kuria traditions and in preserving customary social values and institutions, including the importance of a large family. Some days before the planned event was to take place, he sent out invitations to lineage members living some distance away. Written on small scraps torn from a school exercise book, the message received by my former assistant read:

"TO [Zachariah Magaiwa]

YOU ARE REQUESTED TO ATTEND THE CIRCUM-
CISION CEREMONY OF MY CHILD ON 12/18/98. AT-
TEND WITHOUT FAILURE.

YOUR BROTHER [Chacha Jonas]."[2]

Invited relatives and visitors come on the eve of the initiation day to *okorea obosamba*, to sing praises for the girl, to encourage her to be brave. These are the escorts who will take the girl to the genital cutting on the next morning.

When I arrived, all the women in the homestead were busy with the many tasks necessary to welcome and feed a large gathering of visitors. The initiate's paternal grandmother was working in her kitchen, grinding finger millet for obosara, using traditional grinding stones (*ensoa* and *orogena*). She mixed in bits of dried sweet potato with the sprouted grain to sweeten the flavor. Girls of all ages made trips back and forth to the river, bringing water on their heads in a continuous supply. The candidate's paternal great-grandmother (father's father's mother) entertained early-arriving visitors in her house, serving refreshments and keeping an eye on the youngest children. A young daughter-in-law of the homestead, the candidate's aunt by marriage (father's brother's wife), was sweeping out her house. Young men busily cut down a hedge between some of the houses to facilitate movement and enlarge the space available for the gathering. Other young men rounded up chairs and stools. Despite the hubbub of activities, the homestead was peaceful and the yellow flags of circumcision flew at three points above the thatch roofs, communicating that the initiation celebration would take place there the next day.

Chacha Jonas's younger brother arrived with his family from their temporary home in the market at about 8:00 p.m. and the event began in earnest. First on the agenda was the slaughtering of the goat for the evening's feasting. Chacha's two younger brothers slaughtered and butchered the animal, a job that took them some hours. While the elders (abagaaka) sat around witnessing the activity, giving advice, gossiping, and drinking, young people danced in the cattle enclosure to the music of a boom box (iritiingo). Women cooked ubukima for the meal and prepared obosara for next day's visitors.

At midnight, the roasted goat meat was ready, tantalizing appetites as the aroma spread around the homestead. All ate with gusto. Cauldrons of goat soup were also cooking, and women were serving everyone steaming portions of ubukima. Following custom, men and women ate separately. Men generally eat where the meat was slaughtered, whether in the cattle enclosure or a room inside the house. Women and children take meals in the kitchens. After eating, at about 2:30 a.m., the singing and dancing began in earnest, taken over from the youngsters by mature women. Singing outside in the darkness, they loudly and insistently enjoined the candidate to be brave and to be a credit to the people who raised her and to the larger lineage. The singing and dancing continued until about 4:00 a.m. Some of the elders went to sleep, while some women just continued with the preparations for the day. In the early morning light, they cooked breakfast porridge for their children, and heated water for bathing.

Eventually, everyone and everything was ready and we left at about 8:30 a.m. to take fifteen-year-old Mary Robi to the circumcision ground, which was rumored that morning to be at Nyahea. An entourage of more than fifty people set off at a considerable clip, hoping to make fast time of the 4 to 5 kilometers between the homestead and the circumcision ground. We started on a wide unpaved road, but soon turned on to shortcuts on small paths, wide enough for only one walker comfortably. It wasn't much longer before we began to encounter multiple groups of candidates and their escorts, rushing along, pushing to get ahead. By the time the path opened up onto the unpaved main road in the southern end of the location, we were part of a huge throng of over a thousand people rushing in the same direction.

The crowd pulsed with singing, dancing, shrieking, and whistling; people pushed and shoved in an aggressive, though not untypical, manner. A woman fell, and was lucky not to get trampled. I worked my way to the edge, walking on the elevated shoulder of the roadway, which gave me a panoramic view of the collective race as the road swung downhill toward the river. Just before reaching it, everyone funneled onto a meadow just across the river from the chief's compound. The girls to be initiated stood shoulder to shoulder in a line, assistants and spectators in front and behind. Young warriors, dressed up for the occasion, were prancing around the candidates, pushing spectators, apparently vying to get the girls they were accompanying into optimal position in line for genital cutting. They pushed, yelled, and threatened the women. At one point they pushed the spectators into a barrier of Mauritius thorn.[3] Some old women (*abakungu*) fell into it, and others went scrambling, trying to save themselves from the thorns and escape the young men's threatening whips. In the crush of people, only those holding the candidates would be able to witness the actual cutting.

But as it turned out, the circumciser was not there. That morning her sons were being circumcised, so she had stayed home to greet them when they returned. Everyone knew that, but they also knew she would come and operate on the girls, and they each wanted to be in an optimal position for that. After about a half hour of pushing and shoving, the word went around that this was the wrong place, that the circumciser would perform operations in a large meadow up the hill. This led to a stampede along the narrow path. The crowd grew and grew, and though people were saying that the omosaari was there, I saw no indication of any of that kind of activity. People around me made all sorts of comments about my presence, some amusing, some bemused, some threatening. Since few suspected I could understand them, I listened to their speculations as to why I was there. Some wondered if I, too, had had my genitals cut and whether in the spirit of the day they might include me in the group of candidates. An educated woman, speaking in English, attached herself to me and urged me to move back, to get out of the crowd. She was also made uneasy by the comments. So even before I had the chance to witness any activity, I was forced to retreat from the circumcision ground. I was clearly not going to be able to see anything from where I was, and having witnessed the actual operation on previous occasions, didn't see my presence there as essential to my work. I retreated to a compound nearby, and saw Mary Robi's paternal uncle (my former assistant Zachariah Magaiwa) already seated there, having escaped the crush of the operating ground. So I joined him.

It was well over an hour before the first operations took place and the newly created initiates (abasaamba) and their escorts began to pour out of the bottlenecked meadow. First, the warriors in the group came running out, trilling and threatening with their weapons. They are the emissaries who carry the word back to the homestead that the girl is now an omosaamba; that the operation has been completed. They shout the news to anyone they pass, all the way back to the homestead. They also make deep, throaty sounds, almost sighs, their swords held high in front of them. After they deliver the message, they return to the omosaamba's entourage, to protect her as she walks home.

The plethora of escorts' costumes and body decorations added to the carnivalesque atmosphere. Many coated their bodies in different clays and ochers. Many men wore women's clothes. Music was blaring in all directions—radios and boom boxes, and also musicians playing ekegoogo, ibiraandi, and iritiingo. Youths were banging sticks on iron sheeting, drumming pieces of metal on soda bottles, and blowing on *irirongoe*, an instrument resembling a plunger, with the deep timbre of a ship's horn. A couple of men were strumming guitars. Many people wore bells of all sizes tied around their calves, jingling and jangling. A cacophony of sounds, punctuated by singing and praise, proclaimed the bravery of individuals. While Zachariah and I sat there, we saw over a hundred initiates emerge from the circumcision ground, get their faces powdered, and set off for home. The pace of movement was dictated by the frequency of groups emerging, and thus when Mary Robi and her escorts came out we immediately set off up the hill on the return journey.

The white powder sprinkled on the initiates' faces serves as a mask, hiding expression, making it difficult to discern their feelings, and disguising them in defense of any bad spirits. Because of all the stopping, greeting, dancing, and praising, the return home is much slower than the journey there. Progress is most uneven, with periods of standing still punctuated by short, running bursts on the part of the entire entourage. The girls were keeping up well, even though by now it was hot midday. Spirits were running high, the crowd giddy with elation. Breaking with customary practice, the initiates were given obosara to drink along the way during the long and very hot walk.

While walking, the group repeated a variety of chants, "Hae, hae, hae," or "Brr, brr, brr," and "Dhuk, dhuk, dhuk." Male relatives repeatedly charged ahead, then doubled back to dance in the face of the abasaamba, temporarily halting their progress. Some were wielding clubs (rungu) with large lug nuts on the tips. Women were slashing the air with switches with only a tuft of leaves left at the end of a stripped branch.

Upon arriving at the homestead, Mary Robi was received with great joy by those left behind, including the lame great-grandmother, the small kids, and her parents. Parents do not accompany their own children to initiation; this is an occasion where the primacy of lineage and kinship relationships reigns over the nuclear family group. She danced in front of the gate along with the crowd. Despite the elation of the moment, she looked to be in pain. At the cattle gate she recited a poem, and then entered the enclosure. Pictures were taken during a brief pause, then she climbed into her mother's house and lay down to rest on a skin stretched on the floor. Her aunt by marriage (father's brother's wife) had held her head, and along the way had collected quite a bit of money. Customarily, greeters pin money onto the cloth or hat worn by the abasaamba as they make their way home from the operation. This year the elders' conclave (abagaaka binchaama) had forbidden that practice, and cash was handed instead to the initiate's assistant, who also paid the KShs. 151 fee to the circumciser's assistant.[4]

As Mary Robi rested, the festivities carried on. An ox was brought to be slaughtered, but the man supposed to kill and butcher it did not turn up. He was needed at a celebration at his home as well. The process of slaughtering and sharing became confused, with many of the men present contesting the shares being given to them and to others. Ultimately, apparently having resolved to get what they felt they were entitled to no matter what, they cut into the carcass to grab pieces for themselves. Men roasted some of the meat as the women began to boil some. The feasting went on for hours, as did the drinking of beer and liquor.

Growing Up to Initiation

In Kuria communities, a child begins to hear about initiation from the time he or she is five or six years old. Always presented as something to be aspired to—an event that holds the promise of a significant improvement in status—initiation also carries the threat of shame that could fall on the individual, the family, and the lineage were the candidate to cry. Language carries some of the subtleties. The terms for a child, *umuriisia* (male) and omosaagane (female), carry the implication of being young, but also of belonging only to the immediate family, not to the lineage or any larger social or political unit. An umuriisia or omosaagane who dies is not buried, but rather thrown away.[5] The outcome of initiation—becoming umumura or umuiseke upon coming out of seclusion—elevates the individual onto the path to becoming an ancestor, someone whom newborn children may be named after when he or she dies, and thereby "living forever" as his or her name is kept alive. In particular, omosaagane is seen as a term of abuse, designating a completely powerless person. To be called omosaagane is to have this lack of a positive status pointed out, made public. Women say that when a child is called omosaagane, she feels bad. But after she is circumcised, if any uncircumcised girl abuses her, she will simply beat her in response.

The specifics of what is entailed in the initiation process are not usually discussed, especially not the operation. Adults believe that the less aware an initiate is of the procedure, the less likely he or she will build up fear that might lead to "crying" at the event. So for most young people, what will happen and the implications of the operation on future health and well-being are topics generally avoided within family. As it is quite unlikely that young people will see the genitalia of older members of the family, particularly those of their parents, the physical change entailed in genital operations remains a mystery. Children stand in a relationship of respect to their parents, and thus are not free to joke with them or to discuss any matters of sexuality or familiarity on a physical level. Though they stand in a joking relationship with their grandparents, the forums that allow for their exposure to each other's nudity are very scarce in today's society, since bathing in rivers and other public places has become rare. Adults are much more likely to have water brought to the homestead and placed in a bathing room than to bathe at the river. When older men or women bathe in a river, they post child lookouts who deflect anyone going in the direction of the river.

Young people learn that initiation is an essential rite of passage because it opens up the possibility for marriage. In Kuria society marriage is universal, despite potential variables like physical and mental handicaps, age, or even financial status. Strong sanctions exist to ensure that young men gain adequate cattle to pay the bridewealth. And where that does not happen, alternative mechanisms such as elopement exist to ensure that everyone is married. Polygyny puts a premium on girls, and most uneducated girls are married in their teens. Even educated girls are married in their early twenties, and often a feasible alternative for a girl is to marry on completion of secondary school, to bear one or two children, and then continue on to teacher training college (if she is accepted). Though I know a few women who were married in their thirties, they did not reveal their true age, convincing their in-laws that they were as much as a decade younger than their actual age. Because childbearing continues to be the central purpose of marriage, families desire daughters-in-law with a maximal span of reproductive years ahead of them.

Kuria regard circumcision as a culturally distinct practice, and thus it is synonymous with being Kuria. In this way, it is not unlike the circumcision carried out on the eighth day after the birth of a Jewish male baby. The operation ensures membership in the sociopolitical unit and the right to reside in the territory and to enjoy the benefits and responsibilities of Kuria ethnic identity. This is particularly important for girls, since they do not hold a fixed place in the agnatic descent system, and remain peripheral in both their natal lineage and that of their husband. Genital cutting distinguishes Kuria from their Luo neighbors, who do not circumcise at all, and Maasai, who circumcise both males and females but following different, culturally specific rituals and timing. In the past, women married in other parts of Kenya were circumcised when they came to live in Bukuria or at the birth of their first child, practices which are no longer carried out.

Young people keenly watch for the signs that indicate they are ready for initiation. The increasing maturity of the body is a primary criterion. For girls, the growth of breasts and body hair and the onset of menstruation are key signs. For boys, the changing of the voice and the growth of body hair are similarly marked. Youth and parents alike watch for these signs and young people usually insist that they, not their parents, decide when to get initiated when they feel their physical changes have progressed enough. The process is clearly mutual, since the parents are constantly reminding the children of the greater eminence, responsibility, and respect they will enjoy after they undergo genital cutting, thereby whetting the children's appetite to join the initiated. Not all the bantering stresses the positives. Derision and scorn are heaped on the uninitiated, both Kuria and non-Kuria: they are seen as immature, dirty, undisciplined, irresponsible, unmarriageable—in short, not fully socialized. And clearly, no young child wants to remain like that!

When the physical changes have taken place, the elders believe it is time to initiate the youth. The feared specter is a girl who becomes pregnant before being initiated. Though nobody can actually recall this having taken place, the punishment for such a transgression is for the girl to be thrown out of her clan, to be banished from the ikiaro into which she is born and within which she expects to live the rest of her life. So the adults watch the way a girl's body is maturing, the way she walks, and the attention she gets from boys and men.

Because a candidate cannot return home without having been operated on, a transgression of any taboos has to be rectified before or during the operation. In the case of a known sexually active girl, the circumciser would stop and tell the girl's escorts that the child is spoiled. While the circumciser operated on others, somebody would run and tell the girl's father that the operator had skipped his daughter. The messenger would then be given a goat to take back to the operation site to give to the circumciser. After accepting the fine, the circumciser would operate on the candidate. Throughout the ritual process, a tension exists between the norms, or the understanding of what is normative, and the actual behavior or sequencing, which is dependent on the exigencies of life.[6] So for example, the norm that is articulated is that children are not supposed to be sexually active before they are circumcised. But if they are, there is a mechanism to compensate for that. Another example is the norm for hosting a consolation feast for an initiate that calls on the mother's brother to be a sponsor, but allows others to host the feast if the mother doesn't have a brother or one in a position to do it. Whoever hosts the feast will be given cattle from the bridewealth paid on the girl's marriage.

The timing of initiation also depends on factors other than physical maturation because an orderly progression through the ritual cycle reinforces cultural norms at other levels. For example, the initiation of a firstborn promotes his or her parents' progression through the age-based hierarchy, from being young married people (*omosaacha* and *omokari*) to elders (*omogaaka* and umukungu), which in turn creates pressure from parents for earlier initiation. In another example, boys usually depend on the bridewealth brought in by their sister's marriage for their own marriages, so pressure is especially strong on girl children to be initiated and married young. Additional pressure exists in poor families, which sometimes count on bridewealth generated by the marriage of their daughters to improve the family's economic well-being. Similarly, if a girl's father is looking to take a second wife, he might pressure a daughter to be married, and thereby gain the bridewealth for taking a second wife for himself.[7]

As initiation for girls marks a crucial transition from childhood to adulthood, the candidate is required to show courage during the operation. For girls, too, crying garners stigma, though it has a less lasting effect for them than for boys. Girls nonetheless aspire to make their families proud by showing courage and fortitude, to not even roll their eyeballs, startle, or faint when they are being cut. Like boys, girls are also taught the tricks of stoicism: staring into space, focusing on one spot, remaining immobile, expressionless, and behaving like a stone. Sanctions exist for girls who commit the most serious offense—touching the hand of the circumciser. Her family must pay a goat to make up for that. In such a case, the candidate is not allowed to leave the circumcision ground while a suitable animal is sought out and brought in payment. The bravery of the candidate is lauded in songs sung going to and coming from the circumcision ground. By the time the initiate is walking back, all the people along her path and in her home know how she behaved. Those who have cried go back home with minimum fanfare, having let their families down.

Kuria attest that the ancestors set the standards articulated and upheld throughout the communities during the initiation season. In the following interview, Pacifica Mokona takes us back to the time she underwent initiation in the early 1930s, offering a detailed account of the practices and expectations of her time.

Initiating the Abamingisi (1931)

Sitting in the shade of her thatch-grass roof, leaning against the rough daub of the outside wall, Pacifica spoke to me about initiation as we shelled the beans she grew amidst her maize.[8,9] A vocal, expressive, and articulate great-grandmother, she enjoyed speaking. Often, when our interviews were over, she would shout to her grandchildren, daughters-in-law, and grand daughters-in-law, inviting them to come listen to the recordings, much to their entertainment, often stirring up their amazement with tales of how things used to be. She had recovered from the swelling of her legs that had made her lame in the late 1980s, and her energy and enthusiasm for life were quite inspiring.

Pacifica Mokona's Story

When the Abamingisi were being circumcised and a girl was ready to be initiated, her parents prepared for the occasion by brewing beer and slaughtering an ox. The circumciser came from Tanzania to her father's home, so people were telling each other that the omosaari would go to Maroa Mwita's home to operate on his daughter on a particular date, so the girls to be initiated would go there. On the eve of the initiation obosara was cooked.

At 6:00 a.m. I woke up and went to the stream to bathe. Returning to the homestead, I entered the cattle enclosure through the gateway [ikihita], and stood inside it. Though I was wearing my regular clothing, my mother was dressed in *igisiiriiti*, a special outfit colored with red crushed stones [*etaago*] and decorated with very many beads. My father came and anointed me with oil kept in a cow's horn container. The oil resembled vegetable shortening used nowadays; it was quite solid. After anointing me, he anointed my mother and everybody present. I ate no food, but was given medicine to place under the tongue, a red seed called *ehete*, to prevent excessive bleeding. I kept it in my mouth throughout the operation.

I had matured physically and had already begun menstruating.[10] Consequently, special ritual steps had to be undertaken. A goat had been slaughtered before sunrise that morning, and after having been anointed with oil I was then anointed with chyme [*ubuhu*] from the goat before I could proceed to the operation. The goat was cooked to feed the escorts. The need to be brave was emphasized throughout the preparations. Prior to initiation, the candidates were told that even if they felt terrible pain during the operation, they should not say "Oh mother," or "Oh father," because if they did, the parent mentioned would die. This taboo was stressed.

Six girls arrived to be initiated at the homestead, but because seven is an unlucky number, one was asked to go elsewhere. The operation took place under a tree outside the home. The circumciser was my relative, a sister-in-law to my father. He had brought her to our home, paying her KShs. 5 for the service she performed on me. The other girls paid KShs.10 each. She used a different knife for candidates from each generation class [irikora], anointed the initiates' faces with flour made of finger millet [oboroe] that had been brought by a woman into the enclosure, and then the omosaari moved to a different operating ground.

In those days, after the cutting, a girl was given a small decorated gourd [ekeraandi] with a handle made of skin or a rope to hold. She put leaves of esaaraara and inyamunsi in it. Coming to the circumcision ground, a girl would also hold a stick from the ikirundu bush, while a boy would enter his circumcision ground holding a small bow. Five days after circumcision, boys were given big bows, along with a blunt type of arrow called ikuno. Four days after their operation girls were given a stick of a type of tree called egeseemi. On arriving home, both ikirundu and ekeraandi were taken away from the initiate and kept as she was led to the goats' room in her mother's house [eheero] where she was given her ritual first meal [ogokomboora] and expected to go to sleep. The gourd and the stick were put by her side.

The difference in timing—five days for boys and four for girls—reflects the general ideology that genders are unequal. In this context, the different length of time corresponds to the commonly held idea that boys' circumcision is a more arduous operation than female genital cutting, and thus boys need longer to recover.[11] The five/four difference also applies to the length of time a mother rests after giving birth: five days for a son, four days for a daughter. This basic gender asymmetry is regarded as natural and normal, and does not stand, in people's minds, as contradictory to the construction that esaaro is the same for boys and girls.

A gendered difference in delivery of songs and praise poems also exists. Males tend to perform solo, creating their own lyrics and stepping up to sing by themselves, presenting an individual voice to the assembled group. Females, on the other hand, tend to follow the call and response style of singing. An initiate intones the first line and that is repeated in unison by the assembled females. The caller usually has a strong and powerful voice, and knows the appropriate lyrics. In this form, each line is repeated, and often the repetition introduces an extra word or phrase that carries the original line's message one step further. Their expression through song is thus collective, rather than individual. We will see this again as we discuss singing performed during seclusion.[12]

The walk home would be filled with jubilation. People came up and greeted the column of initiates walking together, greeting individual members with songs of praise and admiration, lauding their accomplishment in being stoic, showing no fear or pain. For the initiation of a firstborn, musicians are often hired to accompany the procession, playing the ekegoogo and the ibiraandi. Customarily, family and escorts sang songs even if no musicians were accompanying the crowd. One such song follows:

I greeted the child but she didn't respond [x2]
My child, I greeted her but she didn't respond [x2]
I gave her 5 shillings [to entice her] *but she still didn't respond*
My child still didn't respond
I gave her 11 shillings [to entice her more] *but she still didn't respond*
My child still didn't respond
I put 30 shillings in her hands but she still didn't respond
My child still didn't respond
When I gave her 100 shillings she responded and shouted [x2]
My child responded and shouted
Lo! A child, I greeted but she didn't respond [x2]

This song, as well as many other practices of the initiation season, interrogates the norms of everyday life. Like carnival events in Europe, a number of mechanisms are invoked that transgress everyday norms; mechanisms that are meant to confuse evil spirits or to deflect negative energy from the vulnerable. These mechanisms include noise, cross-dressing, borrowing headgear styles from adjacent ethnic groups, masking, and painting faces and exposed skin in different colors. The basic rules of social intercourse are often violated, as this song shows. Young people are expected to greet anyone senior to them. To not initiate the exchange is a transgression of norms, and to not respond when greeted is an even greater one. The song alludes to the fact that the initiate has moved up the social ladder from a child to an adult. Unlike children, who may be easily enticed to do certain things, she cannot be easily influenced. She didn't respond until the stakes were high enough (from 5, 11, 30 to 100 shillings), when she finally shouted in bravado.

While the omosaamba rested, the celebrations went on in the homestead. The escorts were given obosara to drink. An ox was slaughtered in the cattle enclosure. People drank beer, cooked, and ate. Cuts of meat were distributed. If a young man had intentions to marry you, explained Pacifica, his friends would drive his cattle into your homestead after you had come back from the operation. The cattle were said to have come to console you. The boys bringing the cattle were fed and then went back to their homes, taking the cattle. The women of the suitor's home would reinforce the gesture by coming to make the fire in the eheero where the girl would sleep for the duration of seclusion. Though in actuality the woman who held a girl's head during the cutting lit the fire, the female kin of the suitor reinforced his interest by their gesture. After the seclusion period ended, the suitor and his kin would come in courtship. Sometimes, the girl would agree to be married to that home. At other times, the suitor and his escorts would have to go look for a bride elsewhere.

The fire was treated with great care. Whenever the omosaamba went out for a walk, a big piece of wood had to be put on to keep it burning. People in the home would repeatedly remind each other to check on it so that it would not go out, which was regarded as bad luck, and an omen that the initiate would never bear children. If the fire did go out, it was kept a secret, because if the truth were known nobody would come to marry that girl. This was also true if the ikirundu or ekeraandi broke. For boys, the small bow they had to keep for five days after circumcision carried a similar portent. If that broke, it was said that the boy would marry up to seven women and they would all die. Only the eighth would survive.

When other abasaamba came to comfort the new initiate, they stood by the entrance to the cattle enclosure and asked in a song whether she had cried, implying that if she had done so, they could walk away, pretending to be just passing by. The initiate would respond in a similar form, praising them and saying:

Eeh, come in, eeh he [x2]
Boys of our land come in, eeh [x2]
Eeh ehe, boys of our land come in, it has climbed
Eeh ehe, it has reached the peak, eeh ehe [x2]
It has climbed to the peak, eeh he [x2]
It has climbed to the peak, and reached maximum height [13]

Women from the homestead would cheer the visitors, trilling "aririri," and the abasaamba would enter. If the initiate or her family did not reply, the visitors would conclude that she had cried, and walk away. But prior to their departure, they sang songs teasing the home, saying that the daughter of this family had cried, that she would go to the forest and be killed by a leopard. Or, they sang that the homestead had fallen badly—it had fallen toward the cattle enclosure. The disgraced initiate would not dare go where other abasaamba were present, but those who had been brave came by the homestead and insulted the coward.

Many prohibitions and taboos shaped the period of seclusion. Walking was the only activity allowed and initiates wandered through the neighborhood in a group. Flour was applied to the faces of the initiates for several days, even as they began to leave their homesteads to go for walks, usually the day after being cut. They were not allowed to go far. Boys' faces were anointed for five days, girls' for four. If for some reason it wasn't done at home, it would be done in the next home they visited.

Working in the *shamba* [garden] or doing any other work was prohibited, including cooking, so mothers had to rush from wherever they were working to cook for the initiates. As a part of rambling around the neighborhood, the abasaamba went to different homes and were fed. Often, the feeding would be a special occasion, one where an initiate's maternal uncle came to console [*okohonia*] the initiate. Then they were served meat and other delicacies. The abasaamba were not allowed to bathe for the duration of seclusion; they could only rub themselves to scratch off dirt. For instance, they crushed boiled potatoes, mixed them with fat, and smeared the paste on their bodies. Later they rubbed off the paste and were cleansed. Because they were not allowed to carry anything on their heads, the abasaamba were exempted from carrying water.

The initiates would sleep on a skin placed in the sitting room [eheero] that opened up to the cattle corral in the house [*iriburu*] where they spent seclusion. Because candles were unknown in those years, they saw by firelight. The skin just stayed on the floor where it was; it was not taken out of the house. The same was true for the utensils the initiate used. The *ekehe* and *ekebakuri* remained inside the house. All the utensils were placed or hung in the iriburu. Nobody else could use them, and they were discarded at the end of seclusion. During that period, none of these items were supposed to be moved even into the adjoining bedroom [*irirungu*].

During the Abamingisi initiation, *orosohani* was one of the initiation ceremonies, but it is no longer practiced. As female initiates began to recover, initiated women [*abasubaati* and abakungu] gave them bead necklaces [*emesaanga*] to wear during the five or six months of seclusion and then they were returned to their original owners. For each one returned, the owner offered the gift of a dance. At the time of returning the necklaces, the young women would request carved staffs, to be made by their friends or any male asked to do this favor. Because initiates in seclusion were not allowed to bathe, they were filthy when they returned the necklaces. For orosohani, an initiate would ask someone to come and smear mud onto her body. The mud would be beaten and smoothed before smearing. The initiates folded their clothes upwards so they looked like underwear. The rest of the body remained bare. After they were covered with mud, they went home and scraped it off in the seclusion house as they weren't allowed to do it in public. They scraped off the mud flakes with the dull edge of a knife, then they recited poems.

Another celebration of the initiation season was a dance called *isiibi,* meant to recognize and praise the person who was circumcised first in the set. Initiates would invite others from as far away as Makararangwe, Itiirio, or Kebaroti, neighboring villages 5 or even 10 miles away. The abasaamba would dress up in tree branches and pieces of cloth cut out by knives, and dance, praising their circumcision set. At the dance, women watched as the boys dropped their *isungu* (batons) on the ground and danced together in a circle while the circumcised girls served them obosara they had brought and plucked leaves to wipe off the male initiates' sweat. When done dancing and about to leave, the boys picked up their batons. Singing would praise the *umuturiani*, the first boy operated on in the circumcision season.

Tradition indicates that this practice began with Mukwaya, who fathered Mosabi.[14] An elder of the inchaama had dreamed that if someone gave a bull to be castrated and it healed, it would be an indication that the initiation ceremony would be successful. They asked Mosabi to donate the bull. He gave one of his two, the one that was castrated and healed without problems. The inchaama thus decided to proceed with initiations. When the abasaamba were circumcised, they praised the ox and sang:

We want to know our white ox
Mukwaya's white ox
We want to know our umuturiani [x2]
It is Kerabu Mukwaya

During the colonial era, these dances drew the initial Western disapproval to initiation rituals. British administrators and missionaries regarded the dances as lascivious and a waste of energy and time. Especially missionaries saw the extended period of seclusion and its revelry as an element of "native" life that needed to be stamped out (Murray 1974, 101–3). Over the course of the century, the dances have disappeared, partly because most of the initiates are Christians and partly because the seclusion period has shrunk from six months to six weeks, corresponding to the school break. Further, to a large extent, the period of seclusion has lost its primary focus as a time of finding a marriage partner.

Constructing Tradition

People stress the traditional character of initiation and seldom talk about the elements that have changed in initiation ceremonies over time. No doubt this is at least partly because what is significant about initiations is the transitions they enable, the orderly movement of individuals and their families through the social structure and hierarchy of Kuria society. On that level, little has changed: "By encompassing the complex combination of communicative resources in a ritual event, shifts in some details can be subsumed within the continuity of general practice" (Kratz 1993, 55).

According to Kuria informants, circumcision is a tradition because it was done by the ancestors of people alive today. Performing the ritual is a quintessential part of being Kuria. Because genital cutting practices persist despite a century of attempts on the part of outsiders to bring them to an end, my primary focus is on continuity, though I do examine changes over time in subsequent chapters. I record the changes I have witnessed and those pointed out to me by knowledgeable Kuria observers. The important point is that this set of rituals is not unchanging and does not follow a primordial mold, even though people connect the acts of today with the practices of their ancestors. Instead, the rituals are a part of people's lives and are always responsive to the exigencies of everyday life and the various influences on the practice. Like Okiek Kratz (1993) describes, Kuria interpret and incorporate changing circumstances into their initiation practice (51). In the late 1990s, circumstances were changing in many aspects of Kenyan life. Those changes were grappled with in the activities and contexts of Kuria ritual process.

Most observers of initiation have a short-term horizon. Though overseen by Kuria elders, genital cutting is generally attended by people of recent circumcision sets, whose experiences are most likely to be replicated closely. The fascination and jubilation is carried out by those who have recently undergone initiation. Because parents do not go to the circumcision of their own children, the focus of activity for them is in the homestead. They receive their initiated child and her or his escorts when they return home, and entertain their kin throughout the initiation period as a way of negotiating the transition into their own new status within the family, lineage, and community.

Continuity implies neither uniformity nor rigidity, though Western notions of tradition sometimes conflate them. The continuity and tradition of Kuria initiation respond to and incorporate changing circumstances of personal, regional, and national life within ceremonial performances (similarly for the Okiek; see Kratz 1993, 61). Beginning in the next chapter, I trace some of the most important influences leading to change, and explore the variety of adaptations local practitioners have made in response to the criticism channeled through a number of sources as well as the funding intended to eradicate the initiation practices in Kuria society. In the current chapter, I present a number of stories of women's experiences at various points in the past century, with the intention of providing another lens onto changes and continuities in practice.

At the time I interviewed her, Klara Robi was nineteen years old. She had completed Form IV the previous year, and was currently staying at home with her widowed mother and six younger siblings, helping out in her mother's retail shop as well as at home.[15] At the time, I was also staying at her mother's home and Klara Robi became curious about my work and came to visit with me, to find out what I was doing. I explained the purpose of the interviews I was gathering on the subject of genital cutting, and she quite eagerly spoke of her own experience, when genital cutting was not locally controversial.

Klara Robi's Story

Klara Robi was eleven when she was operated on in 1992, joining the Abatamesongo set. The firstborn child of her mother, she felt pressure to make the transition from childhood to adulthood, and thus enable her mother to make the parallel shift towards the initial stages of elderhood. The third wife to her husband, Klara Robi's mother Mogore Maria was the only one of the co-wives without initiated children at that time. Leading up to the time of initiation, Klara Robi was aware of physical changes taking place in her body, especially the budding of her breasts and the appearance of underarm hair. She listened to her cousins making plans for their own initiations, and began thinking about it too. That she was only eleven years old didn't worry her because she held the common local belief that the younger the initiate is the less pain she feels from genital cutting. As excitement grew in the community about the upcoming initiation season, her mother came to her and told her that young people were talking about being circumcised, and that her cousins were planning to go.

Klara Robi's mother asked her what she thought about going for circumcision. In response, Klara Robi told her she would go, but that she feared she might cry. Her mother reassured her, telling her there is no need to fear, because there is no pain. Nowadays, she said, they don't chop all of it (the clitoris) the way they used to cut everything, they just remove a bit of it. Besides, the woman doing the operations was a good friend, and Klara Robi's mother would tell her not to remove all of it. A month later, Klara Robi took part in initiation.

Being a firstborn, she was setting an example for her younger siblings. Nobody explained to her what was going to happen, what exactly would be removed, or why. Klara Robi just imagined for herself. Nobody told her what the consequences of the removal would be, or how it would change her body. But she was not questioning the tradition. She knew the practice had been done before, that it would be done in the way the ancestors did it, and she was doing what every girl was expected to do. "In being circumcised, the youth are following the culture," she explained.

Though there was no forum in the community for discussing genital cutting, Klara Robi and some of her cohorts had the opportunity to discuss the pros and cons in a debate at school.[16] She learned there that removing "that part" prevents a woman from enjoying sexual activity. The discussion at school moved on to whether or not genital cutting makes childbirth easier or more difficult. The girls who had been operated on argued that at the time of childbirth a woman feels a lot of pain, but if she has been cut she will have an easy time giving birth, or, at least she already has practice enduring extreme pain from the genital cutting she underwent earlier. The girls who had been operated on also upheld the position that genital cutting makes a girl mature and allows her to join adulthood. In response, Luo students argued that once girls are operated on, they are not so bright. That is why the Luo students are always leading in everything. Kuria girls responded by asserting that by having their clitoris cut, they did not run the risk of it growing so long that it would tear their underwear.

Wanting to have some sense of what was to come, Klara Robi asked her cousin, who was also going to be a candidate, how the operation was done. The cousin showed her how people sit in order to be operated on, and told her where they use the razor blade. Klara Robi began to feel afraid, but was reassured, "That is normal, and there is a cure for that." As her cousin told her, the candidates are not supposed to sleep the night before their operation, because they might dream about it and cry in the morning. So Klara decided to be quiet and keep her thoughts private. A cousin came from another Bwirege community and reassured her that there was no pain, the cutting happened so quickly that the initiate didn't know what was happening. Klara Robi decided she would go the next morning.

Just before the day of Klara Robi's initiation ceremony, her
mother had to travel to Nairobi with a delegation to meet with the
president of the country. As an elected leader in the district, she had
to discharge that obligation. Klara Robi's grandmother and an aunt
were left to preside over the initiation activities. They prepared the
obosara, while cousins who lived nearby came that night to sing
obosamba. The youths did not sleep at all that night, instead singing
outside and teaching each other the songs they knew for giving the
candidate courage. So while mothers prepared obosara and young
children slept, the youth sang songs of initiation. Klara Robi's younger
brothers stayed up and danced the whole night. People ate but Klara
Robi didn't feel like it, thinking of what was going to happen.

The next morning Klara Robi went at 8:00 a.m., walking to a site
about 5 kilometers from her home. She was accompanied by her aunt,
grandmother, brothers, and cousins. Everyone was singing the same
obosamba as were sung the night before.

Ee ee hehe ee hee [x2]
The blade for the firstborn, be calm ee
When she holds you, let her stick you in
Ee he heye he ee ee hehe ee
Your fathers are wearing headdresses and are made up [x2]
He he made up he he made up he he ee
With shields he hehe he
Your kin are dancing, with shields [x2]
And warriors [abamura] *he he he he* [x2]
That they will run he he [x2]
If they are caught they will run he he he
If they are ambushed in Maasai they will run he he heye [x2]
I encourage you he ee he he [x2]
Fearless girl, I encourage you he ee he [x2]
I encourage you he he he
Nyamagera [circumciser] *he he ee he*
Take me to Nyamagera the woman he ee he ee [x2]
You look beautifully made up
Your kin are dressed beautifully he ee
They look beautiful he he ee ye

On reaching the place where the operations were being
performed that day, they were instructed to go to the latrine to

urinate. To do so inadvertently during the cutting is a transgression, the same as crying or flinching in reaction to the cut. They then stood in line, and waited while the earlier arrivals were operated on. There were eight girls. When they were cut, they stood up and left. Then the next eight were asked to sit down and were cut. Then they stood up and left. The initiates sit only while they are being operated on.

Klara Robi's paternal aunt acted as the *omogotamotoe*, or head holder, who sits with the initiate between her legs, holding her head to steady her as the initiate leans her head back and holding her hands to prevent her from touching the circumciser. The omogotamotoe directs her charge on how to sit. And though most girls sit that way willingly, some struggle. Some feel embarrassed or shy about sitting with their legs spread that way. "You find that some girls may have played sex before, some may be on their monthly periods, so it takes time for them to sit. Once they are found that they will not sit, they may be told to pay a cock, or a goat, for the girl to be circumcised." It is embarrassing for everyone, because there are many people in the audience, even young boys who have come with the women, elder men (abagaaka) whose task is to chase the boys away, and many, many women.

Five girls from Klara Robi's lineage were initiated with her, two aunts and three cousins. They sat down according to their generation class (irikora). Two aunts went first, then Klara Robi, then her cousins. As the group sat down, the omosaari began her work. Klara Robi's holder gave the circumciser a brand new razor blade. The circumciser came close and bent toward her. She held the razor blade in her right hand and Klara Robi's genitals with the left and made a single cut. Klara Robi didn't even feel it, she was tired and sleepy. The reaction from the escorts was immediate and loud, as they ululated and sang out, saying:

She has become like a stone [she didn't flinch], *hayi* [x2]
She has been circumcised like a man [bravely] [x2]

Individually, after the cutting, each girl brings her legs together and waits. When a group is circumcised, all stand up together. Moving in unison is necessary because people believe that if three stand up and two remain sitting, the pain the three feel transfers onto the two sitting. So the initiate and the woman who holds her head both have to be attentive to what is happening around them. When the initiates stand up, the women escorting them immediately cluster around them. The *abagotamotoe* collect all the blood and the excised part using the cloth that was spread for the initiate to sit on. The parts are put into a paper bag and later thrown into a latrine. A kanga is tied around the initiate's neck. The omogotamotoe sprinkles powder onto her face, and the walk home begins. The men are informed whether the initiate has cried or not and runners are sent to bring back the news to the compound.

Klara Robi remembered that she noticed all the things going on; she was not solely focused on the cut. She didn't feel like crying. She felt something normal had happened. At the circumcision ground, she didn't feel any pain. "I never felt anything. I felt among the best girls that year. In fact, the circumciser returned the money I paid her. She gave it to the woman who held my head. I don't know why exactly, but she said it was because I never feared."

She walked back with the same five people with whom she was operated on, and they walked in the same order as they were cut. The first to be cut was the first to be dropped off, so her aunts were dropped off first. Then Klara Robi and the escorts went with her cousins. On the walk back, they were greeted all along the way by happy people, jumping and praising the initiates. Men and women rushed up to dance next to individual initiates, to pin money on their hats, and praise them. Every time they stopped the initiates felt proud, because now they were adults. Klara Robi didn't even think about how long the walk was taking; it felt fast, as there was nothing to fear now. And all the way home she felt no pain.

Upon reaching home, the escorts brought her to the cattle gate. Klara Robi stopped there. Because Klara Robi's father had died some years prior to her initiation and her mother was out of town, the omogotamotoe welcomed her into the house saying "*tasoha inyumba*" (welcome to the house). She went in, with the omogotamotoe holding her up. Before going into the home, she would have recited a poem to honor her parents, had they been there to receive her. Here is an example she shared with me:

Aee ee I am going through it [the cattle enclosure] *aee*
The homestead of the father that I am going through should
overflow with milk [be abundantly blessed]
Aee ee, and oil, ee
That it should overflow with milk and oil, ee aee
That it should overflow with milk and oil; meat with honey.

The homestead of my father is widely spread [firmly established], *aee*
The homestead of my father is widely spread like a mushroom from
Kiribo
From Kiribo
Like a mushroom from Kiribo
Like a mushroom from Kiribo haee haee
Like a mushroom from Kiribo, the one with a long root.
Haee I bless you haee haee [x2]
The homestead of the father I bless it haee [x2]
Haee I bless it to overflow with milk.
Eee and oil haee haee [x2]
Overflow with milk and oil haee haee
Haee overflow with oil, meat with honey.

Klara Robi went into the house without reciting any poems. By the time she arrived home, Klara was tired, sleepy, and felt faint from blood loss. Her relatives spread a mattress in the sitting room for her. She drank obosara, placed a piece of plastic sheeting on the mattress as she had bled a lot and did not want to spoil it, and lay down. She fell asleep immediately, and did not feel pain until about 4:00 p.m., when she woke up. She was then told to go bathe the wound, and walking she felt the pain. Urinating, she felt more pain. Penicillin powder was applied to the wound and throughout the recovery period so she did not develop an infection. She was washed the same day because she had bled a lot. Those who don't bleed a lot may not be washed until the following day. The wound took about two weeks to heal. A scab formed and had to come off before being completely healed.

Asked how she saw genital operations eight years later, she responded, "I have not yet reached the stage where I can decide. When I am married, have a kid, I will be at a stage to decide."

Age and Gender as Identity Markers

Despite the increasing importance of education and wealth as status markers, age and gender continue to underpin the status hierarchy of Kuria families and, by extension, the communities and the society. At the birth of a child, the parents, family, relatives, and even the local

neighborhood welcome the newborn with joy and immediately a series of distinctions based on gender begins. Both sexes are valued and
welcomed with jubilation, and parents seek the contribution of both
genders to the work of the homestead. Language praising the mother
reflects the expected contributions of each gender: giving birth to a
boy might be praised as "she brought us a shield and a spear," whereas
giving birth to a girl might be "she brought someone who will collect
firewood" (Kjerland 1995, 63–64). Though both are important, they
are not appreciated in the same way.

During the course of a lifetime, each individual is accorded a status
and role in the community on the basis of gender and age. Status
changes are usually marked and celebrated with the performance of
specific rites of passage. Within the overall social structure of a Kuria
community, the age-statuses are fixed and the members of the society
pass through them on their way from birth to death (Ruel 1959, 118).
Each stage carries specific responsibilities and expectations. The
stages are outlined in the following chart:[17]

Male	*Female*
umuriisia	*omosaagane*
umumura	*umuiseke*
umuguru	*omorekari*
omosaacha	*umusubaati*
omogaaka	*umukungu*
umusubi	*umusubi*

Children, boys and girls alike, assume responsibilities according to
their abilities and gender. Around age five or six years, young boys
(abariisia, uncircumcised boys; literally "herders") begin to look after
livestock. Initially, they are entrusted to graze calves, then goats and
sheep, until they have acquired enough skill and sense of responsibility
to look after their father's entire herd. Young girls can perform these
tasks too, if they have no brothers of suitable age. Usually, young girls
(abasaagane, or uncircumcised girls) perform tasks for their mothers,
and through imitation, play, and instruction, they learn the tasks they
will be called upon to perform in adulthood. These include looking after
younger siblings (young babies are often tied to their backs and the
girls ferry the infants around much of the day), fetching water from
the river, collecting firewood, sweeping, and helping to hoe the garden.
If there are no female children in the home, young boys are expected

to help, especially in looking after younger siblings. Young children of either gender are expected to run errands and to obey their parents' orders without back talk or sullenness. Children have a junior status in the homestead, lacking the rights and independence of adults. They are under the authority of their parents, and most importantly, they should not engage in sexual intercourse, marry, or bear children.

In the past, girls were usually married soon after being initiated, while boys socialized with their cohort of both genders and began to develop their leadership skills.[18] These days, most of the newly initiated youth go back to school after coming out of seclusion, and marriage is delayed for some years. They continue to work on perfecting the skills necessary for maintaining a homestead and family.

In the 1950s, Ruel remarked that the post-initiation, pre-marriage stage of life had the greatest glory attached to it, and was marked by a relatively greater independence from parental control (especially for the young men) than any other stage of life. Eager to show themselves off to the opposite gender, both abamura and abaiseke took special care in their appearance, as they were now expected to find a spouse. This was especially true for girls, whose adult roles centered on marriage and reproduction. By presenting herself well, the umuiseke was expected to be finding a husband (*ogokemba*), and her marriageable status was the most short-lived period in her life. In a few months or a year or two she was expected to be married, at which point she would either be called a bride (*omorekari*) or continue to be called an umuiseke until the birth of her first child. By giving birth she became a young married woman (*umusubaati*). At that point, her sphere of life became centered in her married home (Ruel 1959, 120). Nowadays, most initiated girls spend at least a few years completing elementary school education, at which time, unless called to a secondary school, parents begin to direct their daughter's attention towards marriage. Today, most newly initiated young women consider marriage proposals following initiation to be the worst fate possible, as often their genital cutting takes place between Standard 4 and 5, when they are in their early to mid-teens, and are reluctant to end their education there. But because of generally weak results in the national standardized tests that determine opportunities for going on with education, for most Kuria youths— male and especially female—continuing into secondary school is not a real option.

The status of young men (abamura) generally lasts longer than that of young women (abaiseke). Early in the twentieth century, it used to be their responsibility to herd and protect cattle. Their primary role was fighting to protect the clan (ikiaro) and its resources, or raiding other clans for cattle. The qualities of courage, loyalty to age-mates, deference to elders, sharp appearance, and ability to work hard on the farm were the most greatly admired. In their leisure time, abamura wandered (ogotaara) about visiting friends, courting young women, and getting involved in fights and other escapades (Ruel 1959, 120). Even today, the abamura have their own bachelor huts (*isiiga*) within their father's homestead where they can socialize with friends as well as sleep. Nowadays, like female initiates, most male initiates are still in elementary school and return there following seclusion, still wearing their school uniforms. Boys no longer wear shorts after circumcision, instead dressing in long trousers.

Kuria cultural norm is for everyone to marry and to begin a family. Though young people are said to be free to select their own spouses, a number of constraints influence the decision. A young woman may be pressed into accepting a suitor because he offers bridewealth that a brother needs in order to marry. Conversely, a young man may be pressured into finding a bride because, following the marriage of a sister, cattle are available and his father is unwilling to risk keeping them too long for fear of raiders. Potential spouses consider personal characteristics and family reputation of their suitor. Qualities such as obedience, docility, and disposition to work hard are highly sought in a bride. From the bride's perspective, a husband should be from a good family, generous, kind, hard-working, and not prone to heavy drinking. Both sets of parents usually demand that there be no witches in either family. Accusations of witchcraft, or even a rumored association with that form of activity, imperils negotiations.

Residence is virilocal and following marriage the bride (omorekari) moves to the homestead of her husband's father. Initially, she is not allowed to have her own cooking hearth so she shares her mother-in-law's until after she gives birth to a child. During this time her primary role and status is *omokamona* (daughter-in-law, literally "child's wife"). Her mother-in-law directs her in farming, cooking, and carrying out household chores. She is responsible for opening up the cattle corral gate (ikihita) every morning, and closing it up in the evening. Given the complex nature of interwoven logs that serve as the closure for the ikihita, this is a time-consuming and crucially important task.

With the birth of a child, a married couple (omosaacha and umusubaati) start its own umugi (in the sense of family, not of a homestead). Though they remain under the ultimate authority of the homestead head who owns the land they farm, they both have more freedom to take charge of their affairs. They decide what crops to grow, how to allocate their income, what kinds of endeavors to undertake, and how to bring up their children. The transition to family head or elder (omogaaka) is a gradual one that unfolds over time as a man's family grows and he consolidates his position as a head of a homestead and family. The honor of his position is a reflection of the number and status of his descendants. In Ruel's words, "In seeking to ascertain a person's status Kuria ask a series of questions: has he married? has he had children? has he circumcised or initiated his children? has he married a 'son's wife' for his home? It is only when all these duties have been completed that a man is truly an elder" (1959, 121).

When their firstborn is of the age to be initiated, parents begin the penultimate stage in their own life cycle. Usually at this stage the parents split off to form their own homestead, and with it, their autonomy increases tremendously. One of the most important ceremonies for parents is their first child's initiation. According to Ruel, when Kuria speak of "having a descendant" (*ukubiuka*), they imply that the child has become or is about to become mature (1959, 121). Most significantly, at the initiation of his oldest child, a man becomes fully recognized as a parent and family head. Men can begin to build their own herds from bridewealth received for their daughters, from inheritance from their father's herd, and from any purchases of livestock they make from their own earnings. Adult sons do not usually own their farmland and homestead area until they inherit, but their fathers allocate land to their son(s) when the son's firstborn child is initiated.

As sons marry and bring home daughters-in-law, the homestead population expands and the status of the parents rises. They are now omogaaka and umukungu, respected by their children, grandchildren, in-laws, and community members. They allocate much of the work of the homestead to the younger generation. There is only one higher status attainable within the society, *ubusubi*, which is achieved only by a small minority. Clan elders are the protectors of its traditions and of clan and territorial harmony. They make up the councils and the public assembly and are expected to use their experience and concern for the clan to restrain hot headedness, arbitrate disputes justly, and generally maintain clan well-being. They sit on the chief's baraza and apply local standards to settling disputes. In a sense, they offer a counterbalance to the state power embodied in the office of the chief. *Abasubi* are elders who have undergone the ceremony of *isubo* (often translated by English-speaking Kuria as "jubilee"). This is another extremely important ritual transition, and the ceremony can be performed by any elder whose parents have also undergone the ceremony. The isubo ceremony requires a great deal of wealth to perform, since a number of cattle are necessary to give as additional bridewealth payments to in-laws, as well as to be consumed during the rituals. Flour for ubukima and yeast for beer are needed in large quantities, and thus not everyone can afford to sponsor the event. Following the ceremony, the participant is endowed with the symbols of ubusubi, including brass hoop earrings (*ekegara*) and wristlet (*egetaanke*), a cow-tail flywhisk (*ekewaasi kieng'ombe*) from a ritually slaughtered cow (*eng'ombe yi inyangi*) that is later replaced by the more prestigious wildebeest-tail flywhisk (*ekewaasi*), a container for drinking straws (*ekegaancha*), and a more prestigious wristlet (*igituang'a*). Traditionally, this was the greatest of Kuria rites of passage as it served to formalize attainment of full status as family head and progenitor.

Though the ritual is not performed as often as it was in the past, elders continue to be depicted as the clan's guardians, the protectors of its traditions and of communal harmony. Elders who have performed isubo have further duties and privileges, some of which surround the slaughter of cattle and distribution of meat. They are the only people to perform the piercing of a slaughtered bovine's stomach. They are given their own portion of meat (the tender fillet), occupy a specific place of rank at a beer party, and are the only ones who have the privilege of carrying their beer-drinking straws. Ritual elders are respected and feared, believed to be closer to the supernatural or religious forces and thought to know more about 'medicines' and herbal magic than others.

The levels of status through which an individual moves in the course of his or her life are by definition ascribed, since every individual falls into them as she or he develops and matures. There is, however, an achieved element to all of them, depending on individual qualities and abilities. Generally, during the progression from youth to elderhood, both genders command increasing respect, simply on the basis of age, although males always take a superior position to females. They are the leaders, women the followers.

This chapter focused on the experiences of ordinary females undergoing the initiation process in rural Bukuria. The experience of one girl evoked from participant observation and two paraphrased stories of past initiations convey details from the early 1930s and the early 1990s. Through the three perspectives, I have highlighted the common experiences, exposed the differences, and reflected on concepts of tradition and innovation in the context of Kuria cultural practices. These narratives also allow for an exploration of the values of Kuria culture that are embedded in initiation rituals, particularly age and gender as two important criteria for marking identity that are defined through the performance of genital cutting. This investigation allows us to view and experience from a more critical, experientially based perspective the commonly held belief that male and female genital cutting are equivalent.

In the next chapter, I continue to explore continuity and change through the ordinary experiences of individuals. It begins by exploring the dynamics of behavior change, focusing on the case of Leah Mokami and her decision-making process in regard to circumcision. Then the chapter examines convention theory, social norms and expectations, and two elimination strategies: medicalization and legislation. These outsider perspectives are part of the global furor over genital cutting in the late 1990s and have impacted practices in Bwirege, giving rise to new alternatives to genital cutting that have been added to the cultural repertoire.

Female initiate leaving circumcision ground

Escorts on hillside encountering living bushes

Musicians with *ekegoogo* and *ibiraandi*

Escorts in marketplace

Female initiate walking home with escorts

Father, grandmother, and relatives waiting to greet initiates as they return home

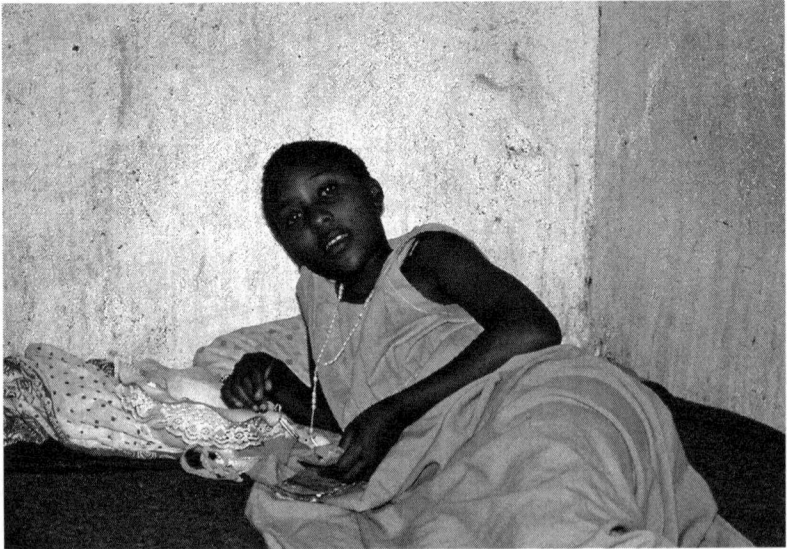
Omosaamba resting upon returning from cutting, counting up her money

4

Something Different

Leah Mokami's story began for me on the day I moved into her family's homestead in 1998. Klara Robi, her oldest sister and the firstborn child of their mother, told me that Leah Mokami, who had turned twelve a couple of months earlier, had decided not to get initiated (Prazak 2000).[1] Though at that point the whole initiation season had been canceled, Klara Robi nonetheless spoke of Leah Mokami's decision in quite disparaging terms. Their youngest sister, Esta Nyamburi, was held up as an exemplar of Kuria virtue because even at nine years of age she was already interested in and willing to undergo genital cutting. Leah Mokami, a tall, thin, serious, and quiet girl, was deeply Christian, wore a sizeable cross all the time, and in an unassuming way seemed quite intransigent. Though initiations on the community level were called off, her mother had accumulated, sprouted, and roasted sufficient finger millet to provide plentifully for the entertainment of visiting revelers. Leah Mokami, however, was quite clear about her preference not to undergo genital cutting. Public awareness of the purported dangers and irrelevance of the ritual had arisen from a widespread government campaign, which also promised to help individuals not willing to follow the traditional path. As more and more risks were discussed publicly, the inevitability of the practice was increasingly being questioned. Some Seventh Day Adventist (SDA) churches in the community declared that girls should not be operated on at all.[2]

Discussing the practice, Leah Mokami argued to her immediate family that she could become an adult without having her genitals cut. But when the initiation season was finally declared open for boys, and then for girls, the pressure on her to conform to the traditional path intensified. Within the homestead her sisters and mother mounted pressure. If Leah Mokami was sitting outside when an initiation group passed the homestead, her sisters would tell her to run inside and hide, or she would get kidnapped and forcibly operated on. If a group of women stopped by, her sisters would tell her to go hide lest the women mock or tease her about being omosaagane. Her sisters always delivered these ostensibly thoughtful comments with great hilarity, signifying to me that they were mocking Leah Mokami. If their mother was home, she would usually join the sisters, making Leah Mokami feel that her choice was the wrong one. When I asked the girls why they were tormenting Leah Mokami so, they replied that this was nothing compared to the lifetime of mockery she would receive as an uncircumcised female going into her late teens and beyond. And when Leah asked me about my stance regarding genital cutting, I told her about the millions of adult women in other parts of Kenya, Africa, and the world who had not had their genitals operated on who led normal adult lives. Even though I have known Leah since her toddlerhood, my voice clearly came from further beyond her realm of experience than any she had heard.

Some days later, Leah Mokami told me she had made up her mind to undergo the ritual, but I remained skeptical about her commitment. She asked me to accompany her to the circumciser and I felt quite torn. Should I continue to give her reasons not to undergo the operation, or should I accompany and support her by my presence? In either case I felt responsible for ensuring her well-being. But I was profoundly disappointed that she had changed her mind, that she had been unable to withstand the pressure from the community. Despite the president's assurance that he would back any girl not wishing to be operated on, the reality of daily life made that assurance an empty gesture. Preadolescent girls simply have no power.

Leah Mokami's mother, Mogore Maria, made the decision to have Leah Mokami operated on at the mission. She had learned assertiveness both as an entrepreneur and as a widow supporting seven children, of whom the youngest was six months and the oldest nine years when her husband died. As a community leader she was often called forth to represent the interests of women within local government. Acutely aware of the HIV/AIDS epidemic that had been officially acknowledged just the previous year and the need for hygienic operations, Mogore Maria's decision to go to the mission showed both a way of upholding traditions important to the people of her community and a way to move with the times. She was able to provide progressive leadership by example, taking her daughter to a clinical setting rather than a traditional omosaari.

Around 11:00 p.m. on the night before Leah Mokami's cutting at the mission, the kitchen hut in the homestead became a center of activity, the hub of preparations for the big event taking place the next day. The kitchen was a large, round, mud-smeared, grass-thatched structure. Other than a couple of the four-legged stools (ibituumbe) emblematic of Kuria furniture, the only other furnishing was the traditional three-stone hearth (*iriiko*) where a fire was roaring underneath a huge cauldron of obosara, the sine qua non of entertainment beverages.[3] Mogore Maria and her neighbor and sister-in-law were cooking, drinking bottled beers, and gossiping as they prepared for visitors the next day. They were happy to have me join them and add to their topics of discussion. Leah Mokami occasionally came in from the courtyard and sat in a darker spot within the kitchen. With the only light emanating from the fire, she listened to the banter but didn't contribute. Her siblings were in the courtyard, dancing to a cranked-up radio. Though this revelry in preparation for the operation is supposed to last throughout the night and involve many guests and kin, only immediate family members celebrated in this home. Also contrary to what is described as customary, everyone, including the candidate, went to bed by 2:00 a.m. The short hours remaining until the morning were broken up by the noise of initiation parties walking to a cattle corral circumcision place down the path, aiming to be early in line.

By 8:00 a.m. we were ready to set out from the home. Leah Mokami had bathed early in the morning and seemed quite collected, although a bit nervous, and was dressed in her orange school uniform and a little white crocheted hat that might have been suitably worn to a baptism or an Easter Sunday church visit. She was being accompanied by two sisters from a neighboring family who were also to be initiated. The two girls had been orphaned two months earlier, and Mogore Maria was paying for their genital cutting alongside her daughter's. The mission was nearby, a distance of half a mile or so from their home. The walk there was short and uneventful. I stayed close to Leah Mokami, trying to give her courage and support despite being filled with irreconcilable thoughts and emotions. Leah Mokami had asked me to escort her, so I wanted her to feel I was there to support and encourage her. Yet my being there was proof, in my mind, that I could not support her and had not been able to help her maintain her original stance against the community in wishing not to be operated on. I walked silently next to her. One of Leah Mokami's older sisters ran off a few times during the walk to inform people of what was happening, and thereby increased the size of the group. By the time we reached the mission there were four candidates and about a dozen escorts.

As we were the first group to arrive at the circumciser's, there was no wait. The girls were taken inside an outbuilding at the mission, and seated side by side in a small anteroom. The operating room next door was exceedingly small, only able to accommodate the candidate, the person holding her head, those holding her legs, and the nurse doing the cutting. The nurse came in and started organizing the tools of her task. Once ready, she led everyone in prayer, and then took Leah Mokami first. She collected the KShs. 300 fee from Leah Mokami's paternal aunt (father's brother's wife), then led Leah Mokami and her attendants into the tiny operating room, largely filled by the table on which she reclined. She struggled to keep her legs together as the attendants tried to pry them open, and the woman holding her head admonished her to cooperate. The nurse closed the door so those in the anteroom wouldn't see the struggle. Not wanting to add to Leah Mokami's sense of discomfort and shame at publicly revealing her private parts, I left the little room. In fact I left the whole building, fighting tears as my mind kept returning to the thought that the child, a twelve-year-old, was being altered irrevocably by this event, her life never to be the same again. My mind was overrun with values and judgments from my own culture—thoughts of castration, subjugation, altered reality, and so on—fighting in my brain with the ideas current in the community and the notions about cutting, described to me so often as a step toward respect, the transition from childhood to adulthood, the pride and the proof of strength and courage. I teared up nevertheless, glad my dark glasses afforded me at least some privacy.

The most closely concerned and inquisitive escorts crowded around the window, looking on to ensure that the operation was performed properly. As the excised part dropped a cheer went up from the watching women, and the men and women of the escorting group started singing and praising the initiate. Leah Mokami did not cry. The entire procedure had taken no more than five minutes. As the nurse finished with her, Leah Mokami came out and resumed her seat in the anteroom. By the time the four operations were completed, there was a pool of blood under each of the chairs. Though not fundamentally different from the trails of blood that marked the routes from circumcision grounds during that season, the pools on the wicker seats and concrete floor of the clinic seemed in my scattered thoughts much more dangerous and sinister.

Maybe a half hour after arriving, we were ready to leave. In unison the girls stood up. Their escorts knotted the kangas they would now have to wear until they came out of seclusion behind their necks. They sprinkled baby powder on their faces, and the girls, dazed but impassive, lined up in the order in which they had undergone their operations and set off on the walk home. In the meanwhile, a very large and noisy group had arrived at the mission escorting another candidate, dancing, singing, and playing a variety of instruments, including a guitar. Most of the men were wearing women's clothes. And even before Leah Mokami's group could exit the compound the next new initiate came out. The circumciser was working steadily that morning.

Women sprinkled powder in the faces of the initiates throughout the walk, and many individuals eagerly stopped the column to greet and praise the abasaamba, to thrust money in the hands of their assistants and to pin it to the hats and clothes of the initiates. As we walked along, the crowd grew, as did the jubilation and exuberance of the escorts. Each of the initiates carried an umbrella that offered some respite from the sun beating down on the procession. They progressed by fits and starts toward their homes, blood trickling down each one's legs. In the marketplace the frenzied celebration swelled as many people came out to honor the initiates, give them money, and dance in their faces. As the daughter of a prominent community leader, Leah Mokami received much attention. Her three brothers popped up at various locations, looking fierce and vigilant against any dangers, whether physical or spiritual, that might lurk in the crowd and harm their sister.

A distance that usually took five minutes to cover took at least an hour to walk. Before being allowed to enter their homes, the initiates had to dance. Leah Mokami had been first in the column of initiates, but was the last to get home. She did not perform the traditional recitation of the initiate before entering the cattle gate. Her homestead does not even have the symbolic cattle gate. She came into the house, went to her room, and lay down on a foam mattress that had been placed on the floor. The accompanying celebrants were served obosara as they rested in the cool living room, perched on couches richly covered in crocheted doilies.

Soon after having gone to lie down, Leah Mokami was served a meal of ubukima and meat soup, which she ate propped up on her elbows, lying on the mattress. She was counting her money. On the walk home she had been given over KShs. 600.[4] She lay down and napped but her sleep was frequently interrupted by visits from other abasaamba, both boys and girls, coming by to see her and give her money, to praise her, to commiserate with her, and to support her. During the afternoon at least a dozen age-mates came to visit.

Dynamics of Behavior Change

How does an individual decide to buck a practice that the rest of her community considers essential to defining personhood and belonging? The pressure that enforces conformity, coming from various members of the community, including her family, is difficult to ignore or overcome. In such a situation, does a girl really play a big role in the decision-making process, or are her peers and elders the ones with more say? And further, if one family opts out of a practice, do its members pay the price of being ostracized? For some time these questions have been the topmost concerns of NGOs, governments, activists, and policymakers concerned with bringing about the demise of female genital cutting practices in Africa. They have also been addressed in academic literature.

Mackie's writing on strategies for changing social conventions (1996, 2000) has been used to refine strategies endorsed by the biggest funders of elimination of female genital cutting (see, e.g., WHO 2008, 2010; UNICEF 2010). His premise is that social conventions get changed not by individuals but rather by groups committing to a shift in behavior (Mackie 2000, 253ff). If the most widely articulated reason for FGC is that it is necessary for marriage, then people in a series of intermarrying communities need to commit to their children marrying uncircumcised partners. If the reason for adherence to the practice is intergenerational peer pressure, the opinion of peers across generations has to change (Shell-Duncan et al. 2011). Thus if girls undergo FGC in order to gain admission into a network of women that gives them access to positions and resources within the society, the elimination efforts need to be focused on getting the network of elders to allow intact females to join their ranks.[5] Change is predicated on coordinated abandonment of social conventions by groups.

Before the widespread articulation of the social convention theory, those concerned with the elimination of female genital cutting initially focused on ameliorating the health risks associated with cutting practices. The medicalization of cutting practices is discussed below. A repositioning of the anti-FGM campaign into a human rights framework shifted the focus from protecting girls' health to improving their standing in their families, communities, and societies (see, e.g., An-Na'im 2002; Merry 2006a; Shell-Duncan et al. 2013). This entails a principal shift to moral norms—behavioral rules motivated by personal values of right and wrong, rather than communal ones (UNICEF 2010, 8).[6]

Genital Cutting at the Mission

The day the initiation season opened to girls, just after Jamhuri Day, one of the religious missions in Bwirege began offering girls the genital cutting services of a medically trained nurse from Kisii. The innovation entailed in medicalized cutting at the mission was multifold. As this was the first time such a thing had happened in the area, it reflected a willingness to accept something new that would have been unbelievable just five years earlier.

In part, the government's message regarding AIDS was being heard, and parents were worried about the possibility of infection by traditional methods in which sterile procedures were not followed. Customarily, all the boys were operated on with the same knife.[7] But as I had witnessed already in the late 1980s, each girl provided her own razor blade, to be unwrapped by the circumciser just prior to the cut being made. The option of having girls operated on in an allegedly "sterile" setting had not been available in this administrative division previously. In part, the decades of government opposition to the practice of FGM (as it is popularly termed in Kenyan and international media) were yielding to skepticism about the practice, which was increasingly seen as an outmoded and dangerous tradition that forward-looking people should question, at least to limit the health risk. One of the local mission leaders, Clergyman Murimi, brought this innovation to the easternmost division of Kuria District in 1998 by hiring a trained nurse and allocating a small outbuilding at the mission as the operating arena. Though he saw this move as the perfect compromise between allowing people to hold on to their traditions and protecting the health of the girls being initiated, medicalization, both in Kenya and globally, quickly became a highly debated topic.[8]

Although the adverse health consequences of genital cutting for females formed the basis of opposition to the practice, anti-circumcision activists as well as many international medical associations largely opposed measures to improve its safety (Shell-Duncan 2001, 1013). Medical intervention had been attempted in various forms, ranging from promoting precautionary steps such as using sterile razors, dispensing prophylactic antibiotics, performing genital operations in clinics or hospitals by trained personnel, and training traditional circumcisers in antiseptic procedures and the use of latex gloves. The impact of these interventions received little attention, and without consideration of the health improvements resulting from various forms of medicalization, these approaches were strongly criticized by anti-circumcision advocates (1014).

The staunch opposition to medical intervention rests on one central assumption: that medicalization counteracts efforts to eliminate female genital cutting. This assumption is not based on empirical evidence (Shell-Duncan 2001, 1014). The potential benefits of adopting a harm-reduction paradigm seeking to minimize health hazards by encouraging safer alternatives have been categorically refused by the main anti-FGM campaign funders and sponsors, despite its potential avenues for yielding favorable outcomes for females undergoing genital cutting—reducing the risk of medical complications by improving hygienic conditions and reducing the amount of cutting. The introduction of genital cutting at the mission in Bwirege was stimulated by both of these considerations.

Opponents of medicalization efforts in Kenya maintain that active participation of health staff in advocating against the practice is essential to reduce their perceived support for its continuation (Njue and Askew 2004, iv). They maintain that the Ministry of Health needs to strengthen its facility-level supervision mechanisms to stop its staff from performing the practice. Further, education on existing policies and laws is needed so that providers and community leaders can understand and discuss FGC issues competently, and so that punitive measures can be taken against those practicing FGC (22). On the global level, a consortium of United Nations agencies, the Donor's Working Group on Female Genital Mutilation/Cutting, and a number of other key stakeholders have articulated the "Global Strategy to stop health-care providers from performing female genital mutilation" against medicalization of FGM, spelling out global goals, global realities, and the challenges that need to be addressed (WHO 2010).

The Circumciser from Outside

While Leah Mokami was resting at home from her operation, I walked back to the mission and spoke with the nurse, Sister Rosaria.[9] She had been performing operations at the mission for three days at that point. Not Kuria herself, she usually worked at a hospital just outside Kuria District in the neighboring Luo area. By Leah's turn, she had operated on twenty-five girls at the mission, and both she and the clergyman who had brought her interpreted the turnout as a very good showing by those supporting the change to new, more hygienically conscious methods. She didn't see any particular pattern to the people who opted to have their daughters operated on at the mission. Some of the community leaders, especially teachers, did not have their kids operated on in the "modern" way at the clinic, while some of the "traditionalists" did. She speculated that maybe the success of the mission alternative was because the traditional circumciser was swamped, causing candidates to wait for hours to be operated on. Or maybe what led them to the mission was the desire to be seen as progressive, as being willing to innovate in this particular way.

Sister Rosaria described the procedure she employed. First she gave the girl two injections: vitamin K against bleeding mixed with B-complex for strength, and an antibiotic. Then she swabbed the girl's genitals with alcohol and excised a part of the clitoris. (From her point of view, she was unlike traditional circumcisers in that she did not cut the labia minora or majora. Traditionally, according to her, the labia minora and the entire clitoris were excised. It was not clear to me whether that was the tradition of the Abagusii or of the Abakuria.) She followed antiseptic procedure by using gloves and surgical scalpels, and washed the plastic-covered exam table on which all the girls would recline. She then covered the wound with a bandage, which the girls were instructed to remove in six hours. She expected the girls to have healed in two to three days. The blood underneath the chairs and on the legs of the girls walking home seemed to challenge at least the bandage part of this story.

Because the nurse came from Kisii, where both boys and girls undergo genital cutting operations as well, she compared the customs of Kuria with the customs of the Abagusii, and was surprised to find much more pageantry, dancing, and feasting in Kuria initiation ceremonies. In her opinion, in Kisii the operations are treated as routine. Another point of difference was the age of the candidates, with the candidates in Bukuria being much bigger and older than those in Kisii, where most have undergone the operation by ten years of age. In Bwirege, she noted, twelve to fifteen seemed to be a much more common age for girls, and fourteen to eighteen for boys. Aside from operating on the girls, she had been called to assist several abasaamba, particularly boys, who had been circumcised and were experiencing problems. Most of them had been circumcised traditionally, but one had been circumcised in a clinic. In his case, Sister Rosaria exclaimed, "The 'doctor' had not sutured the incision, so he might as well be the traditional omosaari!"

After a quiet night, Leah seemed to be doing fine in the morning, and was walking around the house a little bit. She claimed to be okay, and certainly looked so even if her movements involving the lower part of her body were rather tentative. Her family remained close by, although she was excluded from the daily activities of home. Unlike most abasaamba, she chose not to wander around the neighborhood with the band of initiates from the area, but instead spent much of her time at home with her younger sister.

The Head of the Mission

Three years after I witnessed Leah's initiation at the mission, I spoke with Clergyman Murimi, a Kuria from another ikiaro, who had come to Nyankare when the mission was established there in 1990 as its head and the principal clergyman for the Bwirege and Nyabasi locations until early 2002. He spearheaded a number of projects in the area, including a school for the deaf; a private, mission-sponsored primary school; and medicalized female genital cutting, which was performed at the mission in 1998–99 and at the neighboring mission-sponsored primary school in 2001–2. On both occasions he brought trained and experienced nurses from outside the district to perform the operations. In his late thirties or early forties, physically fit and vigorous, he eagerly communicated his ideas.[10]

An ordained minister, Clergyman Murimi was nonetheless keen to preserve tradition, but simultaneously wanted to minimize the potential for harm befalling the initiates. "I saw the need to assist our girls. It [genital cutting] is not something we would like to encourage. But the way it is done outside there, it is not that good, it is dangerous, it is a risk. The young girls bleed; the traditional [circumcisers] do it in an unsafe way. People do it, enjoy it because it is our culture, it has been done since we were born." But nowadays, because of the danger of AIDS, he had to rethink the traditional methods: "People approached me; they wanted us to have it done in a safe way. They asked me to bring a nurse. We brought a nurse here and we tried to help them. We call it a safe circumcision. It is not something we like to encourage, but I wanted to bring them closer. Our people are deeply rooted in this culture. It is not easy to remove them at once, even though the government is trying to discourage it."

Almost 60 girls had come to be operated on that season (2001–2) at the mission. The previous initiation time (in 1998–99), 54 girls had been operated on at the mission. Even though 114 girls had been operated on in those two initiation seasons, people in the community had mixed feelings about the alternative initiation. Some who came had wanted to go to the traditional circumciser instead because they were afraid of being ridiculed by their relatives and other girls: "Are you pregnant, so you have to be taken to the clinic?" Even if they were not pregnant, some of the girls were deeply embarrassed that the community might think so, and sometimes that was enough to prevent them from going to the clinic. Clergyman Murimi exemplified the transition the community desired by introducing incremental change instead of calling for an abrupt end.

The mission was the first place offering a nontraditional genital cutting operation for girls in Bwirege. The operation was performed differently by the nurse than by the traditional circumciser, as Clergyman Murimi explained: "Traditionally they leave a very big scar by going too deep. Sometimes the girls bleed a great deal. Here, the nurse is a professional, she does it in a professional way. Because we don't want to stop the tradition abruptly but want to make a difference, we ask her to make a smaller cut. The girls come from here after being properly treated. The nurse uses sterile procedures, with gloves and antibiotics. Nobody will be infected by any disease. In future, many parents may want to take advantage of having a safe way to provide this service."

He expressed his satisfaction at how the program he introduced was progressing: "Slowly they are getting to know. At first it is not very easy. Something new, people stay aloof, they are watching. Also they fear the *wazee wa kimiira* [abagaaka binchaama]. Sometimes they [the elders] harass them, they are fined. 'If you go to the clinic, you will have to pay a cow.' So they fear. But slowly they will come to understand. Now that the government is serious and many people are fighting against FGM, before they stop it, I would like to assist. Being a culture that has been practiced a long time we will have to see what will happen."

The clergyman was well aware that the cutting was not the most important element of the initiation for many people. By coming to the mission, people were not being asked to forgo the usual types of celebration: "In fact there are some people who come who are religious and don't like to celebrate, but we don't limit people in their celebration. I, as a Kurian, know that if we say 'no celebration,' people will not come. The celebration is the root cause of why the practice continues: the dancing, the rejoicing (*ukuhuuraania*), the gifts to the girls. The people become resistant because they feel that if they stop it then they will miss those kinds of things."

As he knew, the global leadership of his mission church had not come out strongly on this issue: "I personally don't know of much talk among the leaders about this issue." He saw his own position as having arisen from being approached by people in his congregation. Though he was reluctant to encourage the practice of female genital cutting, he saw people would go to the traditional practitioners if they had no alternative. "So I thought about it again. People need to be educated, to know alternatives. If a girl is not circumcised and she stays around here she is abused, she will not be able to marry, she will be called omosaagane. That is why I chose to offer an alternative, so that girls are not abused."

According to Clergyman Murimi, cultural change is a slow process. People can be taught that marrying omosaagane is not wrong or harmful. Kuria men marry women from other ethnic groups who are intact, so why not marry Kuria women who are not operated on? The issue of female genital cutting is not a consideration for a church marriage; it is not something that is even discussed. Nonetheless, the clergyman did not know any Kuria family in Bwirege in his denomination that had adult, intact girls. He had heard of the problem of grown SDA girls being forcibly cut, despite their birth fathers and pastors opposing the practice. He also knew people in Bugumbe location to the west, including his own uncle, who had not circumcised their girls. With them, he posited, they might choose not to circumcise because of interaction with Luo people, who don't follow the practice. He thought perhaps there were more girls educated, or maybe there were more people from Bugumbe who lived and worked outside Bukuria, so "they don't have any problem with the community abusing them. Staying here is where the problem comes. With education you can be married anywhere. If the government comes with force, the law takes its force, and FGM becomes abolished, then it will end. Otherwise it will take time. With education girls will be free to move outside, to work in places outside of Bukuria."

Clergyman Murimi was happy that nobody gave him trouble about opening the mission to genital cutting. He believed this was because people respected the church. "The mocking of clinic-circumcised children has stopped. In the past, they were not allowed to walk together with the bush candidates. But nowadays, the clinic-operated initiates are many, they could form their own groups." He held a celebration at the mission to honor the initiated youth, to bring them closer to the mission, and to encourage them, as well as to recognize that celebrations were in the blood of the people. "Through the party, the mission gives them encouragement, the candidates feel happy they have someone who remembers them. When they come for the operation they come one by one; at the celebration they have the opportunity to meet and interact."

In 2002 the celebration was held on a Sunday. The clergyman slaughtered a cow for the initiates and brought dancers to entertain them. The entertainers included groups of traditional *imitiambu* dancers with raised platform shoes, and a few groups playing and singing church music. Hundreds of people turned up—abasaamba, parents, family members. They celebrated up to around 5:00 p.m. Clergyman Murimi recounted, "After Mass we had the entertainment, then the meal. The slaughtering and division of the cow were done within the church. All the food was eaten—the soup, the rice we bought, plus ubukima. The abasaamba enjoyed, they were happy to be honored."

In customary style, the abasaamba sang the clergyman's praises, and he reciprocated by giving the singers money. Thinking of a future time when traditional circumcision would no longer be practiced, the clergyman brought in someone to take a video of the celebration to record the tradition and make it available so that in the future people would be able to see what used to go on. At the same time as he was changing the tradition, Clergyman Murimi was also including some of the old practices—like feasting and praise singing—in the celebration, making it alive. He was aware of people having come up with an alternative celebration in other parts of Kenya (especially in Meru).[11] In his opinion, "We are not at that point now. We need to educate people first, so they can accept changes and innovations."

I asked him to comment on the recently passed law that stated that genital cutting should be stopped or at least postponed until after the girls turned eighteen, as called for by the Children Bill of 2001. Would that work in this community? After some thought, he responded: "If they make it a law, and are serious about it, it would work. If they get rid of the circumcisers, there won't be anyone to do it, or anywhere to go. If they go after the parents, they will have to take a big risk. But of course people will do it in secret, as in Tanzania. People come here [to Kenya] to have their kids circumcised. The parents are still doing it, even though there is a law against it." Such a law would be difficult to enforce. "It really will take education, and introduction of something different, a different type of celebration. I have heard in Meru they have an alternative, where the girls come together, then come out of it together, with celebrations as during esaaro."

Clergyman Murimi continued, comparing the mission's progress with progress through the education system: "Whereas in the past, initiation was an occasion for teaching youth about sexual matters, when girls were educated about relationships, and then after initiation were ready to be married, that element is not present today. Even very small girls are being initiated, and they are not being educated about anything to do with adult sexual behavior. The mission is not doing any educating in this arena either. Currently, they are trying to educate the girls about the dangers of going outside [having multiple sexual partners], but we are going slowly, not really doing anything in that direction. Right now, we are in the nursery."

National and international media discourse on genital cutting tends to portray the tradition of female initiation as unchanging and retrogressive, but that image misses reality. Among Kuria and other ethnic practicing groups, initiation is sensitive to the ideas and criticisms from within the culture and from public discourse outside of the culture via media, especially radio. People are acutely aware of the charges made against genital cutting practices, and amend practices in ways they find acceptable to obviate at least some of dangers.

The Circumciser from the Community

As the demand for mission initiations grew following the 1998 introduction of this service, Clergyman Murimi sought a second woman to perform operations for the 2001 initiation season. He selected Rose Wankio. Already in her mid-fifties when she began operating, she sought me out to talk about the work she had been called to take up. Having heard that I was interviewing people about genital cutting practices, she had sent me a note inviting me to talk with her about initiation. As it turned out, she would operate for one season only (in 2001).[12]

In her estimation, she had inherited her role as circumciser. Her grandmother had been one. Her sister still practiced. A number of years earlier Rose had fallen ill, and wasn't able to walk or see. One side of her body was not functioning: her right side from the shoulder down to the leg. When she went for treatment and was injected with medicine, she swelled up to an extent that horrified people and made them turn away at the sight of her. "I did not become an omosaari by choice, it was fate," she said. "I fell ill for four years. I used to swell, my body would bloat and doctors couldn't diagnose a thing. I would see razor blades everywhere; on the road, on the bed, at the granary. But I would point out the blades to other people but they couldn't see them. Then I fell sick." She decided to go to a traditional healer, and he sent her to the council of elders. They told her to become an omosaari. "I recovered, without going to the hospital."

In the year 2000 she went to seek assistance from the head of the local mission. The clergyman baptized her and told her she would be a circumciser and would practice at the mission, not anywhere else. She spoke with the elders as well, and they told her that she would be operating on the Abakehenche, people who live at Wangirabose, Matare, and Makararangwe. Her sister, Nyaroberi, would cut the Abarisenye. Nyaroberi was furious at losing a part of her territory, and the elders intervened in the dispute between the sisters, telling the younger—who had been operating for over fifteen years—that she had to let her sister begin as well. The elders told her she had no choice, since they decide who can initiate and who cannot.

Clergyman Murimi insisted that Rose was to operate on girls according to Christian standards, not according to traditional custom. To her this meant discarding the traditional medicine (charms) that people tie around the neck or hands of an initiate on her way to initiation. She was sent to the district hospital in Kehancha for train-ing. She had been assisting her sister previously, and had learned what to do by observing her. She liked the work, and thought she was good at it. She also saw that there was much money to be made. Though she wasn't sure of exactly how many girls she had circumcised during the season, because she was new she earned about KShs. 10,000, a small amount compared to the KShs. 150,000 per season she thought her sister earned performing traditional operations.

Speaking of the persistence of genital cutting operations despite the negative media attention the custom received at home and abroad, she said, "Genital cutting has been Kuria tradition for ages now. A young girl of today must undergo the same process as her ances-tors underwent. So that tradition is carried on: everybody without exception is compelled to be circumcised." She continued: "Nowadays though, things seem to be changing." In the past, the cutting was much deeper. Now, "Just as long as a little blood is seen to be drip-ping, the operation is seen as sufficient." People have become aware that girls in the past had been injured. The old esaaro was painful, as evidenced in the way the girls walked slowly with their legs apart. "Now that was painful. But these days you see the freshly circumcised girls sprinting back home. The operation is very fast. The omosaari just pulls [the prepuce] and cuts, using gloves and the razor blade the candidate brought. Those who forget to bring their own are charged KShs. 20 and in that case, the circumciser provides a new one for each needy candidate."[13] After completing the cut, she would hand the razor blade to the person holding the girl's head. "My time was pain-ful. These days they call it 'aaruure ubunyinya' (a minor cut to prevent a girl from becoming an outcast). So the tradition is already actually dying slowly, it just can't be dropped all at once."

Parents fear their daughter might become pregnant before she is initiated and consequently be banned from the community. According to Rose, this is the main reason the tradition persists. So they have their daughters initiated, and the parents celebrate. But without ini-tiation there would be no celebrations, which are central to the ritual and to social order. In her opinion, the government cannot succeed in doing away with just girls' genital cutting. The campaign will only be successful if it eradicates circumcision of both boys and girls.

Genital operations at the mission were an innovation that some members of the community welcomed and others opposed. Those opposed would stand guard on the pathways to the mission and try to dissuade or prevent candidates from going in. Those in support argued that following sterile procedures would ensure that the tradition of genital cutting on girls continued. Despite the debate, most everyone I spoke with or overheard discussing the topic was still interested in seeing female genital cutting continue as a basic ritual practice. But most everyone also heard the voice of the president of Kenya, regularly broadcast by the media, weighing in against genital cutting, especially his promise that he would support any girl who didn't want to be circumcised to break away from her parents. Rose Wankio's response to that was simple: "You can't take the bark of a coral tree (*omotembe*) and graft it onto a euphorbia tree (*omosoocho*). What would he do with these children from another culture?"

Excision at a Clinic

In 1992, Matiinde Rosa had been initiated at age eleven in a clinic outside Kuria District. Her well-educated, professional parents were concerned with the risks of the traditional "bush" initiation, and afforded her the same option they had given her brother: to have the operation performed in a medical setting. Since there were no facilities within Kuria District that operated on girls, she was operated on in Kisii District, about 100 kilometers from Bwirege. At the time of this interview in 2003, Matiinde was in her final year of university.[14]

She remembered being eight years old when a cousin began mentioning genital cutting and asking her when she would undergo initiation. At the time, she didn't think she would, but when she turned eleven, all her cousins were preparing for the ritual, and so, she explained, it just kind of happened. She joined in with their plans. Her parents hadn't told her to do it, but it was assumed. Her grandmother kept singing initiation songs to her, preparing her psychologically. Nobody talked to her about the operation explicitly in terms of what it entailed. She simply thought that everybody went through it—there was no cause to question it. And since her cousins were doing it, she thought, "OK, I'll do it." She had been brought up in Kenya outside Kuria society, so her contact with the culture was only partial, through the heritage of her parents. She did know that a younger cousin wanted to do it, but her parents thought her too young. However she insisted, wanting to be initiated with the rest of them. So the cousins all went together to the hospital. Not one of the girls objected.

Matiinde Rosa's Experience

Parents and children don't discuss the cutting before it takes place. Adults assume that young people know about it because they have seen family members experience initiation, and it's a tradition, it just has to be done so they don't really have to explain. The youth certainly don't want to question it. And most often the parents don't need to convince their children to do it. It is just expected that the youth will go along. Most children begin to be questioned when they are quite young, "When are you going to get circumcised?" The idea is instilled from childhood, and children grow up knowing that they will have to undergo genital cutting, it is a part of growing up. If one doesn't do it, she is mocking tradition. That would be the deliberate, marked act; doing it is just going along and doing what is expected. Though talk and speculation take place among peers, questioning those who had undergone the operation didn't yield much knowledge. They wouldn't tell us, they just said "You'll learn when it's your turn."

Matiinde was not initiated within the community, but rather away in a private hospital. Her parents and her maternal aunt and uncle called the hospital and booked an appointment. Matiinde's mother, Nyagonchera Mwita, and her uncle (the father to two of the other girls participating) accompanied them. There was no singing of obosamba the night before, nor any send-off. They simply got into the car and drove off.

My mother's friend met us at the hospital, talked to the nurses who were to operate, and minutes later, came out and asked who wanted to go first. We were circumcised in order of our chronological age, though it was not discussed; neither were amakora—generation classes. Nobody witnessed the operation. Our parents stood outside and we went inside an operating room one by one. When I went in, the nurse asked me to lie on the bed and I didn't even have time to look at the tools they used. When I lay down they asked me to count to ten and before I even started, they were done. I was in my regular clothes, but had taken off my underwear. When done, we were given hospital gowns. Our parents left us to stay in the clinic for three days.

No anesthesia was used during the operation, and it didn't really hurt, except "for like two seconds." Even later the pain was very minimal: "It's nothing like any other pain I have experienced before, you know like real surgery," said Matiinde Rosa. The nurse cut off a part of the clitoris and none of the adjacent tissues—what Matiinde considered to be the clinical way of doing it. It is different from the Kuria way, she said, because "Kuria girls who have been traditionally circumcised...look like they are in pain...and they [bleed] a lot; I didn't bleed. I think I did but not blood gushing out, and I felt better within about three days. For girls who are circumcised traditionally, it takes months sometimes, so I think that the traditional way of circumcising is severe."

The more severe cutting, in her understanding, is the complete removal of the clitoris. But perhaps, she thought, the practice has changed, because in the late 1990s she had seen girls running just ten minutes after their circumcision. "I'm sure it's painful but it means it's not as bad as it used to be."

After three days in the hospital, we returned to Bukuria. My cousins were dropped off at their place, and then I went home. Though my parents were living in another part of the country at this time where my father was employed, this was December and school vacation when I usually stayed in Bukuria. My mother checked how I had been cut.

This echoes the traditional practice of *uguisaabia,* when the clotted blood is washed from the initiate after she has been sleeping following her return to the homestead. By all accounts the washing is a very painful process, carried out by the person who holds the initiate's head and her mother. Some women talk of it as the removing of the scabs, to ensure that the tissues in the genital area return to normal health. The omosaamba usually screams and screams. That's the time the adults confirm the cutting was actually done.

I did not notice much change in the behavior of people in the community toward me. Having spent most of my life with my parents in other parts of Kenya, people didn't really know who I was. To me, initiation was not a major transition that made a difference to my status. But I did think, "Now I am part of the community," despite having been brought up outside of Kurian society. So the initiation was a way of positioning me in the community. This was the only event that connected me to the rest of the community, and that made it meaningful. The people in the community recognized me and said "Well, she was circumcised so she is like the rest of us, she is not a foreigner."

Because of my close relationship with her family, many people of various backgrounds talked to me about Matiinde's initiation. Even if she might not have realized it, people were watching. I heard elders speaking with admiration about how she had learned the initiation songs. Others commented on how skillfully she tied her kanga, showing both adult and Kuria skills. And in the context of the circumcision of her younger brothers six years later (also in a hospital outside of Bukuria), people commented that "these boys know none of the songs, but when their sister was circumcised, she learned the songs." That effort, in the context of a quintessential Kuria ritual, made her a part of the community because they imagined that she understood the deeper traditions surrounding initiation. Though it might not have seemed like a big deal to her, it was meaningful to other people that the communal bond had been reinforced. As Matiinde's mom said to me a year after her daughter's initiation, they had had their daughter operated on because they expected she would live in the community, and not having undergone the ritual would have made life difficult for her.

Matiinde's maternal grandmother and her maternal uncle's senior wife taught her the circumcision songs between the time she was operated on and the time her maternal uncle came to slaughter an ox for Matiinde and her older brother, who had been circumcised in a hospital some weeks earlier. With her brother the firstborn son, and she the firstborn daughter, the *ekehonio* was a large event. Her maternal uncle brought a large black ox, which was slaughtered under the watchful eyes of a related *umusubi*. Her aunt had recited the songs until Matiinde memorized them. After the soup had been cooked and everyone had grouped by amakora and eaten meat, abasaamba from the neighborhood came to eat and sing obosamba. Matiinde led the girls' part of the singing and was greatly applauded and rewarded with quite a bit of money, which was divided after the event between all the attending abasaamba. Because Matiinde had not attended other *ibihonio,* she was instructed and assisted in filling the expectations all the way through.

When interviewed, Matiinde was aware of female genital cutting being regarded as a way of controlling female sexuality, of limiting the amount of sexual arousal girls feel. The aim behind cutting is to prevent women from being distracted and wasting their energies. It doesn't seem to limit sexual activity, or there wouldn't be so many girls pregnant before marriage. "The operation did not make any difference to my sexual drive, but maybe that's because my cut was so minor. I don't feel I am missing something that can never be replaced, or that my physical well-being was altered. But I feel guilty, like the wolf in a sheep's skin...when people are condemning the practice... since I underwent it, I really have no say.... The guilt is more like embarrassment." [15]

Despite that ambivalence, Matiinde thought that campaigns led by nonpractitioners against female genital cutting were valid, though their reasoning was not clear enough. Since opponents have not experienced genital cutting and thus don't know what exactly it entails and what ensues—the consequences, not just to the person individually but to the person in connection to the community—they cannot really say it needs to be stopped. They can argue, as she did, and say that these two body parts, the boys' and the girls', are really different, so what is being done to the boys is not the same as what is being done to the girls, and put an end to it that way: "In my own thinking, I think that boys need it, but for girls, it's not necessary because whatever is cut off is not the same as what is cut off from the boys. They are totally different, I don't even know who thought that cutting off the girls' clitoris would be anything equal to cutting off a part of the boys' sexual organs, and the functions of these two parts are also very different. Therefore I think that they needed to reevaluate this [practice], they needed to have done that before they even started doing it."

She regretted that her parents had never spoken about this with her. I asked her what she would talk to them about if she were to raise the subject. "I would ask them, why did you have to get me circumcised?" was her response. Though they didn't pressure her, it was something she did because they wanted her to. Her first major questioning of the tradition occurred while at boarding school, where only a very small percentage of the students had undergone genital cutting. She felt she was the only one who had. Many functions were held at high school, lectures and discussion sessions, that criticized female genital cutting, and she wondered, "What are my parents thinking, sitting there and listening to this girl reciting a poem against female circumcision?" She never asked them, but she had "awakened to the reality that it doesn't happen everywhere."

Circumcision needs to end but it's going to take a while; it will have to ebb out slowly, so it can't just suddenly stop. People are actually waking up to that reality. It started by the circumcisers cutting off less than they did before. And some girls are not undergoing it at all. I expect that soon parents will say this has to come to an end. I think that Bwirege is still deeply rooted in this circumcision. It's still very elaborate, like they give money, but in other parts of Kuria, circumcision doesn't seem that elaborate and more parents just let their kids be and nobody objects to that. But in Bwirege, maybe it's because it's tiny that everybody knows everybody's business. So they can say "She is not circumcised, she is not circumcised." That's why everybody feels compelled to actually do it.

Progressive Practice, Progressive Parents

In the decade surrounding the start of the new millennium, activity against female genital mutilation in Kenya intensified. The opposition to genital cutting performed on females has a long history in Kenya, beginning in recorded history in the 1920s with missionary and colonial opposition and bans against the practice. These movements generally focused on specific areas, and some parts of Kenya were removed enough from government activity to not be affected by a particular campaign. Periodically, due to pressure from various groups (usually from outside the country), Kenyan and even Kuria voices opposing the tradition are raised in earnest. At the turn of the twenty-first century, President Daniel arap Moi brought his opposition to the practice to the forefront. The net result was that all print and broadcast media—radio, newspapers, and television—carried an anti–genital cutting message that was heard daily all over the country.

In Kuria District this did not stop circumcision, but it made alternative forms of the practice acceptable. Most notably, people responded to the concern for potential transmission of HIV/AIDS via traditional procedures. Local circumcisers were trained in government clinics on sterile procedures, and the alternative of being operated on in a clinic setting by a "traditional" circumciser became fully available for girls in the local community I study. The alternative had been available to boys previously, but the community generally disparaged initiates who were circumcised in clinics, and treated them as if they had cried during the operation. The stigmatization of alternatives to cutting by traditional practitioners receded in the early 2000s, but has made a resurgence in the latest couple of initiation seasons in the 2010s (Bukania 2015).

In the early 2000s, being operated on in a clinic became a vector for identity formation in an unaccustomed way. Parents who opted to forgo a traditional procedure associated their decision with the messages from the leaders—starting with the president of the nation and continuing through the (self-identified) "progressive" elements within the community: the government officials (particularly elected ones), church leaders, the educated, and the employed. The medicalization of the operation allowed this segment of the community to separate from a practice that had been the core of status ascription, to redefine the criteria on which status would be attained. In a certain sense, what had been a more or less ascribed status became an achieved one. Though the impetus for the change came from outside the community, as the terms became available, those who could take advantage of them chose to, separating themselves and their families from the shared experience of the community.

The end of the 2001–02 initiation season brought further changes. By the first half of 2002, an NGO had been formed locally in the hope of getting access to international funds allocated to Kenya to eradicate female genital mutilation. Because the amount of money available for NGOs working to eliminate FGM was unbelievably large for ordinary Kuria, people rushed eagerly to get a piece of the action. And though the ikiaro where circumcisions took place in 2001 followed the usual procedures, a great deal of activity was taking place on the ground to organize against the female part of the practice. People wore shirts printed by an NGO with the slogan "Female circumcision is taboo!" and groups of community leaders attended sensitization seminars to learn the evils of FGM and about alternative rites of passage being enacted in other Kenyan communities.

Those involved in the NGO frenzy adopted the agenda of the external funders and their objective to eliminate FGM, the term that has gained common currency among local translators of the anti-FGM message. Little discussion took place on the impact this innovation would have on the status of girls, particularly if the practice continued to be carried out on boys, and continued to be so closely associated with belonging, identity, and status.

Having focused on the factors and forces of innovation that have introduced new variables and opportunities for initiations in this chapter, I will turn in the next chapter to the theme of how the exigencies of life determine the proper course of action for various participants. Having focused here on the actual cutting aspect of the initiation practices, in the next chapter, the accompanying rituals that establish and confirm bonds between people take center stage.

5

Consoling, Feasting, and Coming Out

The third week of December 1998 was upon us. After the frenzy of the first two weeks, when hundreds of new initiates were created each day, the tempo of circumcisions slowed significantly.[1] Rumors began to circulate that only youth not attending school would be circumcised henceforth due to the short time until school resumed. But girls and boys were still going daily to the abasaari for their initiation, and the celebrations were far from over. In the market and in the privacy of their homesteads, people were commenting on the mixed-up nature of this circumcision season, attributing much of the confusion to the initial delay in opening up initiations. Some children were being circumcised as others were feasting or getting ready to return to school and thus needing to come out of seclusion.

So far, the entire period of initiations was not even two weeks old, with hardly enough time to get all the eligible candidates in front of the circumcisers. Moreover, schools in Tanzania had closed later than those in Kenya, and parents there had had little time to make preparations. Though circumcisers practice in both countries, genital cutting on girls had been outlawed in Tanzania and parents found it expedient to bring their daughters to Kenya for the operation.

As we attended an ekehonio in the home of his relative and my friend, a young Kuria university graduate now teaching in the district described what he perceived as different about this esaaro from previous ones: "This year, everything is so rushed, various homes of the same family had to circumcise on the same day." In the past, he elaborated, when a home would circumcise, people from the entire *omogai* (neighborhood) would come to escort and to celebrate. This year, the celebrations were either attenuated or aborted since relatives often had their own family celebrations to attend to, and thus weren't able to participate in the ones they would have customarily gone to. Or, because the season itself was so short given its late start, youths

141

were being circumcised and the customary feasting was simply being skipped.

Most abasaamba are primary school pupils who return to school once they come out of seclusion at the end of the initiation season. During seclusion—which maximally lasts the whole six weeks of school vacation—they wander all day in groups throughout their neighborhood, engaged in idle chatter as they recuperate. They compare their experiences and talk about how the operation went and how they felt. They are not allowed to associate or eat with noninitiates, nor do any productive work. Accordingly, this becomes an intensely group-focused period in their lives as they hang out together, separated from others, visiting each other and establishing a pecking order that will carry into subsequent life. Within these groups of peers, they begin to establish a group identity, and to see themselves as belonging to a clearly defined circumcision set. They talk about who is having an ekehonio celebration to decide where they will eat that day. In the late afternoon, they descend on the homes of the cohorts they have chosen, to partake in ritual celebrations of consoling and comforting to help them recover, enjoying an extended hospitality ticket. Not all go to each event. Some abasaamba choose not to hang out with the neighborhood group of initiates. Others are attracted by the group dynamic and want to be a part of it. In the process, they are forging ties with other newly initiated youth, and with their maternal and paternal kin.

The abasaamba and their parents are bound by taboos and restrictions. For example, abasaamba cannot be out at night, or sleep away from home. Their parents, also, must return home every evening. Further, abasaamba are not supposed to climb, sleep on a bed, farm, or open a granary. The initiates cannot eat from their usual utensils, and must give away or destroy whatever utensils or clothes they use during seclusion before they reenter society in their new status. They are not supposed to bathe or cut their hair. These aspects of grooming are integral to the coming out (*okoroka*) ceremony and their reintegration into society. The prohibitions emphasize the camaraderie of the circumcision set and the removal of the initiate from the world of childhood.

In 1998, many mothers were apprehensive about the wandering. As abasaamba, initiated youth are in a liminal stage of great vulnerability. Would they receive good food, or would it be unclean and poorly prepared? Throughout this season, daily radio news reported cholera outbreaks all over the country, including in nearby Migori

District. To mothers, this danger was especially real for their children transitioning to adulthood.

The threat of death loomed over the community for as long as the abasaamba were in seclusion. To die before coming out of seclusion meant that the initiate could not be buried within the homestead, or even within the community. The corpse of an omosaamba would be dumped in neighboring communities, because it was believed such deaths were caused by witchcraft, and that usually came from neighboring ibiaro. So when an omosaamba died, the body would remain in the natal home until nightfall, when his or her people would take it and throw it in a different ikiaro. All his or her things—bedding, clothing, walking stick, bow, ikirundu (tooth-brushing stick), *igikuru* (small gourd), and even the utensils would be taken and placed by the body. Many rituals would be carried out by the elders of the secret council. So if neighboring ibiaro were circumcising, people were always on the lookout for corpses. If one was found, the abagaaka of the inchaama would go and cut parts of the corpse and then use them to perform rituals. They would try to send back all the misfortunes to the place from which the deceased came.

In Kuria practice, the group is never secluded collectively, as, for example, in the circumcision camps of the Xhosa. Abasaamba meet with elders of the inchaama only twice during the liminal period to receive instruction on interpersonal behavior during seclusion, but there is no explicit instruction on hygiene, sexuality, childbearing, or other adult roles. Such teaching is done one-on-one by their own grandparents, who stand in a joking relationship to them and are therefore allowed to talk about subjects that are taboo with parents and others in a relationship of respect.

Liminality

Arnold van Gennep defines rites of passage, which include initiation, as "rites which accompany every change of place, state, social position and age" (1909, quoted in Turner 1969, 94). He sees a universal pattern of three phases within rites of passage: separation, margin, and aggregation. Much later, Turner elaborates on the middle phase—margin—and the concept of a mediating period of liminality. He sees it as a period of special and dangerous power, which has to be constrained and channeled to protect the social order. Periods of

liminality are required both to complete the ritual process and to rein-
vigorate the culture itself. His analysis of liminality helps us see what
is happening in the lives of abasaamba. The liminal subject, Turner
says, is ambiguous and passing through a cultural realm that has few
or none of the attributes of the past, or of the coming state he or
she will enter following the liminal period. Kuria initiates are moving between two cultural spaces; their behavior is not acceptable and
normal for the uncircumcised, and they have not yet physically recovered, come out of seclusion, and assumed new statuses and positions.
They socialize only with other abasaamba, and they develop "intense
comradeship and egalitarianism" (Turner 1969, 95).

The liminal period is a blend of lowliness and sacredness, of homogeneity and comradeship. Initiates find themselves experiencing
a "moment in and out of time," and in and out of secular social structure, which reveals some recognition of a generalized social bond that
has ceased to be and another that will be recast in relation to their
new status and position (Turner 1969, 96). Because rites of passage
occur at the boundaries of cultural categories, they provide a valuable
key to a society's social and temporal classifications. In Kuria society,
structural ties are organized in terms of descent and segmentary opposition. Turner continues:

> It is as though there are here two major 'models' for human
> interrelatedness, juxtaposed and alternating. The first is
> society as a structured, differentiated, and often hierarchical
> system of politico-legal-economic positions with many types
> of evaluation separating men in terms of 'more' or 'less.' The
> second, which emerges recognizably in the liminal period,
> is a society as an unstructured or rudimentarily structured
> and relatively undifferentiated *comitatus*, community, or even
> communion of equal individuals who submit together to the
> general authority of the ritual elders. (1969, 96)

Implied within this formulation is that in the state of liminality, an
essential and generic human bond is recognized, without which there
could be no society. But there is a dialectic at play as well, for in rites
of passage, people are released from structure into communitas only
to return to structure revitalized by their experience of communitas
(129). But it is that bond created between youths as equals, as people
of the same experience and commitment to the ritual cycle, which
forms the solidarity that is the basis of Kuria social contract.

Those of the same status share ties of close loyalty and devotion. For example, if men circumcised at the same time maliciously injured each other during the liminal period, it would be regarded not simply as a crime but as a serious magico-religious offense, requiring the full attention of the abagaaka binchaama. Kenyatta elaborates on the teaching of social obligation through the classification of age-groups: "They are like blood brothers; they must not do any wrong to each other. It ranks with an injury done to a member of one's own family. The age group is thus a powerful instrument for securing conformity within tribal usage. The selfish or reckless youth is taught by the opinion of his gang that it does not pay to incur displeasure" (1965, 111–12). He continues, "The age groups do more than bind men of equal standing together. They further emphasise the social grades of junior and senior, inferior and superior." Moreover, "The whole organization of the community again enforces the lesson that behavior to other persons is what matters most" (112).

Seclusion is probably the only stage within the life cycle where the activities of the sexes are not defined by gender-specific work expectations, so during the liminal period, abasaamba become social equivalents regardless of gender. A similar phenomenon is described for the Kikuyu (Murray 1974, 19; Mbiti 1969).

Kin and Affines

Hosting an ekehonio to console and comfort an initiate is also the opportunity to reinforce or negotiate one's status within the kin group and community. A gesture of goodwill, an ekehonio is intended to give strength and promote healing. A mother's brother has a special relationship with his sister's children because the uncle likely married using the cattle brought into the natal homestead by the bridewealth of his sister. His relation to his sister's children is one of affection and support, and a mother's brother is often called upon, for example, to help with school fees. If his sister and her husband pass away, he becomes an important source of support options for his nieces and nephews (Prazak 2012). Called *maamai* ("uncle"), a mother's brother is also special because there are no uncles on the paternal side, as father's brothers in a patrilineal society are called *taata* ("father").

Zachariah Magaiwa shed light on another aspect of ekehonio. I ran into him at an early morning animal auction where he was shopping for goats, having decided to host two ibihonio ceremonies, one for Mary Robi, his older brother's daughter, and one for his wife's younger sister. Zachariah explained that sponsoring ekehonio was nowadays not a good investment. A goat would cost KShs. 1,800 to 2,000. Then when the girl married, she would expect the maamai to give her something like a cupboard. That would run about KShs. 2,000. The girl might fetch a bridewealth of maybe thirteen cattle, because these days, bridewealth was low. Of those, the maamai might get one. That was about KShs. 6,000. A profit, but he would have to wait years to get it, if the current rate of inflation left anything at all. I hadn't heard articulated quite so bluntly before such a practical take on initiations and the ties of obligation elaborated through the involvement of kin and affines. But clearly, the status transition dominates event planning as well as family obligations.

Neither celebration would be a true ekehonio, since he was not a mother's brother to either of them. His true ekehonio would have been for his older sister Muruga's daughter, for whom he had not found a goat, which didn't seem to be pressing too heavily on him. The lack of concern was perhaps due to his sister being a poor widow whose daughters would not likely fetch significant bridewealth.

His sister Muruga's life was filled with challenges. Her husband had died just a few months into their marriage, when she was in her late teens. She had not continued with education beyond primary school, and had left school without getting her certificate. Left child-less, she was encouraged to nonetheless bear children who would continue her husband's line. As is the expectation of all widows, she went on to give birth to four children sired by a close male relative of her husband. When the genitor gained social maturity and married, he no longer took interest in Muruga or her children. Though they were of her husband's lineage, they always lacked the basic amenities that having a living father would have provided for them. And thanks to that, their prospects were not perceived as good by anyone.

Ekehonio at Stephen Wambura's Home

Stephen Wambura's mother hosted an ekehonio at their home on December 31, 1998, for her three granddaughters who had undergone genital cutting two weeks earlier. The girls' father provided the goat to be slaughtered, thinking that the best contribution the "sponsor" could make was cash for the many things the girls would need once out of seclusion.[2] Men sat and slaughtered and divided the meat of the goat. Some VIP visitors sat inside the main house, drinking sodas and discussing topics ranging from idle gossip to agriculture and politics. The women of the homestead paid particular attention to hosting the VIPs, as befitted their status. The rest of the crowd seated themselves on whatever was at hand around the compound, in small groups corresponding to their own age-sets and gender, in the shade of the trees and structures dominating the compound. All were enjoying the plentiful meat and ubukima.

The neighborhood group of abasaamba, twenty-five to thirty boys and girls, arrived around 5:30 p.m., each wearing the requisite kanga. Whereas most girls wear it wrapped around them in the manner of a cape, the boys have more latitude to incorporate it creatively into their abasaamba attire: some wear their kangas wrapped as turbans around their heads, others fold them tightly and thread them though the belt loops of their shorts or trousers, some wear them as a sarong, yet others drape them as shawls around their necks. The decision rests partially on the degree of healing that each initiate has reached, and partially on a desire to stand out and be noticed. The group was noisy and loud, behaving in a brazen, almost rude way that was quite unlike the usual behavior of junior members of the society.

They entered the cattle enclosure and drank obosara. Then the girls of the home brought water and washed everyone's hands and all prayed. Food was brought out of the kitchen and placed in containers on the ground in the oboori. A flat basket (*orohongo*) was filled with pieces of meat, and several *ibihe* had Kuria ubukima made of millet, finger millet, and cassava.[3] The leading abasaamba made food bowls out of ubukima filled with meat and gave them to the *abaramia* who supported them. The abasaamba ate roughly and rudely pushed and shoved, grabbing from the food on the ground. Once satisfied, they were assisted in washing their hands again. Throughout that time they did not sit down, but just stood within the oboori.

As soon as everyone's hands were washed, the initiates walked out of the oboori, only to return a minute later to begin reciting poems—okorea obosamba. As the initiates walked back into the cattle enclosure, the males were behaving in the aggressive, assertive manner characteristic of abamura, speaking curtly and ordering the females around. The girls responded with subservience, hanging their heads and obeying. The initiates lined up, and one boy started the obosamba.

Ee ee ee ee [x3]
Grandmother, father's mother, how big are you?[4]
You are like a thicket found by rivers
One that a warrior cannot jump over
And land on the other side

Grandmother, father's mother
You've slaughtered a he-goat for us
With a nice fold
Grandmother, father's mother, may you be blessed
And sleep on beds with mattresses
From the elite in Mwanza
From the North[5]

Ee ee ee ee [x3]
Grandmother, father's mother, how big are you?
You were once a young girl
Old age that has withered you like the leaves
Whenever they saw you they would arm themselves
To go and fetch cattle from manyattas
Of the Maasai[6]

Ee ee ee ee [x3]
Grandmother, father's mother, how big are you?
You've slaughtered a he-goat for us
Which has a mane on its back
Grandmother, father's mother, how big are you?
Grandmother, father's mother, listen
Today I'll praise you and give you medicine
Take you to the back, it's the farthest
That which you've never seen
Grandmother, father's mother, how big are you?
Grandmother, father's mother, may you be blessed

Ee ee ee ee [x3]
Grandmother, father's mother, how big are you?
What I have left you with is one thing
What I have left you with are bells
Tie them onto weaned grandchildren
So they can respect you

Grandmother, father's mother, how big are you?
Grandmother, father's mother, may you be blessed
Sleep on dried banana leaves and mattresses
And beds

Ee ee ee ee [x3]
Grandmother, father's mother, how big are you?
What I have equated you to is one thing
What I have equated you to is Nyantare[7]
It can never be surrounded by two
Together with Getaboraare.
Grandmother, father's mother, how big are you?
You are as big as Reitindo Nyabikemo[8]
Where lions and rhinos sleep
And young bulls

Ee ee ee ee [x3]
Grandmother, father's mother, how big are you?
You were once a young lady
Whenever they would see you they would arm themselves
They went to bring them [the cattle] *from up there*
Like kiburuuha, kemahaara,
Like kiriimbi[9]

Initiates recite poems and sing songs to praise the person sponsoring the ekehonio (in this case the father's mother) and to show off their composition and oratory skills. At Stephen Wambura's home that afternoon, one initiate was clearly in charge. He was chosen informally by the group because he was articulate and well spoken—two important leadership qualities—and because he had numerous siblings who would come to his support if his leadership were contested. He began reciting individually, adapting elements of his song, as with the invitation poems, but this time to honor his hosts. Two more boys followed, singing praises in a similar manner, and then the girls began in their call and response style, with one leading and the rest chanting in chorus, repeating the key lines. Unique to the praise singing at an ekehonio, the person being praised gives money to the singer when he or she says something particularly pleasing to the audience. At this event, many of the initiates' remarks were met with loud approval from the assembled guests—ululation, shrieks, and *prrr* sounds, accompanied by small gifts of money to those whose praise was most appreciated. One of the initiates from this homestead was given a hen for the quality of the praise she lavished on her grandmother; the elder had not expected her eleven-year-old granddaughter to have learned any songs.

The leader began in a strong, high voice:

Aee ee you've slaughtered for us aee

And the group of girls followed:

Aee ee you've slaughtered for us aee

The entire recitation took this same pattern, with each stanza consisting of two repetitions of the lines:

That grandmother, father's mother, has slaughtered for us aee, aee
That grandmother, father's mother has slaughtered for us, killed for us a he-goat

Aee ee a fat one aee [x2]
That she has slaughtered for us a fat one aee, aee
That she has slaughtered for us a fat one, one with a nice fold

Aee ee how big are you aee [x2]
That grandmother, father's mother, how big are you aee, aee
That grandmother, father's mother, how big are you, you are like Reitindo

Aee ee it's the biggest aee [x2]
That you are like Reitindo, it's the biggest aee, aee
That you are like Reitindo, it's the biggest, where lions sleep

Aee ee you've slaughtered for us aee [x2]
That grandmother, father's mother, has slaughtered for us aee, aee
That grandmother, father's mother, has slaughtered for us, killed for us a he-goat

Aee ee may you live long aee [x2]
That grandmother, father's mother, may you live long aee, aee

That grandmother, father's mother, may you live long, and sleep on beds

Aee ee and mattresses [x2]
That you sleep on beds and mattresses aee, aee
That you sleep on beds and mattresses, these ones for modern people

Aee ee come out aee [x2]
That grandmother, father's mother, come out aee, aee
That grandmother, father's mother, come out, I am praising you

Aee ee you are hiding yourself aee [x2]
That I am praising you but you're hiding yourself aee, aee
That I am praising you but you're hiding yourself, as though I bite

Aee ee she's the best aee [x2]
That grandmother, father's mother, is the best aee, aee
That grandmother, father's mother, is the best, she's like ababiriira [10]

Aee ee abanting'uri aee [x2]
That ababiriira abanting'uri aee, aee
That you are like ababiriira abanting'uri, those who cook milk

Aee ee with fat/oil aee [x2]
That those who cook milk with oil aee, aee
That those who cook milk with oil, and honeycomb

Aee ee come out aee [x2]
That grandmother, father's mother, come out aee, aee
That grandmother, father's mother, come out, you were once a young lady

Aee ee a long time ago aee [x2]
That you were once a young lady a long time ago aee, aee
That you were once a young lady a long time ago, they used to admire you

Aee ee come out aee [x2]
That grandmother, father's mother, come out aee, aee
That grandmother, father's mother, come out, I am praising you

Aee ee you've grown old aee [x2]
That grandmother, father's mother, you've grown old aee, aee
That grandmother, father's mother, you've grown old, I'll look for a
    support

Aee ee of a hardwood tree [x2]
I'm going to cut a support from this hardwood tree
I'm going to cut a support from this hardwood tree, to come and
    support you

Aee ee go far aee [x2]
That I will come to support you in order to go far aee, aee
That I will come to support you in order to go far, beyond Nyamwaga[11]

Aee ee it's the biggest, aee [x2]
That you go beyond Nyamwaga, it's the biggest aee, aee
That you go beyond Nyamwaga, it's the biggest, it's like a tarpaulin[12]

Aee ee how big are you aee [x2]
That grandmother, father's mother, how big are you aee, aee
That grandmother, father's mother, how big are you, you're like a
    Russian

Aee ee you've slaughtered for us aee [x2]
That grandmother, father's mother, has slaughtered for us aee, aee
That grandmother, father's mother, has slaughtered for us, killed for
    us a he-goat

Aee ee a he-goat aee [x2]
That she has slaughtered for us a fat-he-goat aee, aee
That she has slaughtered for us a fat he-goat, one with a nice fold

Aee ee may you live long aee [x2]
That grandmother, father's mother, may you live long aee, aee
That grandmother, father's mother, may you live long, and sleep on
    beds

Aee ee and mattresses [x2]
That you sleep on beds and mattresses aee, aee
That you sleep on beds and mattresses, these ones for modern people

Aee ee she's the best aee [x2]
That grandmother, father's mother, is the best aee, aee
That grandmother, father's mother, is the best, she's like ababiriira

Aee ee abanting'uri aee [x2]
That ababiriira abanting'uri aee, aee
That you are like ababiriira abanting'uri, those that cook milk

Aee ee with fat/oil aee [x2]
That those who cook milk with oil aee, aee
That those who cook milk with oil, and honeycomb

The recitation lasted about twenty minutes, and it was almost dark as the abasaamba ran off, hurrying to their homes before night arrived fully. The potential for evil seemed all the more present as guests at the event discussed an omosaamba in Tanzanian Bwirege who had died. Allegedly, when his people were taking the body to dump in Nyabasi, they had been attacked by some Abanyabasi and shot by poisoned arrows. People were unsure whether one or two had been wounded and if the wounded subsequently died. Clearly the witchcraft fears of a few weeks ago had not disappeared.

Celebrations of the initiation season include large feasts like this one, where families invite visitors to join them in slaughtering an animal and celebrating the changes in their lives caused by initiation ceremonies. But they also include much smaller events, where people come to cheer up, comfort, or console the initiates, visit them while they are recovering, and give them presents and treats. Some kind of consumption—feasting, as well as drinking obosara, sodas, or alcohol—accompanies each event, constituting a significant outlay of resources by the visitors and the initiate's family. In the context of these social occasions, abasaamba test and establish their new statuses, roles, and relationships.

Customarily, this was also a time when marriage was on the mind, so males and females took note of each other's attributes, looking for potential mates for themselves, their children, or their friends. Arranged marriages are uncommon in Kuria society, but a usual practice is for a father to tell his son to find a wife within a given period of time because cattle are available for his bridewealth. In that case, an umumura relies on his friends and relatives to determine the pool of eligible candidates. Though it is not as common as in the past, some abaiseke will not return to school after seclusion because they will be given in marriage or pressured to marry by their families seeking bridewealth to help meet their needs.

Just the day before this celebration, President Moi had announced on the radio that school reopening would be postponed by a week, from the fourth to the eleventh of January. Residents mulled over the meaning of the delay. All agreed that this would certainly give the abasaamba more time to heal and the abagaaka time to consider when to allow them to come out of seclusion. Candidates continued to be circumcised. But people wondered why, after opposing the initiation season in the media for the prior couple of months, the president had taken this stance.

Comforting Mary Robi

The very next day, on January 1, 1999, Zachariah Magaiwa sponsored an ekehonio for Mary Robi, whose initiation had been the original impetus for my journey. When I arrived at the homestead, the goat was slaughtered and the meat cooked, and the feast was ready for the abasaamba by about 3:30 p.m. So the visitors sat around talking and drinking *chang'aa*.[13] We were discussing cross-cultural perceptions of female genital cutting, when Zachariah Magaiwa expressed his belief that "truly, the real reason for genital cutting on girls is to limit female sexuality." This was the first time a Kuria articulated this view—so common in our society—to me.

When the abasaamba arrived, the boys stood against the wooden fence of the cattle enclosure, the girls against the bare brick wall of the initiate's mother's house. In the cleared space where cattle were usually kept, the food was placed on the ground, and once their hands were washed, the lead omosaamba made a small serving of ubukima and meat that was given to the omooramia. As they ate, the initiates posed for photographs and mingled without regard to gender. Once their hands were washed again, the praise recitation was loud and vigorous:

> *Ee ee ee ee* [x3]
> *Father who sired me, you've slaughtered for us*
> *You've killed a fat he-goat for us*
> *One with a nice fold*

Father who sired me, how big are you?
What I have likened you to is the ocean
The Indian Ocean is the biggest
Whites have been defeated in crossing it
Others running with vehicles
And their small planes
My father who sired me, how big are you?
What I have equated you to is Nyarogooso [14] *[x2]*
Of the Abanyamongo; it is the biggest
They have bought vehicles and planes
And trains too

Ee ee ee ee [x3]
My father who sired me, how big are you?
If I were God I would pray for you
Sire another child called Chacha
Who will go to get them [cattle] *from manyattas*
That belong to the Maasai
Ee ee ee ee [x3]
My father who sired me, how big are you?
You are like a tourist's metal rod
That makes noise up there
Women are seated plaiting their hair
With whites among them
Warriors who slaughter cows have thousands and thousands [15]
Although they do not go to farm
Where they are exposed like finger millet [16]
But that which is not ground but sieved

My mother who bore me, how big are you?
I have equated you to the ocean
The Indian Ocean is the big one
It has made it difficult for the whites to cross
Others use their vehicles
And their small airplanes

My mother who bore me, how big are you?
What have I likened you to?
You're like a white; he's the tough one
He's the one who has stepped on the moon on foot

With shoes that shine
With stars on them

My mother who bore me how big are you?
If I were God, I would pray for you
To get a daughter-in-law in charge of the cattle gateway entrance
And one to fetch water

My mother who bore me, what are you like,
You are like the 'tanker' at Musoma
That guards invited guests
I will go steal their socks
And bring them to the growing children,[17] *to use them*
Sit on the police seat...
And Dar es Salaam

Mother who bore me
If I were God I would pray for you
And give you more days
For the modern people

The praise was received with trills and ululation, and the listen-ers and hosts gave money to the youthful praise singers. Because I was present, most of the abasaamba incorporated something about the mzungu in their poems, so I too gave out monetary tokens of appreciation. As a tremendous thunderstorm rolled in, the abasaamba scattered without finishing the full round of recitations. The hosts and I sat for more than an hour waiting for the storm to finish, but it was getting darker and the storm was starting to lift, so I decided to walk home, arriving thoroughly soaked.

There, I asked Klara Robi about the belief Zachariah had expressed to me earlier that day, and she explained that genital cutting on girls is valued for making women docile. But she was more interested in the latest news that had reached her. The elders of the inchaama had asked initiates to change into their regular clothes so they would no longer stand out, and to stop strolling through the neighborhoods. This was meant as a precaution following the alleged death of an omosaamba in Tanzania, whose body had been dumped in Nyabasi. The prohibition against genital operation on girls—issued locally by the SDA church—was another point of widespread discussion and concern. The local congregations were telling their pastors who opposed female genital cutting that they saw no alternatives for uninitiated girls to be married, since their brothers and the young men of the community were still seeking circumcised wives. Who will marry these uninitiated girls, they asked. Would they have to marry and live outside of the community?

Older people reminisced about the months they had had to recover when they were initiated, when there was no school demanding a quick return to ordinary social status. Pacifica Mokono was one of them.

Pacifica Mokona's Memories

Pacifica remembered the ekehonio her uncle had hosted and the praises that were sung.

The abasaamba would sing, praising the uncle, and then the whole of your family. They would say things like "The family is large, and widely spread," that "Our father's family is as widespread as a mushroom from Kiribo which has a deep root." They might praise the uncle saying he was as huge as Mt. Nyamwaga. They would say, "Uncle we have given you sons so that you circumcise each year. We have also given you shields (sons), cattle, babies, and people." Then girls would sing praising him. Then the initiate who is the omosaamba-host would sing praising her uncle.

Eeh she has isolated herself eeh eh
My uncle's black cow (nyangera) has isolated herself eeh eh
My uncle's black cow has isolated herself eeh eh
My uncle's black cow has isolated herself, she feeds by a swamp
Eeh eh in the white grass eeh eh [x2]
She feeds by a swamp on white grass eeh eh [x2]
She feeds by a swamp on white grass that glitters

Eeh eh they are like thunder eeh eh [x2]
Sons of our land are like thunder eeh eh [x2]
Sons of our land are like thunder, they split trees
Eeh eh with hands eeh eh [x2]
They split trees with hands eeh eh [x2]

Eeh they split trees with hands and fingernails
Eeh eh they will run eeh eh [x2]
If the cattle are touched in Maasailand they will run hee [x2]
If the cattle are touched at Maasailand they will run
and the cattle will return with calves

The men would be cheering "Hiihii" and shouting. Women would be cheering from the doorways—"Arriirriirrii." The girl had told her father that the black cow that her uncle will be given when she marries has isolated itself and is grazing in good pasture, a way of saying the uncle sponsoring the event will get some cattle from her bridewealth. When she marries, the uncle who provided the ekehonio feast is given two cattle, or he could get three or four depending on how much bridewealth he received when his sister (the mother to the daughter marrying) got married. If he received enough he would be given two, one would reimburse for what he slaughtered and the other would be additional. While the abasaamba sing in praise of the uncle sponsor, he gives presents in the form of money when a specific phrase or articulation pleases him particularly.

Variations on the Consolation Theme

An unusual turn of events took place at Stephen Wambura's homestead, where a third day of consolation and feasting was to take place for his daughters, sponsored by his wife's mother, her brother, and the kin living on the other side of Bwirege. Relatives and friends gathered, and the goat was killed, distributed, and cooked. But a heavy rainstorm changed everyone's plans. Since so many of the sponsors had far to go, the business of the ekehonio was concluded inside, during the downpour. The mother's brother handed Stephen Wambura KShs. 10,000 in cash and a promise for KShs. 5,000 more. The money was intended to purchase the necessary supplies for the three initiated girls when they came out of seclusion. The handing over was witnessed by the visitors and the abagaaka, as well as put in writing and signed by all concerned parties. So when the rain subsided, the sponsors of the event left, even though the abasaamba group hadn't arrived yet.

Another unusual celebration was held at the home of Thomas Mokono to recognize the initiation of his first wife's two youngest children, a girl and a boy.[18] Together they had six, and he had five more with his second wife. He and both his wives were employed as teachers. At the time of the initiation, he was in his late fifties, and his first wife was a decade younger. The two initiates had been operated on in a clinic in Kisii, and by the time of this celebration, had mostly healed, though they still dressed in omosaamba attire. A table with a scribe was set up at the entry to the half-finished permanent structure that dominated a compound of several semipermanent houses and mature fruit and flowering trees. All participants in the celebration were expected to make their donation to the scribe, who duly recorded it, giving a very official touch to a celebration that otherwise looked much like the others I had witnessed. Celebrants divided into groups according to age and gender, finding ample shady spots among the coffee and banana groves on each side of the compound where they could share gossip and wait for the food and entertainment.

The elders sat in the shade of a tree on their four-legged stools, apportioning the slaughtered ox. These thirty old men had clearly been there a while and had witnessed the slaughtering and butchering. The sharing of the meat was well under way, with the aroma of roasting pieces wafting through the air. Soon, the serious business of eating would begin. Women were seated in the living room of the unfinished structure, sitting under a roof but with no plastering on the walls, with open holes for windows and doors. The young people were gathering in the old structures, listening to the radio and entertaining each other with gossip and tidbits of esoteric information on current affairs and music, showing off the influence of global culture on their lives.

The most "elite" guests—the teachers, administrators, jobholders, and government officials—started to arrive by midafternoon, and the scribe became busy for the first time since my arrival. Interestingly enough, people were asking him to make change, indicating that the donors had specific amounts to give to each of the initiates and were not afraid to ask for change. Though alcohol was served to the elders, SDA influence led to the absence of neighborhood abasaamba from the activities. The neighborhood gang simply did not come, since the initiates from this home had spent no time as a part of that group. They had not been operated on within the community and had not taken part in any activities of forming the corporate group of this year's esaaro. The initiates themselves recited no poetry, and the occasion simply dissolved as sated visitors drifted off. Though the mother of the abasaamba had described this celebration as an ekehonio in inviting me, the absence of the okorea obosamba marked it as different. As I came to see, some Christian homes—as well as some of the most educated homes—have dispensed with the praising and singing of the ekehonio occasion. Though they host feasts to comfort, console, and give strength to their initiates, they skip the elements that make them uncomfortable and instead focus on preparing the abasaamba for returning to school.

Coming Out of Seclusion

As initiates healed, people speculated when they would come out of seclusion, or okoroka. Many parents worried over the need for money to get new clothes and items for the newly elevated young men and women to return to school and the larger society. Technically, the decision to come out of seclusion is not up to the initiates or parents. Members of the council of elders appoint the time following a meeting with the initiates at which they resolve any disputes that might have arisen between them during seclusion, give the esaaro a name, and declare time for the candidates to okoroka. This is the occasion that establishes the members of the esaaro as a corporate group. This year, the real question was when that would happen. Despite the extension of the school break by a week, candidates were still being circumcised in early January and thus their full recovery was unlikely by January 11, the day schools were to reopen.

While on a walk through the community, I visited Victoria Gaati and Moses Kisito and was quite surprised to learn that Smoky Joseph's abasaamba were about to come out of seclusion. Their father had to return to his job outside of Kuria District and wanted to take his daughters with him so that they could study in an elementary school better than the one available in this community. He needed to leave that day, and thus all four of his initiates needed to go through the final stages of the initiation rituals. He couldn't wait for word from the abagaaka. So I remained in the homestead, and observed the activities taking place.

The abasaamba—males and females alike—were getting their heads shaved as the first step of coming out, as were the young children who had been their attendants through the entire season. When done, they scrupulously picked up their hair off the ground and threw it into the latrine to preclude it being used in medicine to bewitch them. Next they went to bathe. Those who had held their heads during the operation now poured water over them, but the abasaamba washed themselves. After drying, they oiled their bodies and put on their new clothes. As they were anointing themselves, they also anointed everyone who was observing their transition. The two girls were impeccably dressed up, their outfits easily suitable for going to a baptism, church, or wedding. The boys dressed in new finery too, including long trousers, button-down shirts, Reeboks, and baseball caps. Though all the steps of the coming out process are meant to be done inside the oboori, they were not. But when the abasaamba were ready, they came out through the ikihita, and went around the assembled people, anointing them with oil.

Because their father was anxious to get back to his work location, we escorted the small group that was traveling to the road, where they waited for a vehicle to come by. In that time, Smoky Joseph explained to me how important it was to get back to work, since the month of initiations had cost him KShs. 15,000—for the operations, the feasting for his children as well those of his sisters, clothes, and traveling. Soon he, the two newly transitioned abaiseke, and his third wife boarded a matatu that began their journey away. And though these initiates had reentered the realm of everyday society in their new statuses, other adolescents were still being circumcised, and others feasted and treated to ibihonio. Two days later, the abagaaka binchaama held a meeting at Saboke, a market center of the minority Abarisenye descent section. Among other things, the assembled initiates were told that they would come out of seclusion in a month. In the meanwhile, they instructed them to go back to school and come directly home when it let out in the afternoon.

Ritual Culmination in the Past

According to older informants, coming out of seclusion used to entail more activities on the part of the initiates than it does now. Pacifica Mokona liked to compare current practices with her long experience.

One afternoon, looking into the distance, she started to speak of the time decades earlier when, after many months of seclusion, the initiates of her esaaro jointly ended the liminal stage of obosamba.

To begin with, the morning of coming out, they would walk around the family's herd before taking a bath, marking the end of seclusion. Walking around the cattle was slightly different for boys and girls. Men and women would gather by the entrance to the cattle enclosure, men shouting and women cheering. The omooramia (child attendant) would lead the male initiate around the herd five times, while the youth sang and praised his father's family and named his accomplishments as an uncircumcised boy (umuriisia)—maybe he had cultivated crops, or worked somewhere and bought a goat or a head of cattle. The people watching would shout their approval and cheer.

Girls would be led around the herd four times. When Pacifica Mokona's firstborn daughter Gaati sang, she said: "I will not run away from the cattle that will face me, giving them my back. I will face them, we will face one another." In this way she told the spectators that she would marry whoever comes with cattle for her people. If a girl went around the herd four times without saying anything, people would say she is timid, and would not "face" cattle, concluding she would marry a poor man. On coming out of seclusion, she would be attractive to poor men only.

In those days (approximately 1950s), girls underwent genital cutting in preparation for marriage, so their mothers taught them how to respect parents-in-law and how to perform the tasks they would be asked to do. They were taught to respect their husbands, how to cook for and feed them. "You were told to respect your parents-in-law and your brothers-in-law. To do what your husband tells you. To go and do what they do. He is the one who will be guiding, you obey him," Pacifica recalled.

A small ceremony accompanied Pacifica's coming out of seclusion. Her head was shaved in a special style. Women came to bathe her. The woman who held her head came with leaves, dipped them in water, and slapped Pacifica with them. "She would hit your front four times and then turn to your back and do the same. After that you would continue to bathe and scrub yourself thoroughly with leaves. If you had anything, like an extra cloth, you would give it

to her as a sign of appreciation." New clothes (in the form of finely
worked skins) prepared by old men were presented to the initiate, as
were necklaces and belts that had been bought. She was smeared with
much oil. They used a hen's feather to apply the oil onto the girl's skin
and every exposed part of the body would be dripping with it.

A goat was slaughtered to feed visitors. Women cooked obosara
and ubukima. In the following month, Pacifica Mokona, as well as the
other initiates, went to dance at the chief's camp. Nyakemori was chief
then.[19] Or they went to collect firewood. Or they worked on gardens
in collective groups of up to ten new initiates. "Everybody wanted
to marry. There was nothing for us to do, there were no schools, so
the distraction of schooling did not exist. After initiation there was
just marriage. In those days the abasaamba were so big that they just
had to marry after seclusion ended."[20] Some were delayed in being
married by "bad luck": no man had brought cattle or sought them
for marriage, so they continued living with their parents. But if a girl
was wanted, she accepted to be married to gain bridewealth for her
brother to marry with and/or for the family to use. Or her father could
use it to marry. "Today we allow girls to learn if they wish and the
parents are able to meet the cost. Those days there was nothing else to
do," explained Pacifica.

Coming out of seclusion, dancing used to be the principal
leisure activity for the newly created abamura and abaiseke. Though
they were expected to participate fully in everyday productive life of
their homesteads, this stage of life was marked by the need to find
a spouse. "After the youth came out of seclusion they would go to
dance. The following morning the young women would go to the
stream very early in the morning, having passed through the ikihita.
When a girl poured the first drop of water on herself, she would say:
'May I marry a man who will not beat me.' As she washed, she would
say more: 'May I marry a husband who has brothers and sisters, may I
go and find my parents-in-law. That is my prayer to God.'" According
to Pacifica, the girls would do that the day after seclusion had ended.
They would go bathe before sunrise—the sun would appear as they
came home. If a group of girls met, they would say that they wished
to marry a good man, a man who would not beat them, who would
not be quarrelsome, a man who would not disturb them.

"We also wanted a man whose father was still alive," Pacifica
continued, "who would come to the girl's aid in case of a fight
with her husband. We wanted a man whose mother was still alive,

so that the girl could leave her child with her, or whose young
children she could ask to look after her child. We also wished
to go to a home which had enough food so that one would not
go hungry.... May I go to a home where there is food—enough
for me, my brothers-in-law and sisters-in-law. An umugi [home/
family] with children, food, and cattle. That is what we would say."
For her, marriage came soon. She was first of the newly initiated
girls to be married: only one month after okoroka, the engagement
process began, and by the third month, she was married. Luckily,
her husband lived next door, so she did not have far to move from her
family.

But the practice is different now: People have become civilized.
In those days people would go to dance isiibi [the coming out dance
for initiates] and we would take obosara to them. These days the
initiates take [only] a few days before they come out of seclusion,
while we could take as long as six months. Our uncles would come to
slaughter oxen for us. Pamela Otaigo's[21] relatives had wanted to come
and slaughter an ox for Mary Robi but now time has run out. If they
come, Chacha Jonas will prepare food for them with bought meat and
the bull they will have slaughtered will be sold so that things, clothes,
are bought for her. The clothes she used to wear will be given to her
younger sisters so that everything she has is new. In the old days,
if a child was circumcised, his mother would dress properly, with
necklaces hanging, and would have her dress smeared with ocher
and oil so that she looked like a girl. The man would also dress in the
appropriate attire and would remain in those clothes for five days for
a boy. For a girl, it would be four days. That is no longer there.

Circumcision Sets as Identity Markers

The timing and form of the circumcision ceremonies vary from
clan to clan. Currently, the Abairege initiate every three years if
the auguries are propitious. People often speak about the esaiga
named Abagesambiso during whose times people were circumcised
yearly. This period (spanning the late 1950s until the mid-1960s)
witnessed extended warfare between Abairege and Maasai, and thus
young warriors were needed to carry on the fighting. Ruel notes
this anomaly in his fieldwork report, writing that, in the past, the

ceremony was held about every four years, but this varied by ikiaro. He notes that the Abairege "even circumcise every year" (1959, 123).

Initiates of any one year form an esaaro. This group is given a name at the close of the initiation period. In Bwirege, three adjacent circumcision groups (*ichisaaro*) are combined into an esaiga, a circumcision set. This more inclusive set is usually named after the first of the three groups of initiates. Ruel reports (1959) that when the esaiga was constituted, the oldest esaaro in the esaiga gave a celebration to which the younger groups were invited (123). The present abagaaka binchaama made a bracelet (igituang'a) out of the chest skin of a goat. One member of each of the three sets forming the esaiga put on the bracelet, beginning with the most senior set. At that time, the younger groups gave up their names, and were called by the name of the oldest group from then on. This type of group assimilation bears similarity to the process an initiated young woman undergoes when she is married. She belongs first to the circumcision set she was initiated into, but through marriage she becomes aligned with her husband's set.

The solidarity of the circumcision set rests on shared experience.[22] Each set has its name and its own praise-term used when the set is referred to collectively, especially in the recitation of praise poems (*amaibaako*). But more importantly, in a social sense, classificatory kinship rules follow circumcision-set membership. For example, the father of a son belonging to the Abakaramu circumcision set is a classificatory father to each member of that set. The respect relationship between parents and children likewise extends to members of the same esaaro. The status of all members within the group is equal, though personal bravery during the circumcision ceremony can impact individual standing. Circumcision sets stratify the members of an ikiaro into a hierarchy of seniority that generalizes the rules of respect found within the homestead—where juniors always defer to seniors—and thus helps to determine precedent in public and ritual contexts.

Abasaamba form a strong fellowship with one another and with ancestral founding spirits associated with their descent group territory (Bernhardsdotter 2001, 35). The strongest general obligation for all members of a set is to be loyal to each other. "Meanness towards, disdain or rejection of a fellow member may be brought to the notice of the set as a whole who will be expected to punish the offender" (Ruel 1959, 127–28). The sanctions held by a circumcision set in the 1950s included physical punishment, fines, inflicted damage, ritual cursing, and ostracism. As Ruel also notes, the period of most intense collective activity for members of a set was immediately before and after initiation. In the 1950s, some of the collective activities had declined and/or were forbidden in certain locations by the colonial administration. A meeting of the set could be called if the occasion warranted collective action, and throughout their lives, members were expected to uphold the solidarity of the set. This continues even in the new millennium where, at key rites of passage of a man's life, the comembers of his set are provided with food and beer. The initiation of his first child is the primary occasion, followed by the marriage of his son—when they share an ox—and at the elderhood ceremony when they share one of the main beer pots and the first ritually slaughtered ox.

The collective activities of circumcision sets in the past might have included fighting, especially when many warriors were needed. Age-sets provided separately directed groups that played a part in the larger war strategy, with members of different sets ready to cover different parts of the battle. Based on previous colonial and academic reports, it appears that the collective activity of age-sets has decreased over time. However, Baxter and Almagor (1978) caution against interpretations that compare the past with the present, because many of the early descriptions of age-sets and their functions reflect "a bias inherent in the colonial obsession with 'primitive unruliness' and the supposed propensity to raiding and warfare of many African peoples, which was then used to justify their colonization" (3). Thus earlier accounts of Kuria age organization as a source of violent action should be regarded with reservations. Circumcision sets were not political bodies per se. In a report on age-grades in Musoma, Tanganyika Territory, Baker (1927) notes that the so-called tribes inhabiting the area, including Kuria, were, "prior to the occupation of the country by the Germans, nominally governed by councils of elders, but were, in the majority of cases, under the dictatorship of the war-doctors, wizards and rain-makers, whose orders were enforced by the age-grades" (221).

In the 1980s and into the present, age-set solidarity is most frequently invoked for work parties (especially for *harambee* projects), in order to carry out self-help development projects. For example, in the 1980s, Abagimuri in Bwirege were responsible for building the polytechnic, the Abamasa for maintaining the secondary school, and the

Abagesambiso for the clinic. Similarly, in fundraising events, members of a circumcision set are urged to support each other in donating to a particular cause as a group, in order to gain prestige as a social group by being the biggest contributors, rather like graduating classes in high schools or universities in the United States. On a less inclusive level, an individual organizing a work party for his or her own benefit may invite age-mates or fellow members of the same circumcision set to participate.

General Outcome of 1998 Initiations

On December 14, circumcisions were opened for boys in Bwirege, and the next day for girls. According to public opinion, initiations were proceeding in an unusual way. Fears of witchcraft had greatly delayed ceremonies, and initiates were to return to school on January 11. Accordingly, masses of children underwent genital cutting each day, and the celebrations that bring the kin group together were either poorly attended due to overlap or skipped altogether. Throughout, two abasaari busily attended to the boys, dividing the workload based on descent group (egesaku). The mission set up a small operating center where a Kisii nurse operated on girls. So in effect, there were two abasaari for girls as well, and the choice of which one to patronize had a great deal to do with the type of image the family wanted to project—traditional or progressive.

As discussed above, the first collective corporate action a circumcision set undertakes is okoroka, to come out of seclusion. This event is led by elders of the inchaama, who name the circumcision set and, after instructing the initiates on some of the community's expectations, allow the new abamura and abaiseke to go home and perform the steps necessary to reintegrate into the society. Everyone expected the okoroka to happen before January 4, but as that date rolled around, youths were still being cut. The initiates began leaving seclusion as circumstances dictated, without the usual ritual process. The official ceremony to name the circumcision set took place in Itirio, Tanzania, on the 23 of February, and was attended by about 250 abasaamba, only a small portion of the initiates (P. M. C., pers. comm.). The young men and women arrived at the venue by 6:30 a.m. and waited for the elders of the inchaama, who arrived around 9:00 a.m. Of the twelve elders present, only three spoke. They first introduced the *abaturiaani,* the first two initiates to have been circumcised, and then told the abasaamba to sit in a circle, with the abaturiaani and the inchaama in the space formed in the middle. Then speeches began. The elders advised the abaturiaani on how to live. They warned the abamura that they should never start a fight within this group, nor should they go hunting, or steal, or go to live in another ikiaro. Finally, the inchaama gave the abasaamba two names from which to choose for their set: Geteeba or Michale. The abasaamba chose Geteeba.[23]

At this meeting, abasaamba from Kenya and some parts of Tanzania were present, but initiates from other parts of Tanzania had not come, and there were rumors that initiates from those areas were being given a different name by their omosaari: they were called Abakambuni. For an omosaari to name the set was very unusual. But it was said that the inchaama would meet to try to combine these groups to make them only one esaaro. The meeting ended.

Thus in the 1998–99 initiation season, a cohort of children were raised into the beginning ranks of adulthood. Their position within their lineages was confirmed, as was their incorporation into the Kuria ethnic group. But their belonging was not unambiguously confirmed vis-à-vis the middle levels of the sociopolitical organization. At least two aspects of the segmentary lineage organization were being challenged: 1) the fixed apical segment (Abairege), and 2) the alignment of traditional segmentary units with contemporary political, territorially defined, groupings. The confusion that followed led to the granting of two distinct names to the generation set stemming from one circumcision season.

People feared that the double naming was a political maneuver to split up the Abairege into two political units, the Abakehenche and Abarisenye, which would provoke a struggle over land. While the Abairege live within a discrete territory, the Abakehenche and Abarisenye are territorially mixed, and a struggle over land would displace many people. At that point, a decade had passed since the expulsion of many Kuria from the adjoining Rift Valley Province, and no one was keen to undergo such a process within Bukuria. Nevertheless, the 1998 circumcisions, as a locus for negotiating identity, failed to underscore and reinforce the horizontal links which usually serve to counterbalance the vertical ties of descent that dominate the social and political life in lineage-based societies.

The talk of that season, with its many strands of innovations and change, carried through into the first decade of the millennium.

Clearly, at the very local level in rural Bwirege, people were keenly aware of the controversies surrounding their ritual practice of initiation, especially the genital cutting of females. In response, they felt their identity was being challenged. This led to some new divisions within the society, some new lines of differentiation. The desire to be modern, progressive, and responsive to the challenges of the time allowed for the introduction of variations on the customary practices. Most notably, the introduction of medicalization signaled a major change in attitude both in terms of the use of more sterile or more hygienic methods and of limiting the amount of tissue disturbed by the cutting. Though not undisputed, medicalized cutting did become another acceptable form of circumcision, and with it came a broader acceptance of youths operated on in clinics and hospitals as full-fledged abasaamba, in accordance with the solidarity-building activities of the period of seclusion. And though the practice of genital cutting continued, new voices gained prominence, and the variations arising from additional options allowed for a growing variety of practices and understandings to flourish. I turn to those in the following chapter, which extends a number of the themes developed in earlier chapters, including intervention strategies such as alternative rites, the mixed input from churches, debates on the use of legislation as a tool for change and the mixed responses to laws, the proliferation of single-issue NGOs, the effect of secondary school on female genital cutting, and the medicalization debate.

Youths posing/threatening at *ekehonio*

Male *abasaamba* waiting to be fed at *ekehonio*

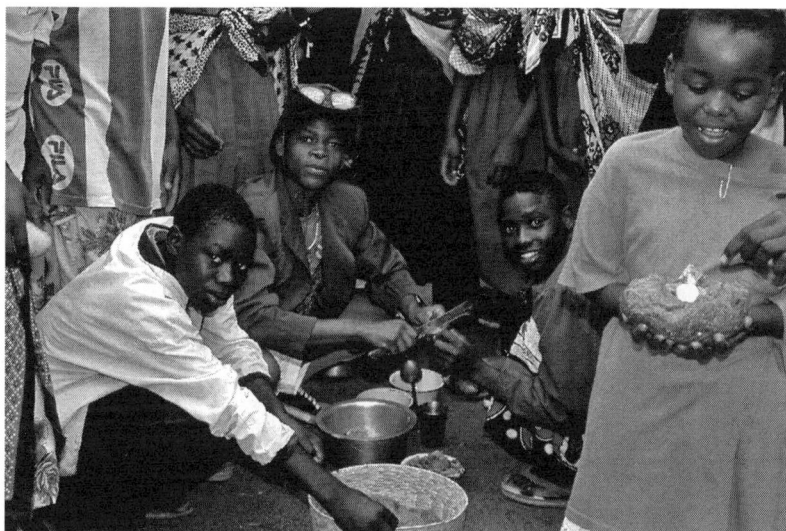

Serving food for the *omooramia*

Female initiates eating at *ekehonio*

Male *abasaamba* eating at *ekehonio*

Males singing praise poems at *ekehonio*

Mother and daughter during seclusion

Abasaamba being consoled at *ekehonio*

Male *abasaamba* at *ekehonio*

Anointing relatives prior to coming out of seclusion (*okoroka*)

Umumura coming out of seclusion (at cattle gate), with ritual supporter (*omooramia*)

Young women (*abaiseke*) with their attendants coming out of seclusion

6

Talk, Talk, Talk

The difficulties of the 1998–99 and the 2001–2 initiation seasons
sparked many conversations, and more generally, an interrogation
of genital cutting, its traditional importance, and the controversy
fanned by the media, the international donor community, NGOs, and
various governmental offices increasingly vocal against the practice.
The issue-shaping power of the media came to upcountry communities on the radio and thus permeated every homestead. Newspapers
also served an important function, particularly in bringing forth the
ideas, opinions, and experiences of other circumcising communities in
Kenya. Though used by a small segment of the population relative to
radio, newspapers were generally the most widely read publications,
and circulated well beyond the individuals who purchased them. Most
of the educated and employed elite within Kuria society read newspapers whenever they could. As a result, the media were and continue to
be a significant voice in the local conversation on initiation.

Voices in the Press

At the time of these circumcision celebrations, national newspapers
were presenting many voices, both pro- and anti-genital cutting.
Those opposing the practice wrote of the health hazards, of the backwardness of tradition, and of the subjugation of females. Those promoting the practice wrote about the educational moment initiation
presents for youths, the value of adherence to traditions, and the need
to hold on to one's own culture rather than copy "everything from
the U.S." (Kigotho 1996). Finally, promoters of alternative rites also
carried out public debate in the media.

Often the news articulated the evolving official Kenyan government position. For instance, the media covered the occasion when

an assistant minister for cultural and social services announced in 1990 that the Kenyan government had banned female circumcision to save women from harmful side effects associated with the practice (Mwangi 1990). For maximum impact, she made the announcement in Nairobi at an international seminar organized by the Young Women's Christian Association (YWCA), held at the Methodist Guest House and attended by over thirty leaders of the YWCA from eight regions of the world. At the time, there was no law on the books banning female circumcision, although President Moi had pronounced an official ban on female circumcision in July 1982. The president made public addresses banning FGC, but these had no legal weight. Banning FGC was debated in Parliament several times, and bills were defeated. Many politicians were averse to supporting a law that ran counter to the cultural norms of their constituents. What appeared as ambivalence on the president's part was in fact a balancing act of avoiding "shame and blame" in the international arena, trying to galvanize political will in Kenya, and at the same time trying to respect local cultural values. Six months later, a one-inch headline proclaimed, "Female Circumcision Irks DC." At the Jamhuri Day celebrations in Meru, the acting district commissioner condemned genital cutting on women in that district, describing the practice as offensive and dangerous, as it could lead to the spread of incurable diseases. He advocated that traditional circumcisers be vetted by health authorities (Imathiu 1990).

As is common in newspapers everywhere, stories of disaster featured prominently. During initiation seasons, stories of deaths were common (e.g., Matoke 1995; *Daily Nation* 1995a, 1995c). Chronicling tragic mishaps, these stories came from the various regions where traditional genital operations continued to be carried out, and they implied that severe injury and death were common.[1]

Local efforts to end the "female cut" also received regular coverage (Nthiga 1994; *Daily Nation* 1995b), as did the story about Nyambene District in Eastern Province, where twenty chiefs participating in a three-day female circumcision seminar raised an action plan to curb FGC by having teachers, church members, political leaders, elders, and NGOs educate the public on the dangers of cutting practices (Nthiga 1994). The seminar report, signed by the Eastern Provincial Family Planning Association of Kenya, identified female circumcision as the major factor leading to poor academic performance by primary schools in this district: "Once girls were circumcised at between

10 and 12 years, they were married off as it was assumed they had graduated to womanhood." A more general statement regarding the practice of genital cutting appeared at the end of the article: "Female circumcision...was the worst form of violence against women as it affected the victims psychologically for the rest of their lives. Other disadvantages were a lack of sensitivity during sexual inter-course, which made sex less enjoyable and the r[u]pturing of genital[s] during delivery" (16).

A short while later, the Family Planning Association of Kenya urged the government to enact a law to ban female circumcision on the grounds that genital cutting was harmful to women's health and was tantamount to genital mutilation (*Daily Nation* 1995b). In the same article, research findings were reported indicating that 71 percent of the 6.3 million Kenyan women who had undergone genital cutting risked being infected with HIV/AIDS because tools were used on more than one initiate without sterilization. Also reported were the myths the Family Planning Association uncovered regarding female genital cutting. Principally, these were "that uncircumcised girls cannot mature or make good wives, and that circumcision enhances marriage opportunities among girls in addition to preserving virginity." The statement claimed that to the contrary, circumcision "suppresses women's sexuality, ensures their subjugation and control (by men) of their reproductive function" (*Daily Nation* 1995b).

Stories of scamming and scheming were also rife. In one typical report, a traditional medical practitioner called for the government to take action against "bogus" circumcisers who were marring the ongoing circumcision ceremonies in Bungoma and Trans-Nzoia districts in Western Kenya (Wanyama 1990). These bogus circumcisers had entered the trade simply to make quick money, seeing the large number of youths (ten thousand) to be initiated. Another story appeared in September of that year, discussing the issue of forced circumcision and reporting an incident from Nakuru, where a mob pounced on five uncircumcised men and demanded they face the knife and be circumcised. Reportedly, four of them ended up undergoing circumcision, and the local market traders collected money for them during their recuperation (Njuguna 1990).

A feature article warned, "Those opposed to female circumcision, impatient that the practice continues to defy the presidential ban, may need to re-assess their position," and reported a new awakening in Samburu and elsewhere that could delay the final collapse of the practice (Naitore and Joel 1994). "In a radical departure from the late 1970s, when the ritual involved extensive mutilation of the female genital, the initiates now lose only a portion of the clitoris!"[2] The main advantage identified with a modified cut was a reduced likelihood of scarring that could otherwise lead to prenatal deaths and/or the rupture of the birth canal and formation of rectovaginal fistulas. The article discussed other innovations, including the use of gloves and a brand new razor blade for each initiate, and focused largely on the meaning of the initiation practices within Samburu society. It presented the view that in practicing communities, people need to be sensitized slowly and carefully to abandon circumcision completely, as "banning orders have failed to achieve the desired effect" (Naitore and Joel 1994).

Whether FGC might die a natural death due to the decreasing number of female circumcisers was taken up in a lengthy study of Samburu practitioners (Sekoh 1996, 6–7). The author provided figures to show the extent of the practice, claiming that FGM was practiced in at least twenty-six African countries, with more than one hundred million women estimated to have undergone genital cutting. While most newspaper stories opposed FGC or depicted it in a negative light, some took the opposite stance.

Vehement support for the value of the ritual practices was also expressed. For example, the "Platform Forum for Discussion" challenged the term "female genital mutilation" and questioned the foundations of the debate: "The debate on female circumcision was started by the missionaries who thought the practice was abominable. They came from countries where even men are not circumcised. They embarked on a campaign to stamp it out using churches and schools to spread their message. The issue of female circumcision is no longer a simple tug-of-war between Protestants on the one hand and the rest of the community on the other. It is now a continental campaign led by highly educated and articulate women who have virtually cowed the circumcised woman into submission" (Muchuku 1996).

In April 1999 a number of articles appeared in the *Daily Nation* broadly publicizing the idea of an alternative to female genital cutting. One reports on a program in Meru called "initiation through counseling," where girls ready for initiation were taught "vital lessons about negative effects of the rite and family life education, among others" (Waruru 1999). Over the course of three years, 360 girls had participated in the program—in an area where, reportedly, 90 percent of initiation-age girls underwent genital cutting. Additionally, the program held workshops to sensitize opinion leaders, including politicians and administration officials, on the need to support the anti–female genital mutilation initiative. Prior to the program, opting out of circumcision was practically unheard of, but local women from Meru who wanted to see the age-old practice come to an end pushed for the changes.

The newspaper report describes the alternative rite as incorporating the major elements of initiation while not cutting the participants' genitals. First, the program identified initiation-age girls and talked to their parents. After parents were convinced their daughters need not undergo circumcision, the girls were taken into seclusion, usually to a school, where they were fed and accommodated for five days. Each child was allowed to choose a sponsor. During the five-day period, the girls were counseled on various issues, including primary health care, family life education, and character building. At the end of the five-day period, the girls attended a graduation ceremony in an open field. Prominent people were invited along with members of the community. The initiates dressed in fine clothes, recited poems, and sang songs in praise of the alternative rite. The previous year, the chairwoman of Maendeleo ya Wanawake had been the chief guest and a banquet was held. "To achieve all that, the group has received support from among other donors the Canadian Save the Children, Care Kenya, and the Global Fund for Women" (Waruru 1999). Similar news stories describe changes taking place—though not uniformly well received—in other areas where female genital cutting is practiced, such as Kisii, Narok, and Uasin Gishu.

Another *Daily Nation* article in 1999 posited that FGM manifests the beliefs and practices of the community, which is why it has been so difficult to eliminate even when so much has been said about its harmfulness (Mwakisha 1999). The article describes each side of the several-decades-long debate: "On the one hand there are medical personnel, gender and human rights activists trying to stop it because the practice is believed to be outdated, inhuman, harmful and a violation of human rights." And on the other "are customary diehards who believe FGM retains the community identity, symbolically endorses the growth of young girls into womanhood. This ties with the objective of cutting girls' genitalia as a way of curtailing their sex urge to control their sexuality" (29). Those who wanted the practice to continue feared communities would lose important celebrations that endorse their identity and value. What would replace such significant ceremonies? A best-practice initiative identified in 1999 at a regional UNIFEM conference in Nairobi responded to the concerns of both sides. Dubbed an alternative circumcision, the initiative kept meaningful aspects of the rituals but omitted the cut. When it was carried out in the Kisii, Meru, and Narok districts from 1996 to 1999, the initiative attracted 1,124 girls (Mwakisha 1999).

Voices in the Community

In Bwirege, the ongoing debate was lively, and took many different directions. Walter Gesabo, a senior officer in the district education department and an ex-headmaster with several decades of experience in primary schools, made the case most prominently articulated by the educated members of the community. In a casual conversation with me, he argued that the Tanzanian legislature's 1998 outlawing of genital cutting on girls meant little to Kuria people in that country, who continue genital operations for initiation.[3] "The law," according to Walter, "must come from the people and not be imposed upon them. When it is imposed, people don't cooperate." He continued, "There is some sense among a few people that it isn't necessary or right to circumcise girls, and some people in Isaroswe [Walter's home community] haven't done it. But for the girls who are not circumcised, it is hard. They get humiliated and scorned by others who call them 'omosaagane.' The people have to be ready to give up a tradition themselves in order for it to be abandoned or replaced by something else."

Between Innovation and Tradition

Stephen Wambura and Severina Nyakorema are parents of nine children, seven girls followed by two boys. Both parents are college educated, both teach, and both engage in various business endeavors in the community. Both were in their early forties at the time of my 2002 interview with them, after their sixth daughter, Trufosa Habuba, had just come out of seclusion and was returning to her primary-level education.[4] A month after Trufosa was born, my husband and I were invited to her naming ceremony, which took place in the family's newly built permanent house. Now, I was sitting once again in the same house, celebrating another transition in Trufosa's life. In the meantime, the house had become the center of the homestead, with newer structures in adjoining areas forming a more typical, interconnected, Kuria umugi. Though the homestead didn't have a cattle enclosure at its center, the improved breed cow that was a new source of income through milk sales lived in a shed within the circle of buildings. Having eaten a hearty meal, we sat back and, with an ease that comes from long friendship and mutual admiration and respect, talked about the changes taking place in initiation practices.

In Stephen's thinking, the changes in esaaro in Bwirege arose out of fear of exchanging blood with others. Stephen noted that quite a number of boys were being circumcised in clinics and hospitals, considered by some to be the more hygienic option. "These are children whose parents have been influenced by Christianity," Stephen said. In his and Severina's opinions, pressure from the church was causing boys and girls to be operated on at much younger ages than before, sometimes as young as eight. "People are preaching against esaaro, especially female circumcision, talking as if it is to be banned soon. So people are being awakened to do it, to undergo circumcision, before it is actually banned. So even younger children have to go."

Stephen affirmed that "people do not want to stop the practice. They are sticking to it." Severina nodded in agreement as he spoke. "I have examples of even girls from homes where they did not circumcise in [the] last esaaro because of influence of religion and this time they were forced to be circumcised. Not by their parents, but by the community. Their peers, other girls, cannot accept them easily. Because of the pressure in school and in the community, they get to know it is a good thing to get circumcised and be able to move among people freely. They are not free when they are not circumcised. And because people believe that uncircumcised girls cannot be married within the community, they call the uncircumcised ones *irinyinya*, which means that one is a rejected one, who would only be married in a foreign community or by other groups of people who do not circumcise. That is a bad thing."

An innovator in the community, Stephen had long challenged the norms in a number of ways, but not when it came to initiating his children. All of his daughters were cut "in the bush" rather than at the mission. "Do you think circumcision is necessary?" I asked.

His reply was somewhat surprising: "It is not necessary as long as you are not bound by the community norms. But if you are bound by the community norms, it is necessary, in the sense that the influence and the people you live with are the same people. So, we don't have much influence from the outside.

"I don't dictate my children to go for circumcision. I give my daughters the option of going for it or not going for it. The girls prefer going for it. So in that case I have no option, what do I do?"

When he realized Trufosa planned to be initiated, he and Severina openly discussed her choice together with her, including all sides of the controversy. In the end she responded, "No, me, I just have to go. I cannot be left out. I will feel out of place if I am not circumcised."

In Stephen's words, "She prepared herself much earlier. That is due to the influence of the environment. Her age-mates had prepared themselves, and she couldn't escape the influence. But I am sure if she was away from the environment, she would have considered the option of going without circumcision."

Severina thought that girls should be older when they undergo the operation, that they should be eighteen so they are more mature, and maybe more able to decide:[5] "Many of them will not like to go when they are eighteen. At eighteen you can make decisions, you can weigh what is the good thing, what is the bad thing. But at the age of eight to twelve, you cannot decide."

Stephen pointed out that many ethnic groups in Kenya perform genital cutting on girls, and in practicing communities, people feel it has become such a big topic because of pressure from NGOs and from developed countries. They hear that the World Bank, the International Monetary Fund, and NGOs from foreign countries make conditions for loans, mandating genital cutting be ended. And though in the West female genital cutting is seen as a human rights issue, a practice that harms African women, "People here see it as a practice which is commonly accepted, not as an abuse of human rights," Stephen explained.

Within the community, Severina continued, "There is a group of people who talk against female circumcision. They talk of the bad side of it, of the disadvantages. Now even those who are circumcised are talking against it. They finished doing their children and now they oppose it. So people are saying, 'They are cheating us'.... [People] know that NGOs can pay them to talk against circumcision, so, in other words, they are using NGOs to make money out of that. What they say is unbalanced. They only talk about the bad side, and say nothing of the good side."

"People believe that uncircumcised girls become easily sexually aroused," Stephen said. "Our custom, circumcision, makes them become a bit sexually inactive. When they talk about the spread of AIDS, that one leaves us wondering. It is not the circumcised that get infected, it is the uncircumcised, for example, our neighbors the Luo. When I look at circumcising, I see it has something to do with the curbing of sexual arousement.... Circumcision does the same for boys. Those uncircumcised like having sex all the time. The Luo can be seen as an example again.... Kuria elders favor the ritual, because they fear their children to become [sexually] loose. And that looseness is what they would not like."

Severina maintained that she herself is not for the continuation of genital cutting, but she thinks it will take time for it to disappear, and it won't be accomplished by forcing people to stop. In her opinion, "The practice has [been] moderated. They are just making a slight chop now. We were just expecting that it will stop. Making just a small mark and calling it a circumcision. But opposition makes it much worse. People are doing it in hiding. No hygienic methods will be used [in those circumstances]. The AIDS disease might get spread."

In the community, people who do not want to operate on their daughters face problems. "Just the other day I was watching a drama [in the neighborhood], where parents who refused to circumcise their daughter were forced by the community to circumcise her," Stephen recounted. The father, a Pentecostal church elder, was against his daughter's undergoing genital cutting. "The *mzee* [elder] had a whole farm of pineapples, bananas, sugarcane. When the people took the girl home after she had been circumcised, all that farm became a field. They cleared everything. That was the punishment they gave the owner of the home. They felt he was going against the norms of the society. Why was he refusing to have the daughter circumcised? Indeed, the daughter was already a grown-up woman, above eighteen."

"They spoiled all the fruits, even the ones that weren't ripe yet. They were just chopped up, spoiled. The mzee escaped narrowly being killed. That was mob justice," added Severina. Before that, the pastor's mother had taken another of his daughters for the operation against his wishes. When he discovered what had been done, he disowned his daughter. "But he was forced to accept them, to even give an animal to slaughter. He had no choice in it," Severina said. Even before that, he had refused to have yet another daughter cut, but according to Stephen and Severina, his displeasure at her disobedience was soothed when the girl got married, fetching sizable bridewealth. "This is a poor family," Severina said. "When they got the wealth [of cattle] they came to understand that it is only through circumcision that the girls can be married off. I think that is what made him accept quietly, though he did not want to show it openly. This man's firstborn, a girl, was circumcised the same way, although he did not want it. The girl became sick with measles. They refused to attend [to] her because she had been circumcised. The mzee was very bitter. The girl passed away. That was the first one."

In another case of family conflict at Wangirabose, a pastor told his daughters who had gotten circumcised against his wishes that he would not let them continue with their studies. "He said no more education for them. 'You are going to be married.' And that is his right," Severina recounted. "He wanted to show the girls they had messed up, and he wanted to punish them. If he is serious, they will have to get married." Severina sees this man as civilized. All his sons are being circumcised in the hospital, and he did not want his girls to undergo genital cutting.

Being operated on in a clinic has become quite acceptable for boys, but medicalized genital cutting for girls is another story. Some girls see the clinic as a place of antenatal care and refuse to go there for genital cutting, saying they are not pregnant and thus don't need to go to the clinic. But generally, people realize that risks are greater with local operations than when they go to clinicians. "The main reason they don't like girls going to the mission is that there isn't a Kuria nurse to do it," said Stephen. "But many people did bring their daughters. Reverend Murimi, who is in charge there, emphasizes that members of his church need to bring their daughters. He uses his influence as preacher to convince his congregation to bring their girls."

Stephen concluded: "People are changing their attitudes. [The reason] we still have the majority opposed is because of the approach. But people are ready to change. I am sure they are."

For their own family, Stephen and Severina say they are ready to accept change as it comes. If a younger daughter says she does not need to go through initiation, they will accept her decision.

Changes: The Perspective of a Male Circumciser

Joshua Maskio was a retired trained community nurse and farmer.[6] He had reached Form II in his formal education and continued on to medical training, where he also learned to circumcise. Until his retirement, he had a clinic licensed by the Church of God in East Africa in the principal market center of Bwirege, and one of his wives still resides there with her sons. He farmed in Rift Valley, where he lived with his second wife and her children. At the time of this interview, he was in his early seventies and spoke fluent English.

Joshua Maskio began circumcising in his clinic in 1959. The process he learned and applied was direct: inject anesthetic, cut, apply medicine, stitch, dress, let the person go. In 1989, he began circumcising in the community (iritongo) at the request of the elders of the secret conclave. Although the general public believes that circumcisers learn of their calling through two signs: by changes in health and by encountering the tools of the trade in the path during ordinary activities, Joshua said the conclave of elders sent a messenger to summon him. By his reckoning, "Some of the elders of the secret conclave are witch doctors; they make medicine, and will use it to entice someone they want for the task. So if they place it in a person's path, and the person steps on it, the person might even fall down." But Joshua was a Christian believer before he became a circumciser. At the first meeting with the elders he told them, "I will not use your medicine, but I will use my faith as a Christian." They agreed. So before he started the work of circumcising even one boy, he prayed. And God helped him, he believed. He felt he did not get a supernatural summons to circumcise because his belief was strong.

Demand for his services increased when people began to recognize the danger of *UKIMWI* (HIV/AIDS), and the elders urged him to continue operating because of his sterile technique, using gloves and one knife for each person. But he did not follow the same procedures in the community that he did in the clinic, due to the demands the boys and their families made: no medicine, no dressing. Also, circumcising large numbers of initiates prevented him from offering the full range of medical steps he had been trained to carry out. In the first two days of a circumcision season, he might circumcise two hundred boys per day. The initiates and their escorts want the omosaari to make the cut very quickly, but even so, operations for one day could take many hours. For example, one morning he was waylaid at 6:00

a.m. while using the latrine, was pressed into duty immediately, and continued circumcising until 8:00 p.m.

In his own estimation, what he did in the bush was more dangerous than the circumcisions he performed in the clinic. Not only is the pain strong when the cut is made, but there is bleeding because no stitches are used. The blood oozes, so it is dangerous. The wound is open, without a dressing, so it takes time to heal. "If using medical procedures were allowed, it would be better. But the abagaaka binchaama and the parents do not accept those modifications. The boys who develop complications, such as infections and heavy hemorrhaging, might go for treatment in a clinic."

In the past, they used to come to him at the clinic. After the chaotic 1998 initiation season, he became the only omosaari for boys in Bwirege in Kenya. There were two more in Tanzania. The boys in Bwirege were free to go to Tanzania if they wanted someone else to perform the operation, and some came from Tanzania to be cut by him. Circumcision of boys is universal in Bukuria, and there was always much demand for his services during esaaro. "The boys themselves want to be circumcised," Joshua said. "The parents want it. In fact, they force it, saying to their sons, 'You have to do it, because it is our custom.' And indeed, when anyone who is alive now was born, they found circumcision taking place. 'The grandfathers were doing it. Then the fathers. Now it has come down to us.' No controversy surrounds circumcising boys."

At least a part of why initiation persisted, in his opinion, was because the elders get money from it. Before Joshua Maskio circumcised anyone, he collected payment. His share was KShs. 150 and KShs. 50 went to the elders.[7] That was their incentive for keeping the custom going. In the course of initiation season he would circumcise about six hundred boys. Some abasaari charge boys who appear to have been sexually active before circumcision a fine, but Joshua Maskio did not. He saw circumcision as being about hygiene, but also believed it was about controlling the behavior of boys. As abariisia, they are supposed to stay away from girls. Once they are cut, they are still supposed to control their sexual urges until the day of marriage. But in most cases, he admitted, they don't do so. Many people see the operation as a step to make boys ready for marriage, and because so many do it, it becomes necessary for everyone to have it done. Once enough people stop circumcising, he thought, it will not be necessary anymore.

Operating on girls is different. On boys just skin is cut. With girls, muscle is cut. They harm the girls. But boys are not harmed. The movement to stop the circumcision of girls is a good thing, because the procedure is a danger to them. Some have even failed to get pregnant because they developed keloids. Medicalizing the procedure at the mission is not an improvement. An improvement would be to make only a superficial cut. The movement to stop female circumcision needs to work with the elders of the inchaama to be successful, to persuade them to let the practice lapse.

Unlike Reverend Murimi, who thought that Kuria culture would end altogether without circumcision, Joshua Maskio thought Kuria tradition would continue even if circumcision did not. In his view, genital cutting was not absolutely necessary for people to be Abakuria, and he was willing to work with groups setting up in Nyankare to stop female genital cutting.[8]

Changes: The Perspective of a Female Circumciser

Rose Wankio's chief curiosity—why people from countries outside of Africa are concerned with this practice—made her reach out to me.[9] (Her work as a circumciser is described in chapter 4.) The abagaaka binchaama chose Rose to operate on Abakehenche girls, and her sister to circumcise daughters of the Abarisenye. In her view, separating the girls by egesaku made sense, so the children from an area did not have to walk far or wait all day to undergo the operation. To me, her reasoning seemed to pertain to the tension between ibisaku and not to the thoughtful convenience for children. The Abakehenche are the larger of the two descent sections of the Abairege, but as Rose Wankio was only permitted to operate at the mission, she didn't actually circumcise most of the Abakehenche girls. Even at the mission she shared duties with the Kisii clinical nurse.

In her view, the younger age of initiates was the main change in the practice:

In the past, girls were physically and socially mature (*ono akong'a*) when they went for genital cutting. "These days we are asked to circumcise younger girls, aged 8 and 10, because if we let them wait, by the time they turn fifteen they could get pregnant. In any given initiation season, three to four older girls are pregnant. As penalty, their parents must slaughter a head of cattle for the abagaaka binchaama, and the girl is charged more money for the operation." Parents use the fear of pregnancy to justify cutting at younger ages. They also fear that female genital operations will be stopped, and waiting might mean the girls will miss the opportunity to be initiated into adulthood, and thus remain undesirable for marriage. Parents hurry their daughters to avoid that fate.

In Rose Wankio's opinion, those trying to start a community group to oppose female genital cutting would not succeed. "This is our culture," she said. "White people's culture allows boys' circumcision but not girls'; Luo culture simply does not circumcise; our culture circumcises both boys and girls. What parent would wish to see their pregnant, uncircumcised daughter thrown away (irinyiinya)? We wouldn't have uncircumcised boys to marry such girls either. It just creates imbalance, because boys would continue to get circumcised." She recalled the Kuria traditional practice of incising earlobes to stretch and elongate them. Both boys and girls stopped doing it and the practice ended abruptly. Similarly, Rose claimed that "if they put an end to boys' circumcision as well as girls', it would truly end. But we actually felt relieved when piercing ears ceased."[10]

She believed that stopping esaaro would happen in a different generation, that she would be long dead. "It is taboo (*mugiro*) to marry an uncircumcised girl. I see such girls being detested by the community: they can't fetch water or have a wedding." She continued, "I think that people have to come together to fight it. Trying to oppose it in small groups won't work because that's just talk, not action. The best way to do it is to discuss with people, share views, exchange ideas." The SDA Church had been preaching against esaaro for at least 10 years. "They won't succeed," maintained Rose Wankio. Naming some of the Kuria ibiaro, she said, "One person has no say against all these people, the Abairege, Abanyabasi, Abagumbe, Abakira, Abangoroime, Abatimbaru, Abanyamongo. We circumcise all those."

As noted earlier, during the 2001–2 season, some in the community opposed performing genital operations at the mission. Men stood in each of the paths going to the mission, telling the girls to go somewhere else. Following the 2001 initiation season, a new head from a noncircumcising ethnic group took over as the head of the mission, replacing the Kuria clergyman who had permitted genital cutting there. The new clergyman discontinued the practice. Medicalized genital cutting was no longer available for girls in Bwirege. Only those with adequate means to pay for transportation to Kisii could afford a safer option for their daughters.

Parents Who Allowed Their Daughter to Refuse

Within the Bwirege communities I study, only one girl publicly refused to undergo genital cutting in 2001. Both parents of this fourteen-year-old supported her decision and protected her from kin and neighbors' harassment. The father, James Weituguru, an adult education coordinator and farmer in his mid-forties, and the mother, Susana Nyaseba, a nursery school teacher and farmer in her mid-thirties, had both completed secondary school. Their daughter Robi Janet was the oldest of seven children.[11] The family had relocated to a small compound comprised of only one house built of traditional materials and some outbuildings. They bought the plot and built their home away from family land, not wishing to live under the rules of patrilineal kin, or near James's first wife and her three children. When newly initiated, he had been pressured by his father to take a wife in return for receiving money for school fees. He has refused to have anything to do with her, but is considered the social father of her children. Living on the outskirts of the market, they have established relative freedom from the oversight of James's mother (the third of his father's wives) and brothers, all of whom continue to live in the compound James's father allocated to them.

James and Susana see themselves as the vanguard of change in the community. They question the need for female genital cutting and the basic premises for it. Their vision for the future is one in which girls are formally educated, youth are released from the sanctions of outdated cultural practices, and individual identity rests on achievement rather than on the parameters of custom. The practices they wish to promote are relevant to a national context, not an ethnolinguistic one. Among the first in Bwirege to abandon female genital cutting, they feel they are going in the direction of the future. "The community, those old *wazee*, they have their right channel to follow," James said. "So we, as the new generation, have also got our rights. We can decide to follow our own channels." He explained that if the elders challenge them, they will point out other changes that have become acceptable, such as not cutting your ears.

When their daughter decided not to go for initiation, they were convinced by her reasoning. She was the same age as most of the girls undergoing genital cutting, but was years ahead of them in schooling. And education, the parents thought, is the key to a good future. They urged Janet to concentrate on her studies, and to do well in school. "If you are educating your kids," Susana said, "they [members of the community] will laugh until they see that there is nothing wrong, the kid is learning." For Susana, education makes a woman marriageable outside her home community, and so it doesn't matter if she is circumcised or not. "So I am saying because I have seen these learned ones even from our tribes here [in] Kuria, when they go to university, they just get the girls there, they marry other tribes. They bring them here and they make a wedding." According to her, the neighboring ikiaro she comes from has many uncircumcised girls. "When a girl is left uninitiated, girls from the community might laugh at her... [but] she will walk with a different group—the learned group."

In James's view, the young candidates don't really understand what genital cutting is about. Parents fear that if they are not operated on, girls will get pregnant and ousted from the community. Both James and Susana argue with that. They think that an uncircumcised child fears contact with boys. "Being uncircumcised keeps her from becoming sexually active.... When they are circumcised, they tend to mature physically, and behave accordingly," he said.

Susana Nyaseba added: "After they have been circumcised, they just feel like now they are ready to get married, they can talk with boys because they are free.... But if you are not circumcised, they [boys] don't even call you [by name], they neglect you, they say 'omosaagane,' they abuse you. But after she has completed her studies, a girl can work. And after she has got a fiancé, during a circumcision season, they [community members] will come and say 'This girl was not circumcised, now she has finished her education. She has got a very nice husband, and now [they will] do the wedding.' They don't feel like calling her 'omosaagane' now. They see that girl is so big [powerful, superior], they just take her as a person who is very important."

Community pressure is still very strong, but James and Susana are willing to take steps to alleviate it for their daughter. They counseled Janet Robi on how to cope with being laughed at because she is not

192 / Chapter 6

initiated. Like Joshua Maskio, they do not worry about supernatural threats because they do not believe in that. Robi's maternal grandmother insisted her grandchild be initiated, but "I told her things have changed now, today is not yesterday, so she accepted. She is not putting more pressure, so I am happy," said Susana. They don't fear she will take Janet Robi for the operation without their approval. They were able to convince all the relatives that they support Janet Robi's decision. If she changes her mind later on, James explained, it will again be her decision. She is certainly young enough to still undergo genital cutting. But they hope she will not change her mind, and will set an example for her younger sisters.

During circumcision seasons, especially during Christmas days, they take their children on a trip, and when they come back, initiations are over. Or Janet Robi goes to visit her aunts and uncles in Nairobi and stays there. Then when the season is over she comes back. They don't fear that Janet Robi will be unmarriageable, and they know "intact girls" who have been married. Further, they reason, if a daughter is educated, she can get married somewhere else, outside the community. Perhaps because Susana was married outside her natal ikiaro, that doesn't seem such a threat. "Boys are marrying girls from communities that do not circumcise girls, they come here, they give birth, and people can see that. The Kurians used to fear that uncircumcised girls would not give birth," Susana chuckled.

"I wish so many people to join me and to join others before us, so I would like to call others to join and set a good example to this new generation.... If we people who are learned don't change the culture, we might be left with others [left behind with the uneducated]," James Weituguru said. "Things are changing! And we can also decide to make so many changes. If the community is trying to threaten us—those who are willing to change the country—we can challenge them about the changes they themselves have made, like taking their children to school."

Susana believed that the opponents of change would gradually learn.

> Nowadays they are taking young ones to school, they are educating them up to university. Everybody now is traveling, so that circumcision, it will reach a time, I know, when everybody will not circumcise girls. They will just let them go to circumcise boys but girls will just continue with learning.

They [the opponents] will just learn from others but if we are not an example, where will they learn from? Nonetheless, it is a very difficult exercise. If we are to succeed, we'd like the teachers and other leaders to help those [like us] who are willing to change.... Governmental leaders, church leaders, are the only people who can make these wazee to change their minds.

The Girl Who Refused to be Initiated

Janet Robi is a self-assured, articulate fourteen-year-old girl, full of ambition to lead a life based on her own accomplishments. A Standard 8 pupil at the time of the interview in 2002, she was the top student in her class. Having come to visit me at the homestead I was residing in, she talked to me about her stand against genital cutting, and her parents' support in backing her decision.[12] She began her argument by stating "that it is not written in the Bible that girls should be circumcised. It's not written anywhere that girls should be circumcised, only boys are supposed to be circumcised." When other members of the community asked how she could buck tradition, she told them that "it's not a must; the girl has [a] choice. Even me, I don't see the need of circumcising girls." Janet Robi's case was strengthened by the fact that she has female cousins, living in Nyabasi, the ikiaro her mother comes from, who are not initiated. One of those girls went to the university, completed her education, and is now employed. She is an inspiration to Janet Robi.

Her position was also shaped by what she heard on the radio and read in magazines and newspapers about the many people around the world, not just in Kenya, who oppose female genital cutting. Though she only knew one other girl locally who chose not to undergo initiation, she felt that her peers did not really abuse her. She had a good comeback to their harassment. When they said "You're not circumcised," she responded, "You are in Standard 3 and you are circumcised and I am [your age but] in class eight.... If you are circumcised and [do] not have education, you are not anywhere." Most of her girlfriends were initiated in the 2001 season. Some decided to break off their friendship because she did not undergo genital cutting. She told those who rejected her that she wanted to be with a friend who was ready to take a stand. "If you leave me, I will be with another friend."

"My mother was the one who was circumcised during her time. They were suffering. But this is another time." When her sisters became old enough, Janet Robi intended to encourage them not to undergo genital cutting. "I will tell them that education is a good thing in your life, circumcision is not essential.... It isn't God." She was aware of influencing the ideas people have by being an example to the community, even though some people were telling her that she was doing wrong. Janet Robi's fervent wish was to go to a national school, like Kenya High, the following year. As the top student in her class, she had a better chance than most to be recruited.[13]

A CBO Perspective

In the first decade of the new millennium, a number of initiatives called for the formation of CBOs to deal with issues perceived as pressing by funders, mostly from abroad.[14] These issues included HIV/AIDS education, testing, and prevention services; care for orphans; and quite prominently, issues pertaining to female children, including genital cutting. A number of educated Kuria discovered the potential of CBOs as vehicles for economic advancement and formed organizations with the aim of registering as NGOs or CBOs with the Kenyan government and thereby becoming eligible to solicit and channel funding from overseas donors.[15] By 2002, a number of groups had formed, but only a few had actually gone through the entire process and paid the cost of registration with the government. Even fewer managed to secure funds from donors. But because so much money was available for projects related to HIV/AIDS, status of the girl child, elimination of female circumcision, and other issues of great interest to the international community, local groups tried to configure themselves and their agendas to meet the eligibility requirements and get funding. In 2003, the only international NGO with funding located in Kuria District was ActionAid Kenya. With the broad mandate to fight poverty, they organized centers for HIV testing and backed alternative rites of passage, among other projects.

The Kuria Development Forum (KDF), an NGO initially created and endowed by a wealthy Kuria banker residing in Nairobi, rented space at Nyankare market. Wilson Kimuamu, the director of the organization in Nyankare, spoke with me about the NGO that in 2003 sought the sponsorship of larger organizations to secure funding into the future. In his early sixties, Wilson was a well-educated ex-teacher and ex-public servant who had decided to leave his employment because of the opportunities afforded by moving into the private sector and the NGO field. He articulated the twin goals of the NGO as ending female genital cutting and ending polygyny in Kuria society. Having heard of my interest in genital cutting, he sought me out on several occasions to discuss his plans for the NGO.[16]

Wilson identified himself as the leader of a small group of educated Kuria wishing to connect with other Kenyans and people from other countries to engage in an effort to stop FGM. According to him, a connection with people outside of Bukuria was necessary in order to develop an approach that would make it seem to Kuria residents that the tradition of genital cutting would come to an end "naturally." In cooperation or in tandem with a number of other groups, such as KenClub and Kuria Girl Child Organization (KOGUO), they hoped to find sufficient funding to craft a plan to actualize their goal.

Unable to articulate how and why genital cutting related to development,[17] and in what way genital cutting made a difference to women, he maintained that the reason to oppose it is "because we are told that it is bad."[18] Wilson Kimuamu saw bringing change to Kuria society as the role of the educated. Since he and his deputy were Kuria, he reasoned they would be in a better position to bring change, because it would be easier for the people to understand that even "if we are against them we are actually doing something. And in any case we keep it open to them to tell us the reasons why they circumcise, the advantage."

The KDF disputes the claim that genital cutting is traditional, arguing that quite a number of Kuria are not initiated. "So a part of what the NGO is trying to do is to make people aware that the practice doesn't make any sense. One of our objectives is to make it known that those who have not done it have been hiding because they are the minority. Now things have changed, they don't need to be isolated any more. We want to speak up and put it in the open."

KDF was pursuing a strategy to change minds in the communities. "We are focusing on the older people because circumcision is not organized by young people, it's done by the elders. So if we stop them, then it will definitely stop," Wilson reasoned. His group was not working to insert teaching about genital cutting into the school syllabus (a national curriculum should not focus on specific "tribal traditions") but was targeting schools as the building blocks of a community-based network for change. "We have arranged it in such a way that we... go to every single school and choose leaders from different areas.... We are targeting to have a seminar... [for] primary school teachers, two teachers per school."[19] In addition, they hoped to include councilors from each location, as well as churches, like the SDA, Catholics, Pentecostal Fellowship of Africa/America (PEFA), and Jehovah's Witnesses. They also wanted to include the person in charge of traditional affairs in the community development agencies in every division, as well as all the chairs of women's groups, two or three per division. "The ultimate goal is to sensitize all these people with regard to FGM, to talk and agree on a strategy, then have each of them go to preach the same in their own seminars." The key, as he saw it, was to secure funding: "If we can have finances to meet them and hold these seminars, then they will understand. When holding seminars, we'll look for [participants] from different areas so that they come and talk. We are thinking that if we can unite in that way then all of Kuria will understand."

Despite his initial assertion that KDF aimed to accomplish change "so that it takes place naturally," Wilson believed that radical, rapid change was possible:

> We have learned from experience that the Kuria people can change overnight. If you came here say in the 1950s, all the Kurians had rings around them,[20] they were removing two teeth, they used to pierce their ears, and you know they stopped at once. And even this circumcision, once we talk to them, they'll stop it. We are taking the responsibility. The church had started much earlier but really mildly, not even aggressively. They should even go a lot further—if you are a Christian and you have circumcised your daughter, you are totally removed from Christianity.... We are also studying the situation and how we can approach it to the level where it takes effect naturally if it can.

Clearly, he contradicted himself over whether change would be rapid or eventual.

A number of people in the community criticized KDF and characterized it as a group of profiteers: highly educated, paid spokespeople for outside organizations. They questioned the motives of KDF leaders Wilson Kimuamu and Nyagonchera Mwita. Both of them had circumcised all of their own children—boys and girls—this despite the fact that neither of Wilson's wives were circumcised, coming from a nonpracticing culture. People felt that the two were trying to mislead them, that they were not sincere believers of what they were preaching. Ordinary people were not swayed or convinced.

A Women's Leader's Perspective

Nyagonchera Mwita, the deputy director of KDF, was in her late forties when I interviewed her. A college-educated, she had previously been an elementary school teacher, a principal, a businesswoman, and the leader of a branch of a national women's organization. Assertive and outspoken, she had a wide-reaching reputation within Kuria District. The wife of a government employee, she was the mother of five children—three sons and two daughters—all of whom had been initiated.[21] At this time we had known each other for almost twenty years, and had shared many of life's milestones. She sought me out to share her most recent activities as the deputy director of KDF.

Through her exposure to national issues as a part of the women's governmental organization, Nyagonchera had learned that Kuria communities lag behind others in Kenya, especially when it comes to educating girls: "Girls drop out of primary school because parents prioritize the education of sons. They say, 'Why should I educate a girl for somebody else, to go and enrich somebody else?' So they marry them off early, immediately after circumcision. Some are married, others are impregnated, and some drop out because their parents are not able to pay their school fees."

Like Wilson, Nyagonchera saw sensitizing elders as key to ending the practice of female genital cutting. This needed to be done by talking with clan elders (abagaaka binchaama) who are the decision makers, with circumcisers, and with the church elders. The NGO would hold a meeting to convince people to help carry the message of abandonment of FGM to their individual constituencies. Another plank in their strategy was to look for other things for girls to do during initiation season instead of taking part in the rituals.

She articulated some of the ideas of the national organization within which she still held an elected position. But she was ready to move on, because "in the national organization people are volunteers; they don't have funds to make them move from one place to another." Through KDF they had made a network of many NGOs in Kuria so they could work together to have an impact.[22] She saw that all had a common goal: "We want to fight women harassment in Kuria and

FGM."[23] They had written a proposal to ActionAid. The group had plans, but had not secured funding.

Nyagonchera's broad vision included building a rehabilitation center where girls who were sent away from home could be helped. To that end, the group aimed to have a center where, in December, they could teach girls how to take care of themselves, especially regarding the danger of AIDS, and also how to make some handicrafts. That center would have a secretary and assistants who would talk to the girls seeking to avoid genital cutting. She rejected the three most commonly used rationales articulated to promote genital cutting: that cutting is necessary so that the girls can be married; that it is needed for girls to transition from childhood to adulthood; and that genital cutting serves to limit girls' sexual activity. Though they held no credence for her, all are articulated in the communities as reasonable rationales.

This is precisely why she saw sensitization seminars as necessary. But their effectiveness depended on careful planning and organization:

> You see…with FGM, we can only talk to individuals and not groups because groups will shout at you. Or [we can talk to] churches where at least they'll get the message, rather than going to a baraza, because they won't listen, they will start asking, "OK, you were circumcised, why are you asking us not to circumcise?" We'll do it slowly by slowly…. We go around and teach them what is supposed to be done, but the most difficult are the clan elders who think they are the decision makers. They decide with the circumcisers … how much they are going to charge each individual [and] … the clan elders are given some of it [the money]. We plan to compensate both the clan elders and the circumcisers. We are even planning to take them to Nairobi on a trip so they can go and see how [educated] people behave.

Nyagonchera believed that female genital cutting could be ended by enticing the clan elders, both by giving them money and by taking them away from the community. Though KDF saw the need to get these issues out in the public, they lacked a forum, since at the usual ones, ideas about terminating female circumcision were scorned and their articulators ridiculed and dismissed.

To reach an end of genital cutting practices, Nyagonchera saw a wider arena of cultural changes that needed to take place. One of these was ending use of the word omosaagane (young, uncircumcised girl). It is seen and used as a term of abuse, so a girl is brought up to know that in being initiated, she can leave the term behind and become an umuiseke. Nyagonchera maintained that a girl should be called umuiseke from the time she is little. Girls are often treated from a very young age as though they are just good for marriage, and Nyagonchera argued that needed to change too. Further, she thought the importance of initiation as a major social event needed to be played down.

A Community Nurse's Reflections

When I interviewed Rucia Mbusiro in 2002, she had been working as a nurse in the community for the past twenty years, initially at a government clinic, now in her own private one. Though not Kuria by birth, she was married to a Kuria man, and had raised four children, all of whom were professionals. She was greatly in demand as a midwife, and had for years been an outspoken proponent of family planning in Nyankare. At the time of this interview she was in her early fifties.[24]

Opposed to female genital cutting, she addressed myths about it one by one. She disproved the belief that genital cutting makes it easier for women to give birth by citing her twenty years of experience assisting women giving birth. "The scar tissue from the cut is tough, a woman's genital region is tight, and when she is pushing, she will tear downwards or upwards but most often, women tear upwards." Since 1978, she had seen a change in the extent of the cutting taking place: "This time they are only cutting the clitoris, which is a bit better. Now when the baby is coming, [one can] easily support the perineum during birth, but when you are supporting the perineum the other tear comes up where the clitoris was chopped."

She recognized that although she and others want female genital cutting to be discouraged completely, the end of the practice will be gradual. Modifying the cut was an important intermediate step. Rucia suggested that "to get around the pressure of the community, mothers should take their girls to clinics. There they can ask the person performing the operation to not cut too much.... Some mothers...will say don't cut the daughter, you just make a mark so they can say she is circumcised."

But not all mothers asked for the same extent of cutting. "You know there are some mothers who say, 'You have done nothing here! What

have you done? You only chopped to say you circumcised this girl!'"
she said, imitating them. "They can go home and circumcise again.
They go home and when they are trying to wash her in the evening,
again they cut." But from her experience, Rucia thinks many mothers
are now deciding not to cut the girls much. Some mothers would
prefer to stop genital cutting, but are afraid of the elders. "People fear
the elders because they have magical powers," Rucia explained. "They
have brought snakes into houses of those who didn't circumcise their
daughters, or hyenas. They shout outside your home, you get cursed.
If you believe in them they can affect you negatively. Otherwise, if you
don't believe in them there is no problem." The example Rucia gave,
as many other people do, talking about the power of elders, is of a
SDA clinical officer who refused to have two of his daughters undergo
genital cutting. Snakes and leopards started coming to his house, and
ultimately he had to give in, and his girls were initiated even though
by then they were fully grown up.

The second myth she disputed is that no one will marry girls who
have not undergone initiation. In her opinion, the boys are deciding
whom to marry themselves, and they do not want to marry circumcised girls. They have gone to other lands and seen girls who are not
circumcised. They have seen the difference. "On the side of sex, it is
said that the clitoris is the center of sex, so some people who have
read books, they know about sex and other things, they know when
they touch such places, a girl becomes on heat [aroused]. Cutting the
genitals of a girl reduces her ability to enjoy sex and makes giving
birth difficult, but also changes her personality, making a girl passive.
It also changes her body. A small girl is circumcised, but after two
years when you meet her, she is an old woman. I don't know what
causes that, I don't know what changes their bodies to make them big
like that—abruptly. Maybe it is the extra care they get. When they
are circumcised they get extra food. In the morning they are cooked
for, around noon again, they are taken care of so much. So I don't
know, maybe that would make them grow."

Though she believed one of the aims of circumcision is to limit the
girls' interest in sex, that does not seem to work. Kuria girls work in
bars all over the country, she said, even though they are circumcised.[25]
"This is the outcome of the curtailment of their sexual drive." The
chain of causation she delineates goes like this:

A young woman is not interested in sex, so when her husband asks for it, she refuses. When he tries to engage in sexual activity with her, she shows no interest, she does not feel like it. So what is the man to do? He moves outside of the home, paying for sex, whether to prostitutes or to girlfriends who welcome him. Or he goes and finds another wife who is not chopped and she is active and is welcoming him. When such a man comes home and his wife says no, he thinks "Why did I marry this lady?" The women are starting to realize this.

Rucia has learned from many years of conversations that men beat their wives when they don't want to have sex with their husband. Since they don't feel a sexual urge, they sometimes choose to go with other men and get presents in return: money or goods for offering their bodies and/or the comforts of home.[26] A man will beat his wife when she declines to have sex with him, but he rewards a girlfriend who will, giving her gifts or money. So, according to Rucia, some women choose to have sex with friends and clients for the material rewards, rather than with husbands who abuse them.

Rucia agreed, however, that the operation and celebration surrounding it are still very important. When some young girls don't undergo initiation at the time their friends do, it is said they are left behind. The girls argue with their parents, saying, "No, I will not be left behind." Young girls enjoy the attention that initiation casts on them: they feel good when they are danced for, given money, and are taken home from the initiation ground and cared for. When they have recovered, their parents buy them new dresses, shoes, underclothing, and hygiene products. "They feel beautiful because they are circumcised, they are now OK, they have bought new things [and are] ready to come out now. So these are the things that make them happy."

Rucia predicted that soon genital cutting as a part of the ritual repertoire of Kuria people will end: "In the other ibiaro they are finished, like in Bukira, girls are not circumcised, even in Nyabasi and Bugumbe, they have stopped circumcising girls, even most of the boys go to hospitals. But these people here, because they are at the border of Tanzania and Kenya, these Kurias of Tanzania are very much into their traditions." Even though circumcision of girls had been made illegal in Tanzania, most Abairege from there were continuing it. "Circumcision is going to be finished soon.... Only our area is tough, and it is tough because of the border, I think."

As someone who had come from outside the community, Rucia was not steeped in Kuria tradition. Accordingly, the paradoxes and contradictions of the initiation celebrations were readily apparent to her.

> The other day as I was going to the clinic, I saw a boy who had been circumcised. People were dancing. I said, "You are dancing and this man is dying, you can see how he is walking, and people are celebrating for his death." People laughed. "Why are you celebrating the death of that boy?" He was bleeding a lot. He was cut very early in the morning and he was in so much pain and he was walking slowly and people are laughing, dancing, jumping, so I made jokes with those mamas, "Bare bakungu, morairi uruku oro omoona ora" [Hey, women, you are celebrating the death of this boy], and they just laughed and said, "No sister, he is OK, he is now a man." He is a man, yes, but he is feeling a lot of pain.

Rucia's thoughts moved to another current issue. The chiefs had told people to stop the initiations so that the abasaamba could come out of seclusion, okoroka. But approaching the end of January, people were still celebrating. From Rucia's perspective, they wasted a lot of money, entertaining lavishly.

> When the visitors leave, their people living in Bukuria are struggling. There is no money even if somebody becomes sick at home, "Now all our money is finished," they say. On what—esaaro! You see, they waste time, money, and energy. Because this dancing, dancing, that is energy, then running all the time, that is wasting time, money, buying all those things for people to eat, where is that shame? Instead of buying for your son who is circumcised, you are buying for the community, for your age-mates. The age-mates are present at the celebrations, but not when there is need in the home. If someone is very poor and has nothing to use for marriage, the age-mates will not bring cattle so he can pay bridewealth. If somebody loses a father or a sister, during the burial you will never see people saying the age-mates of this man are here now, they have got such-and-such amount of money for their home to use. You never see them, but they only want to eat, so they are age-mates of food! I was saying the other day in the clinic teaching mothers, "Don't be talking about

these age-mates!" I said. "When you have problems, did your age-mates come to help? *Hakuna* [no way]! But when there is esaaro, that is when I see you running, claiming you want the whole thigh of the cow!".... But during these other problems they don't attend, even you feel your homestead is burned, every house is burned accidentally, will you ever see any age-mates coming?

In Rucia's view, the solidarity of the circumcision set is there for celebrations, and there for doing group projects, but not when individuals need assistance.

By 2003, two initiation seasons had taken place in Bwirege with significant changes to practice, and a great deal of discussion. Medicalization of the cutting performed on girls was embraced by some as the perfect solution to a number of the internationally and nationally articulated objections to the practice—the risk of infection caused by unhygienic practices, the danger of spreading HIV, and the severity of the cut—were all potentially obviated by reliance on cutting done by medically trained personnel or in a clinical setting. This innovation was welcomed by some. For others, it required too much deviation from norms they were accustomed to, and thus was unacceptable. Ultimately it became moot, as the clergyman who instigated this change was transferred out of the area and the medicalized option disappeared.

But perhaps more than any specific changes in the practice, the conversation about its meaning and importance brought genital cutting out into the open as a tradition being challenged by both insider and outsider forces, and people had to formulate their own understandings and positions regarding the need for this particular set of rituals. In this chapter I have presented a number of voices, of ordinary as well as specially placed individuals regarding genital cutting. The intention was to bring forth voices from within the community whose positions often echo the voices of individuals and organizations from nonpracticing communities, raising similar doubts and concerns, both about the continuation of female genital cutting and about its end.

The position individuals take or articulate often corresponds to their specific relationship to genital cutting practices, including the age of their children, their personal background with regard to connections to outside the locality, and the many particularities that make everyone's lived experience unique. But despite the uniqueness of their experiences, certain themes emerge and sometimes converge with the discourse from beyond Bwirege, brought in by the media, governmental institutions, and nongovernmental institutions concerned with genital cutting practices. The next chapter traces the intensification of the anti-FGM campaign in the first decade of the twenty-first century, bringing forward the main players in the debate locally, examining their positions, their strategies, and their successes. This is counterposed to the realities, considerations, and actions of the main constituents in the ongoing practice: elders, youths, and parents. In conclusion, I return to the opening question and reflect on whose voice is the authentic one.

7

Where Do We Go from Here?

Having spent the year 2003 in Bukuria, I was not present when the 2004 initiation season was discussed and declared. But I was informed about it the whole year, in phone calls from friends and prior assistants, as well as by e-mail. Two of those came from Stephen Wambura. On May 8, 2004, he wrote: "On 23 to 25 April I attended a workshop (seminar) on anti FGM at [a Kuria community in another ikiaro] and I tell you I left the venue convinced that the practice is dying soon. If there will be 'esaro' in Bwirege in 2004 it might be the last major one as things are changing pretty fast. It was organized by GTZ [German Agency for Technical Cooperation] along with some group called KDF [Kuria Development Forum]." This workshop was described by the *Daily Nation* as the first of its kind in the district (Atieno 2004). The three-day workshop brought together clan elders, the provincial administration, teachers, and university students to share ideas and develop strategies for eliminating FGM in the area. Among the many topics discussed, the need for educating girls was prominent.

Another participant at the three-day workshop, Ndera Wairema, was quoted in the *Daily Nation*: "Circumcision was traditionally meant to mark maturity and courage, to serve the community, but we have realized that education prepares people more than circumcision to provide for and support the community." Wairema also suggested that uneducated girls be referred to as uncircumcised. Then, on December 22, 2004, again by e-mail, Stephen Wambura expanded on the genital cutting topic:

> About circumcision, it has been going on, and it started off vigorously, beginning 1st December and has taken three weeks now but it is dwindling. On 6th December, my daughter [seventh-born girl] defied and went for it, and we had

no alternative but to give her the necessary support. This particular 'esaaro' was marred, with some going for what was called 'Alternative rite of passage' sponsored by both GTZ, ActionAid, SDA, and other NGOs but the strange thing is that most of those who went for the rite came back to be circumcised either willingly or by force. We thought the tempo was to slow down but our assessment was that it went up even more than before, with young ones as young as 8–10 years of both sexes getting circumcised.

The ambivalence with which this educated Kuria secondary school headmaster saw the changes taking place came across quite clearly. The dilemmas he was facing epitomize those of the society itself, and his personal experience offers a handy entrée into the developments of the past decade surrounding genital cutting in this society. The performance of rites of passage that include genital cutting serves to establish a man's children unequivocally within their patrilineage; on completion of the rituals, they are recognized as members of their lineage and community. The headmaster wanted his children to be secure in their identity and belonging, able to claim the rights and privileges of their lineage affiliation. Yet he also wanted to be seen as a forward-looking leader, who by virtue of his educational and experiential attainments was in a position to influence youths in his charge, in addition to influencing their parents and promoting modernity. Perhaps due to the influence of the sensitization seminars he attended, he saw the abandonment of genital cutting practices as a chance for transformed conditions of life: a "direction we would like to move in" (Ferguson 2006, 19).

Indigenous activists and anthropologists have often argued for cultural relativism: every culture is to be understood according to its own terms, not judged by outsiders' criteria; the members of each culture should be able to enjoy the right to self-determination, and should have the principal say with regard to their own practices and traditions. But, as case of female genital cutting illustrates, conflict often arises over values—between communities, within a community, and also within individuals.

However, when most Western observers are faced with African practices of female genital cutting, they respond with little ambivalence and no sense of dilemma. With little consideration for the variety of practices and rationales that characterize different societies, female genital cutting has been collapsed into a monolithic practice labeled "female genital mutilation" (FGM). This is a concept with its own ontology (Livingston 2012, 52) separate from "female circumcision." It carries within it ideas of physical mutilation and denial of sexual pleasure, elaborated with adjectives such as *disgusting, revolting, obscene, abusive,* and *inhumane,* and discussed without reference to meanings ascribed in communities of practitioners (Parker 1995, 512–13). Since about the mid-1990s, discourse on genital cutting has aroused increasing interest and concern in Africa, Europe, and America. Within human rights organizations, NGOs, and international development agencies, the practice has been classified as an abuse of human rights, although the basic principles from which this classification stems are by no means new.[1] The resulting universalist stance holds that "oppression of women must cease, always, everywhere, in every culture, as a matter of basic human rights" (Brown 1998, 4). For some opponents of female genital cutting, moral outrage can override scientific objectivity. This is true even among scientists: for example, there was an ironic admission from Peter Brown, who, as editor of *The Sciences,* prefaced an article by Sudanese anthropologist Rogaia Abusharaf by saying that "⌈he⌉ won't hide ⌈his⌉ own sentiments" and will state that female "circumcision" is FGM (Brown 1998, 4).

Though genital cutting on females was banned by colonial powers in Africa in the early twentieth century, Brown notes that the practice has retained a potent grip on many so-called traditional societies. In the prefacing article cited above, he castigates anthropologists for "lapsing into a paralyzing cultural relativism" and advocates that "forces of change"—described as "courageous women and men of conscience"—within societies that practice female genital cutting can prevail if they can introduce suitable cultural substitutes for the practices they seek to eliminate and if they can be assured that in their fight they are no longer alone. For him, nurturing those forces of change resolves the ethical dilemma of imposing external values on a traditional culture (Brown 1998, 4). In assessing FGC in the global context, Hernlund and Shell-Duncan highlight the tendency for analysis of female circumcision to fall into the rights-versus-culture dichotomy. Alternatively, analysis that moves "to the middle" reflects the fact that human minds operate generally between the extremes of universalism and relativism (2007, 2).

My work is situated in the middle ground as well, articulating grassroots views and experiences that reflect the spectrum of global discourse as it shapes understandings and local realities. What are suitable cultural substitutes for female genital cutting and who is to decide? How are those substitutes to be introduced into societies where genital cutting is practiced? These issues have remained at the heart of the controversy in sub-Saharan Africa for the past century. I begin with a look at the efforts of multinational NGOs and their local partners (government branches, Kenyan NGOs and CBOs) engaged in the effort to eliminate female genital cutting.

National and Global Campaigns

It should be clear at this point that the people who want to continue female circumcision and the people who want to end FGM are talking past each other, looking at the issue from vastly different perspectives, each "side" applying logic that simply doesn't account for the fundamental realities recognized by the other. For starters, it is not agreed by all that female genital cutting is, indeed, a violation of human rights. This means that women who abandon the practice often have a lot to lose: their position in the community is affected, they are less desired as marriage partners, and often the bridewealth offered for them is reduced. To them, it does not appear that ending female genital cutting will improve their rights and status in the community. Development policy and programs that intend to stop FGC will need to move far beyond the indictment of customs.[2]

While the local level of discussion has increased greatly and brought into question the necessity of the rites for shaping girls' futures, rates of female genital cutting have declined in some areas but not in others, including Kuria District, where they remain at historically high levels. Given this failure to speak a common language on the issues of female genital cutting, it almost goes without saying that strategies to move forward, whether to retain tradition or stop it entirely, will accordingly be limited and piecemeal. For example, alternative rites of passage have not been particularly effective in providing much of an alternative for girls in Bukuria.[3] The analysis of major donors presented at a Nairobi conference in 2004 indicates that many FGM intervention campaigns had little to no impact, and some may have contributed to further entrenching the practice (Richardson 2005).[4] Governments that criminalize female genital cutting often do not formulate enforcement approaches, which has ultimately

embarrassed governments and undercut the law. Governments rationalize that the law itself is not going to make a difference until the
people are educated. Meanwhile, the work of educating people is left
to NGOs. As Faiza Mohammed, director of the NGO Equality Now
points out, "As long as the work is left to NGOs, we will make changes
here and there, but will be defeated by the lack of political will.... The
NGOs can raise awareness of the issue among girls, but when they
run away, they are sent back [by local authorities] and get mutilated"
(United Nations 2006).

The classification of female genital cutting as an international
human rights violation has been a subject of ongoing debate, cen-
tering on whether or not FGC actually falls under the purview of
international law, and on which of the possible claim areas it should
be framed: the rights of the child, the right to sexual and corporal integrity, or the right to health (Hernlund and Shell-Duncan 2007, 12).
Over time, international activists have backed away from the right to
health and have added instead the right to be free from torture (26).
As activists, legal experts, and policy makers debate the best strategies for indicting FGC as a human rights violation, some academics
have been concerned with the process by which any transnational
notion of human rights is enacted in a local setting in rural Africa
(Merry 2006a, 2006b).

In the first decade of this century, a number of multilateral part-
nerships and networks were established both within Kenyan districts
where female genital cutting practices continue and with global
partners. For instance, the Federal Republic of Germany signed an
eight-year bilateral agreement with the government of Kenya to
encourage the abandonment of FGM/C, subscribing to a number
of international conventions and action plans supporting the implementation and protection of human rights within which concrete
measures against FGM/C were formulated (Evelia, Sheikh Abdi, and
Askew 2008, 2). With clear-cut objectives, five districts were identified for implementation of projects: Kuria, Kajiado, Transmara, Meru,
and Garissa. In each district, the interventions were to be specifically
developed and tested for conformity with different sociocultural conditions in the different areas.

The first phase of the project entailed conducting research to support the development of appropriate strategies. In Kuria District, research found that FGM/C was a deeply rooted cultural practice. There
was a low level of awareness of the negative medical, psychological,

and social consequences of cutting. Cutting was being done mainly by traditional circumcisers, and over time, the tendency for cutting younger girls was observed (Evelia, Sheikh Abdi, and Askew 2008, 4). The study recommended reaching out to groups already opposed to cutting, such as churches, educated families, provincial administration, and schools, empowering them as advocates to encourage abandonment of the practice. It also recommended the sensitization of clan elders to the range of risks to young girls and the introduction of alternative rites of passage. Because of limited funding, the second phase (systematic evaluation of the interventions begun under the first phase) did not reach Kuria District (7–8).

Current Practice in Kuria District

Rituals of initiation, including the practice of genital cutting on both males and females, still serve as the hallmark ritual event in Kuria society today. These rituals have come down to current generations as customs carried out since time immemorial, far longer than anyone living can remember or know. Specific ritual practices have changed as they were passed across generations, and recent social and health concerns continue to reshape them.

As discussed in chapter 4, beginning in the mid-1990s, in response to the danger of HIV transmission, sterile procedures were introduced to circumcisers by the Ministry of Health. Then in the late 1990s, a clergyman, wanting to preserve the ritual which he saw as key to maintaining Kuria ethnic identity, brought a trained nurse to his mission to operate on girls.[5] In 2001, she was joined by a Kuria circumciser who also performed female genital cutting at the mission, obviating some of the concerns about interethnic and interclan witchcraft, which are always prevalent in a season of heightened ritual tension (Prazak 2000). In each of these seasons, about sixty girls underwent genital cutting there. Circumcision of boys had been available in local clinics since the 1950s, and though elders and initiates alike had once frowned on it as the "weakling's choice," by the late 1990s the youths so circumcised were no longer ostracized from the gangs of initiates that wander the community during the period of seclusion (obosaamba).

In the 2004 season, "traditional" genital cutting began in December, and I learned about its innovations through emails and phone calls from friends and former research assistants. Approximately 3,500 Kuria boys and girls went through the ritual.[6] In addition, 289 girls underwent an alternative rite of passage, introduced in the area during this season after several years of campaigning by international NGOs, including ActionAid Kenya, GTZ, the Pentecostal Fellowship of America, the Seventh-Day Adventist Church, and the Kenya Alliance for the Advancement of Children. Female candidates from three of the four clan territories (ibiaro) that comprise the district were brought by their relatives to workshops at a secondary school. Teachers, doctors, and "priests from different denominations"[7] educated the candidates on topics such as "culture, female genital mutilation, empowerment, adolescence, legal rights, youth peer counseling, effects of FGM, myths and misconceptions, religion, communication, problem handling, the reproductive system, peer pressure, STD/HIV, and gender."[8] The workshops and knowledge sharing were intended to replace the customary rite of passage. No cutting or any other alteration of the genitals was involved. Such alternative rituals have been held in other areas of Kenya, including in Meru, Kisii, Samburu, and Maasai communities. The structure, intentions, and outcomes of alternative rites differed radically from those of indigenous practices.

All 289 girls completed the alternative rite process and received certificates of attendance for anti-FGM, witnessed by their parents, community leaders, government officials, and two foreigners from Germany.[9] Subsequently, events unfolded differently from what both the sponsors and the girls had expected. Going back home, all but 80 of those girls were forced by their relatives or pressured by their peers to undergo the cutting, most before they were allowed back into their homes.[10] Although the Kuria member of parliament threatened lawsuits against parents who took part in this, no official charges were filed: "His words were a storm in a tea cup," one Kuria observer noted.[11] Mogore Maria's youngest daughter, Esta Nyamburi, was one of the girls who remained intact. Given that both her parents were deceased by then, her siblings supported her decision not to undergo genital cutting. This was, in part, a tribute to their late mother, who had attended a number of the sensitization seminars in the years since her daughter Leah Mokami had undergone initiation in 1998, and used her public office as a platform to campaign against genital cutting. To withstand the pressure of patrilineal kin, her siblings encouraged Esta to pass the initiation season following the alternative rite of passage with their maternal relatives in another ikiaro.[12]

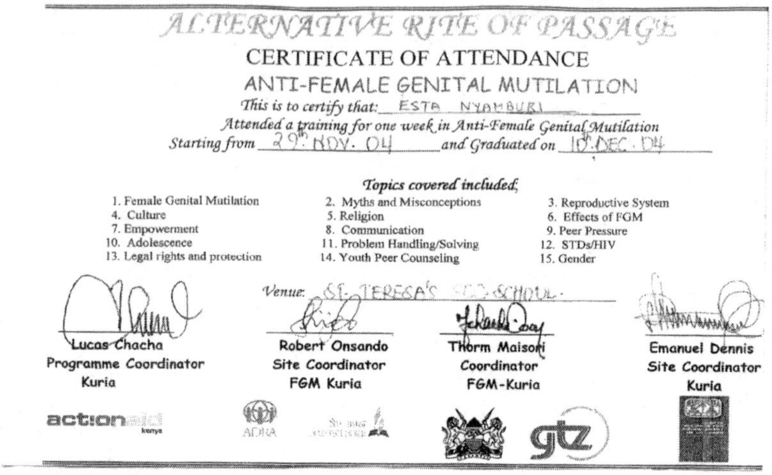

ALTERNATIVE RITE OF PASSAGE
CERTIFICATE OF ATTENDANCE
ANTI-FEMALE GENITAL MUTILATION
This is to certify that: ESTA NYAMBURI
Attended a training for one week in Anti-Female Genital Mutilation
Starting from 29ᵗʰ NOV. 04 *and Graduated on* 10ᵗʰ DEC. 04

Topics covered included:

1. Female Genital Mutilation	2. Myths and Misconceptions	3. Reproductive System
4. Culture	5. Religion	6. Effects of FGM
7. Empowerment	8. Communication	9. Peer Pressure
10. Adolescence	11. Problem Handling/Solving	12. STDs/HIV
13. Legal rights and protection	14. Youth Peer Counseling	15. Gender

Venue: ST. TERESA'S SCHOOL.

Lucas Chacha	Robert Onsando	Thorm Maisori	Emanuel Dennis
Programme Coordinator	Site Coordinator	Coordinator	Site Coordinator
Kuria	FGM Kuria	FGM-Kuria	Kuria

actionaid kenya   ADRA   gtz

Figure 3. Alternative Rite of Passage Certificate.

How can we best understand the ambivalence or different perspectives prevalent in the community? As Oboler (2001) reminds us, cultural continuity requires competing interests to reach a consensus about which items of traditional behavior are to be dropped and which maintained because they are deemed central to cultural identity. Her prescription for "an appropriate approach to the eradication of female genital modification is to find those in the community that have a strong interest in eliminating these practices and, having found them, to work diligently with them to formulate a program that draws on their insider perspectives. The program will be most effective if the major impetus for change comes from within the community rather than from outside it" (313).

This perspective is very similar to Brown's (1998, 4), noted above. But Oboler goes further and identifies two other key elements of particular relevance to this case study of Kuria genital-cutting practices: "It is essential to respect the motives of the people participating in the maintenance of female genital modification," and a "rhetoric of blame and shame must be avoided at all costs" (2001, 313). Unlike the injunction proposed by Brown, asking the community to change in response to outrage from outsiders, these suggestions focus on responding to voices and opinions from the inside in a way that allows people to embrace new ideas and meaningful change. The most recent manuals for social change published by donors have adopted the caution that Oboler sounds, recognizing that the blame and shame strategies have not brought about the elimination of genital cutting, and that abandonment is more likely to occur and be sustained where an understanding and appreciation of the complex social dynamics associated with genital cutting informs elimination efforts (see, e.g., UNICEF 2010, 48).

As NGOs formalized more sensitive approaches to eliminating female genital cutting in the later part of the first decade of the twenty-first century, the media continued its narrow focus on blame and shame narratives. The lack of success of anti-FGM campaigns in Kuria District was brought to global light in 2009, and genital cutting in Kuria District reached a worldwide audience, when the program *Worldfocus* aired a segment on it.[13] Broadcast on March 9, the day after International Women's Day, the timing of the release was intended to highlight that "something disturbing is still going on in many parts of Africa." Identifying Kuria people as living along the border between Kenya and Tanzania, and asserting that the practice of female circumcision, now more commonly known as female genital mutilation, is outlawed in Kenya, the news anchor described the district as a place where "the old ways persist and the young girls continue to suffer" (Worldfocus 2009).[14]

Dramatic footage of female genital cutting rituals and their accompanying celebrations serves as a backdrop for a poignant articulation of a perspective addressing a primarily Western audience: "For hundreds of years, music has been able to bring Kuria people of southern Kenya together. Despite modernity, initiation dances like these have stood the test of time. Just like their forefathers did, this village is preparing its young people for adulthood. Circumcision is done once every two years and is the biggest social event for many Kurias. The dancing will carry on until the next day when many young initiates will begin new lives. Every home with an initiate proudly flies a flag on their rooftop. Chacha Kemega's household is one such place. He is preparing a huge party for his daughter, who will become a woman today. Since time immemorial Kuria girls have had to undergo circumcision to earn respect" (Worldfocus 2009).

The program depicts the experience of two girls, Chacha Kemega's daughter who undergoes cutting and a neighbor who has refused to participate. "She feels circumcision will not prepare her for the challenges of adulthood. Her decision may make her the laughingstock of her community." Speaking for herself, she says: "When I was told the badness of being circumcised, I stopped it. Until now, I am not circumcised and I will not be circumcised." The segment concludes with the narrator saying, "It may be years before female circumcision can be rooted out amongst the Kuria people. Like those before them, many young girls will have to go through the practice for the sake of their community" (Worldfocus 2009). Produced by a Kenyan company, the video is keen both to the issues that affect local communities and to those that appeal to the Western media outlets this company targets for distribution of its documentary work.

Though the above program turns genital cutting into a sensational story that plays on the preconceptions of international audiences, it does, nonetheless, highlight the three main categories of players within the genital cutting arena. It is due to their enduring importance and centrality within the ongoing genital cutting practices that I turn to these people who constitute the most important players in initiation and genital cutting in Kuria District: elders, youths, and parents.

The Elders

The rites of initiation are integrally tied to the elders in the community, as the inchaama has to activate the ritual season and guide it to a safe and successful completion. The men in the inchaama have reached the highest level of the age-based hierarchy, and have performed the elderhood ceremony. They are responsible for the ritual or spiritual well-being of the society, and it is their job to study the auguries that determine whether a particular year is propitious for initiations to be held. They closely follow the genital cutting of the amanaanai, and if all signs bode well, they declare the ritual season open. As the most traditional element in the society, the elder council upholds values and norms.[15] They order and articulate the reasons for initiation, including the introduction of the initiate to the corporate community as an active member (described by Mbiti [1969, 121] for African societies generally).

But all elders hold domain over the ritual life of the community. Kuria, like other Kenyan peoples, observe initiation and puberty rites that represent key moments in the rhythm of individual life and resonate with and restore the corporate group, of which the individual is a part. Whatever happens to the single youth happens as well to the parents, the relatives, the neighbors, and the ancestors (Mbiti 1969, 121). Through the rites surrounding genital cutting, the initiates are introduced to the art of collective living. In seclusion during the liminal stage, they experience the withdrawal or removal from mainstream society; afterward they are introduced to adult life, and upon rejoining society are allowed to share in the full privileges and duties of the community. "They enter into the state of responsibility: they inherit new rights, and new obligations are expected of them by society…. The initiation rites prepare young people in matters of sexual life, marriage, procreation, and family responsibilities" (121–22). Perhaps most important, undergoing initiation anchors each youth within the descent structure of the community, firmly establishing his or her identity within a descent group (Prazak 2000).

Though it is often stated that initiation rituals serve an important educational purpose, this learning is implicit in Kuria experience, where no explicit teaching is carried out in preparation for the rituals or during the period of seclusion. As is always the case, children learn through imitation of the people they work alongside and through stories and events recounted by peers and grandparents. Mbiti and others have described the attainment of initiation as the beginning of acquiring knowledge otherwise inaccessible to those who have not been initiated. The initiates learn to endure hardships, interact with one another, and obey the constraints of liminality. With Kuria, as with peoples everywhere, there is a generational tension because acquiring access to norms and meanings most significant in the lives of elders and the society of the past is probably less useful today than it was in the past; learning about human rights, NGOs, and the laws and policies of governmental institutions might prepare youth better for contemporary life.

The contest between generations is not new. During the colonial era elders appealed to "tradition" in order to defend their dominance of the rural means of production against challenge by the young. Men used it to ensure that the increasing role women played in production did not result in any diminution of male control; chiefs used it to maintain control over their subjects; and indigenous populations used it to ensure that migrants did not achieve political or economic rights. In a situation of increasingly complex relations, managing these tensions was a function of the elders' control of traditional knowledge (Ranger 1983, 255). In Kenya, as the historical record shows, initiation rites have been subject to controversy for over a century—yet in many areas, Kuria District included, the practice persists *because* of elders' commitment to ensuring successful transitions into adulthood for their children and grandchildren, and thus ensuring the continuation of the social status quo. In the courses of their lives, elders have seen few benefits of modernity, and strive to protect the advantages seniority gives them in age-old communal practices. As modernity remains elusive to many, traditions are embraced in part because they give access to the larger moral community within which people's lives unfold.

The elders invoke the necessary protective magic to keep the initiates and their communities safe for the period of heightened ritual tension. They get a share of the fee collected by the circumcisers from each initiate, collect fines for transgressions, and enjoy food and drink served at feasts that parents host to celebrate the bravery of their initiate(s). Quite conspicuously, the leaders of the move toward alternative rites of passage and the banning of genital cutting do not come from this group. They are not abagaaka binchaama and none of them have performed isubo. These "alternative leaders" are less senior in the age hierarchy. In Bwirege, the leaders behind the alternative rites of passage are of the first generation of formally educated people; they are retired government officials, aging teachers and headmasters, and previous employees of banks and multinational corporations. Some of them have attended seminars sponsored by NGOs and become aware of the dangers and implications of genital cutting. They have learned the language of the NGOs and see their own involvement as an avenue for remunerative employment. Some have started their own NGOs or CBOs and receive funding from international NGOs to disseminate their sponsor's message within the community.[16]

Many members of the community question the motives of alternative-rite leaders, as most of them have previously circumcised their own children, male and female. People of the community wonder why they now want to interfere with other people's efforts to adhere to tradition. Part of the hostility evident in the struggle stems from the fact that the leaders use the language of the NGOs and churches in their rhetoric, branding their neighbors as backward, undeveloped, engaged in mutilating their children, and performing taboo acts; they are seen as having cynically assessed the opportunities within the communities and recognized that foreign aid projects, whether externally or internally generated, can earn them income. In attending seminars hosted by NGOs, many educated leaders have learned a language to unlock funding. Accordingly, locally organized NGOs and CBOs have proliferated and registered with the government with vague aims and agendas that can easily be channeled in the direction of donor interest. This fluidity of purpose is evident in many contexts. The following example is from Bukuria in 2003. In response to a rumor that a group of European sponsors might visit the community, a large group of alternative leaders sat around for a day at a school, waiting for the donors to come meet with them. The donors never made it, and at dark, when the group finally broke up, I asked one of the men who had attended what he thought of the day. Sagirei Amos had not lived in the community since before independence, and had returned to it on retirement. He was pleased that despite the donors' absence, the group had talked among themselves and determined what the problems of the area were and what the solutions ought to be. He felt they had accomplished a great deal. To the question of what the next step would be, he responded, "Finding a different set of donors." Nothing could be done until someone from the outside invested in the improvements that needed to be made. Though elders desire political and social activism and seek solutions for community problems, talk and funding do not necessarily translate into meaningful outcomes, nor do the elites of any community necessarily know the constraints or values by which the majority of the people live. The generally held perception that the means for making changes will have to come from outside support is a reflection on the legacy of Western development efforts in rural Kenya, whereby insiders tend to look to outsiders to fund the meeting of local needs—a dependency mode of economic activity that enriches a few locally who may serve as catalysts for neoliberal-style growth and translators for outsiders' agendas.

This understanding is supported by scholars who describe the proliferation of NGOs in Africa as the direct result of structural-adjustment programs and the evisceration of African governments' abilities to provide basic human services (Nugent 2004, 348–52; Adelman 2008, 512). Humanitarian aid is welcomed, but it raises problematic issues; these include equity in remuneration for expatriate and local workers and the usurping of state functions which might infringe on national sovereignty. The average person in Kuria District does not see the attempts toward personal gain via an NGO as problematic, as the history of foreign or outside intervention has created respect for an individual who figures out an angle for personal benefit; however, people do object to being vilified for maintaining their community traditions.

Efforts to introduce change through NGOs in the early 2000s for-
sook the grassroots approach to social development, whereby local
communities formulate their own solutions by developing the practice
and cohesion of self-directed leadership. Wilson Kimuamu, a leader of
the alternative rites of passage movement introduced in chapter 6,
was amazed when I shared with him the findings from four opinion
polls that I had taken over the previous twenty years, showing that
many youths have, since the late 1980s, accepted the idea that female
genital cutting is unnecessary (Prazak 2007, 32). His astonishment
arose from the fact that as early as the 1980s, people in the community were seriously thinking about opposing female genital cutting. In
fact, young people had already been rethinking the cultural necessity
of female genital cutting at the time he was circumcising his own
daughters![17] There was no NGO involvement then. And now, the emphasis of NGO action is on changing the opinions of the old, not on
strengthening the position of the young.[18]

Kuria language and views on genital cutting become curiously distorted as the local community borrows perspectives from NGO and
international discourse. For example, when an eighteen-year-old describes events following an alternative rite of passage by saying "most
of the celebrants were infibulated on the way home," the statement
reflects not a shift in practice (in recorded history, Kuria have never
practiced infibulation, nor do they do so presently), but an adoption
of rhetoric that does not acknowledge (or want to understand) local
customs, instead lumping together all related practices under the acronym FGM.[19] In the same curious way, many Kuria community leaders
refer to the genital cutting performed on their daughters in the past as
FGM, seemingly oblivious to the harsh moral tones the term implies,
and their own culpability in perpetrating heinous acts on their children.
They simply use FGM as a direct translation of esaaro. How do we understand the rhetoric of blame and shame being employed by the very
people who have subjected their children to genital cutting?

Aside from the power of language, what role have NGOs played
in changing practice? How has the influx of sponsor money into the
community affected the genital cutting controversy? It is common to
provide stipends for attendees at sensitization seminars, along with
meals, transportation, per diems, and other perks that make it worth-
while for people to attend. Moreover, those who form CBOs and forge
links with national and international NGOs gain access to substantial
monetary resources. For some, this access is their most significant

source of income. Ironically, the tradition of esaaro makes possible for some to benefit from well-endowed organizations. For these paid participants in the NGO agenda, ending the tradition would end their source of income. In that sense, modern community leaders are in the same situation as the elders—their income depends on the continuation of FGM.

The Youths

Initiation benefits for a young person begin with an elevation of status within the age-based hierarchy. The widely articulated position is that uncircumcised children are "despised"—they have no standing within the society, perform the most undesirable tasks, and gain no recognition for their contributions to daily life. Undergoing the ritual allows them to take the first step in elevating their status and gives them a perch in the entrenched hierarchy needed to look down on others. What does the physical element of initiation signify? According to Mbiti, writing about Kenyan practices in general, the cutting of the skin from the sexual organs symbolizes and dramatizes the separation from childhood. It is parallel to the cutting of the umbilical cord when the child is born:

> The sexual organ attaches the child to the state of ignorance, the state of inactivity, and the state of potential impotence (asexuality). But once that link is severed, the young person is freed from that state of ignorance and inactivity. He is born into another state, which is the state of knowledge, of activity, of reproduction. So long as a person is not initiated, he cannot get married and he is not supposed to reproduce or bear children. The shedding of his blood . . . is the blood of new birth. The physical pain which the children are encouraged to endure, is the beginning of training them for difficulties and sufferings of later life. (1969, 123)

No doubt these aspirations and connections are important to many young people, but not to all—at least, not all choose these criteria to define their identity. Educated Kuria youth have been opposed to genital cutting for almost twenty years. Written opinion polls solicited the opinions of Standard 8 students in community schools on a range of issues in 1988, 1993, 2003, and 2007 (see tables in Figures 4A and

Girls	1988	1993	2003	2007
# Surveyed	26	62	138	159
Average Age	15.5	15.3	14.8	13.9
% Approve	58	29	20	7
% Do not approve	42	71	79	93

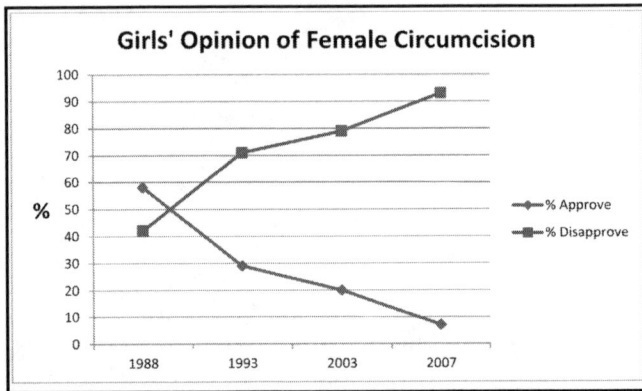

Figure 4A. Opinion poll findings on girls' opinions of genital cutting.

4B). One true/false item stated: "It is good for girls to be circumcised." The percentage of both sexes finding this assertion false has grown significantly over the years. In 1988, about half the respondents selected "false." In 2007, it was 92 percent. This is true for both boys and girls.

How representative are the data on schoolchildren? In 1980, only 12 percent of the female students who had started school in 1974 graduated from Standard 7, which was then the completion of primary education. Later, in 2002, only one-third of the girls who started school together in 1994 had reached Standard 8. Potentially, nearly two-thirds of this latter cohort had been initiated and married (data obtained from Area Education Officer, Ntimaru Division on May 5, 2003). But practice does not necessarily parallel responses to an opinion poll, and no doubt some of the girls removed from school for genital cutting and marriage would have expressed their disapproval of the practice, as many of the stories appearing in the national press, from Kuria District and elsewhere, attest (see, e.g., Atieno 2003, 2004; *Daily Nation* 2005a, 2005b; Ombulor 2004; United Nations 2008).

Boys	1988	1993	2003	2007
# Surveyed	106	134	192	232
Average Age	16.8	15.9	15.1	14.9
% Approve	45	19	17	8
% Do not Approve	55	81	83	92

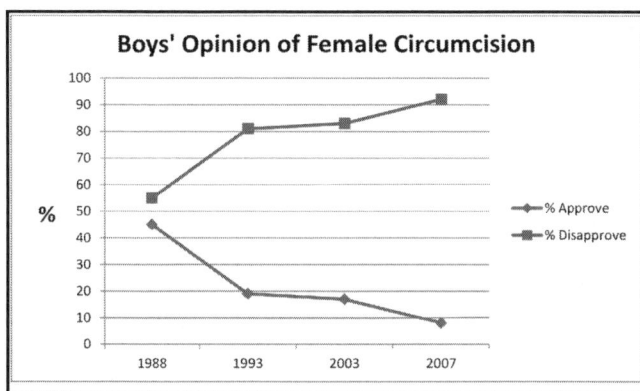

Figure 4B. Opinion poll findings on boys' opinion of genital cutting.

The attrition rate during primary school is high for boys and girls, and only a minority of youth remain in school through Standard 8. This is particularly true of girls, who experience a precipitous dropout rate, especially in upper elementary years. Genital-cutting rituals catch most girls during the break between Standards 4 and 5, and some do not return to formal schooling after that, since they are seen as marriageable—or indeed, married—upon recovering from the operation. The young people responding to the opinion poll are the most educated of their cohort, and are perhaps the most attuned of their age-mates to alternative perspectives. There was no ready mechanism for identifying nonschooling peers or dropouts; therefore they were not polled. They—not the educated—represent the majority of the cohort. It's a reasonable assumption that the majority are more conservative in wanting to keep the tradition; however, that research remains to be done.

Among young women in Kuria District who had been married shortly after being operated on, interviews yield little information regarding their attitude toward genital cutting. They see that their education ended because they had been operated on and were

consequently marriageable, but on the other hand, being initiated allowed them to take on adult roles of wife and mother. According to
the role models available to them locally, even educated women are
primarily wives and mothers, and thus these abaiseke, even if they
may feel they have taken on their adult roles early, see that their lives
are moving in the trajectory idealized in Kuria values. Though some
of the young women expressed regret at having ended their education
in Standard 3, 4, or 5, not one expressed regret in having been initiated and operated on. And not one expressed a desire for that outcome
to be different, now that they were married with children. While they
are in school, girls may idealize becoming educated and gaining paid
employment, but once initiated and married with children, they adapt
to the social identity they fit most easily—they become the *abakari*,
young, married mothers, establishing their households and their husband's homestead. There are no real alternative trajectories available
to young women in rural areas.

Stambach identifies two categories of womanhood that circulated
in popular discourse in the neighboring Chagga society in Tanzania—
"women of the house" and "big sisters of the city"—that conformed
to the culturally and historically constructed polar ends of tradition
and modernity (2000, 60). In Kuria society, the traditional/modern
dichotomy has yet to be distilled into such clearly specified models to
which girls aspire, and for which they are prepared, in the course of
their upbringing and education. Lived experience directs them to the
wife-mother role, and for most, genital cutting continues to be the
threshold they must cross to attain it. Given what they know from
experience, it is not clear in their eyes what empowerment would entail. NGOs and the anti-FGM discourses have not provided a feasible
alternative way to envision their futures.

The Parents

As noted in chapter 5, Stephen Wambura was characteristic of many
parents in his ambivalence toward female genital cutting. An educator, he had attended sensitization and awareness seminars, yet faced
with some regret the possibility that change could leave his last two
daughters intact. Though he says his daughter defied her parents
when she underwent traditional female genital cutting, she was following in the footsteps of her six older sisters, operated on during

the past decade. In each case before hers, it had been clear that the girls were doing something expected of them, endorsed by family and community. A girl who has undergone genital cutting is usually portrayed as well-behaved, courageous, brave, and respectful, a role model (Ikamari 2002, 39).

Adults fear that uncircumcised girls may be unmarriageable within their own community, and this is enough to stymie parents who would otherwise consider abandoning genital cutting. They fear that their daughters will have to be married away from the community, to people who do not operate on girls, and therefore they will move far away from home. Further, the vast majority of beliefs about uncircumcised girls are negative. They are seen as outcasts who cannot keep secrets and will have loose morals; they won't be able to maintain good hygiene at home; being cowards, they remain children, and thus cannot be respectable, and lack self-esteem and confidence (Ikamari 2002, 49). As among the Kikuyu in 1973 (Murray 1974, 29), an "uncircumcised" woman in Kuria society today is regarded as a social anomaly, less than mature and consequently unable to participate fully in adult relationships. Given these beliefs, it is unsurprising that parents are ambivalent about encouraging their daughters to skip genital cutting. An element of confusion arises when male genital cutting continues to be promoted at the same time that female genital cutting is scorned and agitated against (Ahlberg et al. 1997; Caldwell, Orubuloye, and Caldwell 1997; Soori et al. 1997). For a people who see the two as equivalent in the functions they serve, promoting one at the same time as dissuading people from the other makes no sense.

In the media, the usual story about FGC portrays a young girl who defies her parents' attempts to circumcise her and marry her to a man much older than herself, often a polygamist. The story depicts the marriage to be driven by the family's greed for bridewealth cattle (see, e.g., Ombulor 2004; *Daily Nation* 2005b; Atieno 2003, 2004; Kago 2004; J. Otieno 2004; and many more). That makes for heart-wrenching copy and is an excellent motivator against both genital cutting and polygyny. However, greed for cattle is not what usually motivates parents to encourage their daughters to conform to community values. In a society where marriage is an essential element in attaining social adulthood, parental support for genital cutting can be seen as an effort to maximize their daughters' chances in life. The concern that their daughters will not marry satisfactory partners if they do not undergo genital cutting is real, as is the fear their daughters will have to abandon their home communities to find a man whose family will not insist on female genital cutting. Adult women recognize that there are not many options open to their daughters, and they support the practice more strongly than adult men, just as girls support the practice more strongly than boys. Parents recognize their daughters will need to marry and bear children in order for their lives to proceed along a socially sanctioned, ritually confirmed trajectory, regardless of educational accomplishment. And though education is a prerequisite for off-farm employment, it has not been sufficient since the 1990s, as finding paid employment has become more and more difficult. This has been especially true for females, for whom "tarmacking" was not an alternative unless they were being helped by already employed kin.[20]

In past decades, the issue of consent had proved to be a long-standing dilemma for the opponents of female genital cutting as they looked for a way to weaken parental authority and control over the matter. "What the missionaries wanted was a provision which would enable a girl to refuse, even if her guardian wished for her circumcision, but which would also give parents a right to prosecute if a girl opted for circumcision against their wishes" (Murray 1974, 290). The dilemma faced by missionaries was how to encourage disobedience in regard to traditional custom if the parents were "heathen," and how to encourage obedience, to the extent of going against the deepest traditions, if the parents were Christians. The delaying of initiation until age eighteen by the Children Act requires a female to have reached the age of legal majority to decide to undergo genital cutting.

What are parents' attitudes about alternative rites of passage programs? Overall, they are ambivalent. They don't want to be seen as backward, which is how national and international media describe them for continuing female genital cutting. Local leaders of the movement for alternative rites are using this term as well. A significant percentage of youths oppose the idea of female genital cutting, and therefore, it would seem, welcome the opportunity to do something else. But even parents who support ending female genital cutting do not necessarily support the alternative rites of passage. Those attending the three-day sensitization workshop in Kuria District described at the start of this chapter concluded that alternative rites were expensive and unnecessary (Atieno 2004).

Most parents see that circumstances in their communities are changing. The material well-being they had in the past is disappearing,

and the paths to social and material attainment have become compli-
cated. The genital cutting controversy unleashed additional anxiety
over change. In their words, as reported in the national media, some
men regret that Kuria women have been left behind as a result of
limited educational achievement, genital cutting, and early marriage.
Some of those willing to eliminate female genital cutting from the
culture explain that "the value of bride price has drastically gone
down and girls are no longer considered a major source of wealth"
(Atieno 2004). Those men interviewed by the media say the girls can
stay uncircumcised and go to school, and hopefully, gain employment
that will help them support their (natal) families. Certainly parents do
not see the genital cutting controversy to be about empowerment of
girls, their self-determination, making their own choices, and so on.

The complex range of opinion over genital cutting among Kuria
parents can be categorized into four types of reaction to the controversy (Murray 1974, 362–66). The accommodators are people making
an open break with the custom of female genital cutting. They have
the most contact with Western influences and have summed up the
pros and cons of cooperation. They are the innovators whose alignment with NGO agendas may be a matter of enlightened self-interest.
The second group are the well-educated dissidents (such as the father
whose emails begin this chapter) who don't believe it is necessary to
leave Kuria traditions behind to be considered progressive and who
openly question why people would need to do so. They value Kuria
tradition and are distrustful of the accommodators. The compromis-
ers, the third group, are not quite dissidents; they accept with little
question the traditional customs while also accepting the logic of new
ideas, especially of development and progress. For them, the solution
offered by the mission-sponsored genital cutting was ideal.

The fourth group is small, and holds the most dogmatic minority
stance, strongly influenced by an outside perspective. These people
are ready to stand against the majority of people in the community,
who prefer to compromise, and virtually pull out of local society in
order to associate for the most part only with like-minded individuals
for mutual support. Members of the dogmatic minority are rigid on
several issues, totally committed to a cause, and separated and alien-
ated from the rest of the community. Typical of this group is the pastor who refused to allow his daughter to be operated on and refused
to allow her to return home after the operation was sponsored by
her grandmother, his mother. This so incensed the members of the

community that they attacked his home and destroyed both it and his gardens in protest; he, however, did not demur from his refusal to accept the initiated daughter back. Another example is the SDA pastor's wife who was seriously beaten and admitted to hospital after being attacked in her home for having allowed her two daughters, ages fourteen and fifteen, to undergo the alternative rite of passage. A crowd of some thirty villagers with circumcision equipment stormed her home, and while her daughters managed to escape, the attackers clobbered the mother and stripped her naked to force her to allow the girls to undergo the traditional rite. Luckily, the assistant chief heard distress calls and intervened; the girls managed to escape a forcible cut and the mother was taken to hospital for treatment (E. Otieno 2004).

Currently, all these groups are represented in Bwirege. Though very few individuals represent the dogmatic minority stance, their activism connects them closely with others fully committed to the cause of eliminating FGM in other parts of the district.

The Latest Caveat

Despite finding that legislation is a poor tool for evoking behavior changes that might lead to the elimination of FGC, human rights NGOs regularly publish reports on a government's human rights performance, and some require for its human rights report that countries produce evidence of legislation or bans against FGC (Hernlund and Shell-Duncan 2007, 35–36). These are scrutinized by the international community. In September 2011, Kenya passed the Prohibition of Female Genital Mutilation Act making illegal the practice or procurement of FGM or taking somebody abroad for female genital cutting. The law was recognized as a massive step toward changing attitudes; it gave strength to those who oppose the practice, and rapid implementation was called for (Boseley 2011; IFHHRO 2011). "The government of Kenya has firmed up its commitment in fighting FGM such that the law provides that the Government shall take necessary steps within its available resources to protect women and girls from FGM by providing support services to victims of FGM and undertaking public education to sensitize the people of Kenya on the dangers and adverse effects of female genital mutilation" (Yassin 2011).

In December 2011, before the year's initiation season got under way, Dennitah Ghati, a women's rights activist in Bukuria with the

Education Center for the Advancement of Women (ECAW) operating in Kuria District, wrote to the provincial administration asking them to ensure full enforcement of laws that promote girls and women. "As we play our part in sensitizing the community to abandon FGM, you should play your part in enforcing the law and bringing the perpetrators to book," Ghati said in her letter. She continued, "This cruel practice still goes on unabated in many communities, Kuria included. It is also unfortunate that just a few months since the President of Kenya signed the anti-FGM bill into law outlawing FGM, this practice is still going on" (*Nairobi Star* 2011).

The adoption of new legislation didn't appear to make a great deal of change immediately; certainly this was the case during the 2011 initiation season. In an e-mail I received toward the end of January 2012, Samwel Ragita updated me on the events of the 2011 initiation season.[21] Because his family is intricately involved in the events he describes, Samwel's account offered a close rendering of what transpired from their perspective, as well as his view of it. The following is a paraphrasing of Samwel's words.

> In early November (2011), even before schools were closed, boys began to run around inviting people to escort them to their circumcision, a customary activity at the outset of an initiation season. At the same time, so-called voluntary groups were positioning themselves to gain maximal access to the resources to be made available by the sponsors of anti-FGM activities. First, a meeting at Kegonga, Kuria East district headquarters, took place between religious leaders, community elders (the usual opinion and political leaders), and government representatives. The aim was to build support for an alternative rite of passage for girls. These groups included VYOPEC Kenya, ECAW, World Vision, AFYA Nyanza, and the Children's Welfare office. Approximately seventy-eight girls were taken to St. Simon's Secondary School, where Samwel's older sister was to be a coordinator.[22] She was removed from her position in short order when she disclosed that the organizers had received funds and failed to issue the candidate girls with enough food or adequate security. A girl was taken from the group and forcibly subjected to the traditional cut, and no action was taken to protect her or to punish the perpetrators. No facilitator was present for

the girls in the first two weeks to talk to them on the various topics that were to constitute the alternative rite, which had been budgeted for and funds set aside to meet the cost. Samwel's sister was relieved of her duties by the group without pay.

Almost 76 percent of these girls were later either forced to go or willingly went for genital cutting. Despite the area district commissioner sending heavily armed administration police officers on day one of the rite, their tear gas canisters were so old as to be ineffective and they were not allowed to shoot people, especially considering the mass of people that could overpower them. No arrest was made and things worked "the African way," of having decided to follow new ideas and [instead] doing the same old things in the same old ways.

Despite the trouble people in Bwirege were experiencing with the alternative rite/rescue center in their midst, evidence from the Demographic and Health Surveys (KDHS) shows that the overall prevalence of FGM in Kenya declined from 38 percent in 1998 to 27 percent in 2008–9. Older women were more likely to have undergone FGM than younger women, further indicating a decline in prevalence (Oloo et al. 2011, 4). Further, this case study identified the approaches used with varying degrees of success to encourage communities to abandon FGM. Included in these were some health risk/ harmful practice reduction measures, educating and providing alternative sources of income to circumcisers, holding alternative rites of passage, addressing FGM through religious institutions, adoption of legal and human rights language, and the promotion of girls' education and empowerment programs. All these approaches, promoted by government bodies, individual NGOs, and local CBOs, shared the common goal of unseating genital cutting practices.

These measures seemed to have a very limited success in Kuria District. Prevalence of FGM remained high, with 96 percent of females having undergone genital cutting. This placed it on par with Kisii (also at 96 percent), slightly lower than in the Somali community (97 percent), but higher than the Maasai communities (93 percent). These four populations had the highest FGM prevalence rates in Kenya (Oloo et al. 2011, 4). In Kuria District, the anti-FGM network has been deemed "extremely active" in coordinating the efforts of all agencies working to combat FGM, yet the incidence of abandonment is most limited. The rescue camps organized during initiation seasons are run by a committee drawn from the local anti-FGM network, which actively promotes collaboration between agencies, and pools resources to support the camps and raise awareness of their existence. Girls are mobilized from all over the district, when funds allow. They are given accommodation for the entire circumcision period in a camp away from the community. While in the camps, girls receive training on life skills, sex and sexuality, FGM, hygiene, career choices, and so on (Oloo et al. 2011, 21). Nonetheless, changing of attitudes has been limited.

An Authentic Voice

As mentioned in the introduction, Christine Walley (1997) discusses the controversy surrounding female genital operations in terms of specific interest groups and their competition for authenticity (428–29). Some female African scholars and professional women working for the abolition of genital cutting argue that Western women distort the issues and do not speak for them. Other female African scholars and professionals criticize their counterparts, saying that female African scholars who oppose genital cutting are also removed from the realities of the ordinary women in Africa and do not represent an authentic voice any more than the Western feminists and activists they criticize. They argue that if the aim is to stop female genital cutting, they should join forces and "focus on how to tap into international goodwill to stop this suffering of our girls" (428).

Both groups continue to attach importance to "authentic voices" and the presumed ability of such voices to speak for others. The paradox lies in the fact that those who speak most loudly in Kuria communities, claiming to represent the inside voice working for change, are principally articulating outsider messages. They ignore that the language is disrespectful, that it shames their neighbors and kin, deprecates communal values, and avoids steps needed for creating meaningful change. Why is the perspective of outside interests being adopted uncritically by the self-appointed leaders of alternative rites? What is the modus operandi of NGO and church sponsors? After all, improving women's lives is a multifaceted task, and few, if any, Kuria would put the end of female genital cutting at the head of that list.

How are transnational ideas—for instance, human rights approaches to violence against women—adopted in local social settings? How do they move across the gap between a cosmopolitan awareness of human rights and local sociocultural understandings of gender, family, and justice? Answers are needed in order to improve the efficacy of anti-FGM campaigns. As Sally Engle Merry enjoins (2006b), by exploring the practice of human rights, focusing on where and how human rights concepts and institutions are produced, how they circulate, and how they shape everyday lives and actions, it is possible to conceptualize human rights in practical terms and focus on the social processes of human rights implementation and resistance. Then, instead of framing the issue of FGM in terms of a universalism-relativism debate, Merry argues that the focus shifts to understanding the real differences that human rights might make in a community. For example, what difference does eliminating FGM actually make toward emancipating women from poverty and social inequality and conferring specific rights and benefits? Might it lead instead to an outcome where women are further disenfranchised from full rights and social standing (39)?

In Merry's approach, the key is to understand how human rights are remade in the vernacular by people who translate the discourses and practices from the arena of international law and legal institutions to the specific situations of genital cutting and other applications of national and international laws. As social and political actors, these translators are both powerful and vulnerable (Merry 2006b, 40). Serving as knowledge brokers, they channel the flow of information but are often distrusted, because their ultimate loyalties are ambiguous. Their power derives from mastery of the discourses of the interchange, but they are vulnerable to charges of disloyalty or double-dealing as their translation skills can undermine the communities they represent. Usually more knowledgeable of and committed to one side than the other, they add to the inequality of power within the domains in which translation takes place. Translators' work is influenced by the interests of those funding them; their ethnic, gender, or other social commitments; and institutional frameworks that create opportunities for wealth and power.

In addition, translators are not always successful. New ideas and practices may be ignored, rejected, or folded into preexisting institutions to create more hybrid discourse and organizations. Further, vernacularization falls along a continuum depending on how extensively local cultural forms and practices are incorporated into institutions. It can take several forms: replication, whereby the imported institutions remain largely unchanged from their transnational prototypes; adaptation, which is superficial and primarily decorative; or hybridization, a process that merges imported institutions and symbols with local ones, sometimes uneasily. But imported ideas and institutions may be rejected outright, or subverted, seized, and transformed into something quite different from the transnational concept.

To achieve a successful elimination program, Merry argues, continued data collection is necessary, so that campaigns can be tailored specifically to the communities targeted for the eradication of FGM.[23] Two areas often receive too little attention: first, the community's standing conceptions of the rights and obligations of women and children and the standard practices through which these are taught and enacted, and second, opposition sponsors need to understand more fully their translators—the people on whose agency the introduction of often radically new and different ideas rests. In Bwirege, they are people of various backgrounds and personal agendas, differentially committed to bringing change. Some are seen as problematic figures, since what they preach is not what they have practiced, presenting at best an ambiguous message.

So what did the alternative rites of passage alter? Given that most of the girls in Kuria District who received their certificate for attending the camps in 2004 underwent female genital cutting soon after, the one thing the alternative rites did not accomplish was sparing the girls from the cut. In some cases, the alternative rites spurred parents to have their younger children operated on, in fear that the practice might be banned before those children would come of age. This dynamic has in fact been repeated in subsequent initiation seasons—2005, 2008, and 2011. But significant changes have been introduced, primarily shifting the discourse on genital cutting, both in terms of who participates in it and what is being said. That is no trivial accomplishment, given Kuria culture and the stranglehold the elders had, until recently, both on the discourse and on the practice of genital cutting. By being sidestepped in this process, their authority has been seriously undermined. That holds the potential for opening up channels of change, and for the demise of other customs that have been seen as crucial to ethnic identity until now.

It is difficult for many in the community to support a campaign to eradicate genital cutting if it belittles those who practice it and posits the tradition as irrational, ignorant, or backward. To anthropologists, elitist and ethnocentric attitudes do not offer much hope for productive dialogue or the mutual understanding for which Gruenbaum calls (2001, 17). When Kuria proponents of alternatives to genital cutting articulate, as cultural insiders, the same deprecating language and attitude toward genital cutting that is leveled by cultural outsiders, they create an upheaval that stands in the way of "community self-determination," which, as Oboler suggests, would be a process of advancing a dialogue between community members who could identify alternatives to fill social functions and satisfy needs now related to genital cutting (2001, 314). Perhaps more is to be gained from focusing on that minority who did not undergo the physical operation, for whom the alternative rites truly did provide an alternative.

If NGOs and the local leaders they support rethink their efforts to make changes, they could integrate a process of community self-determination which has been used successfully in other Kenyan settings to bring about the end of FGC (Oboler 2001, 313). For all concerned in Kuria—parents, elders, and youth—the first decade of alternative rites of passage did not fulfill social functions and satisfy needs related to genital cutting. But that does not diminish the importance of the dialogue taking place. In Bukuria during the first decade of this millennium, the FGC debate increasingly reflects issues of modernity and development. This is the current language being employed to motivate parents to forgo the genital cutting of their daughters, and to prepare them better to improve their own and their family's lives through education and employment.

Subsequent to the 2004 season of genital cutting, the alternative rites of passage became rather haphazard in Bwirege. In an unusual move, the abagaaka of the inchaama called for another initiation season in 2005, arguing that since 2007 would be inauspicious on account of the seven, there was a need to perform genital cutting in 2005. Alternative rites of passage were held that year as well, but clearly the preferred option was to undergo the customary rites of passage. The year 2008 began with widespread election violence, and Kuria District was not spared from involvement. It became the host location for hundreds, if not thousands, of Kikuyu people displaced from the adjoining Luo areas, including the town of Migori. Though initiations were held that year, the dislocation and insecurity stemming from Kenya's larger issues overshadowed any local excitement, and the organizing of alternative rites of passage was not a high priority.

Why do genital cutting practices continue to flourish in Kuria areas? The NGOs articulate that Kuria society continues to have too great an adherence to traditional values: the council of elders exercises an undue hold on the initiation seasons, and people fear the repercussions of going against the wishes of the council (Oloo et al. 2011, 30–31). From the perspective of funders, more interventions are needed to challenge the authority and power of the elders. Such interventions include a variety of programs aimed at furthering female empowerment and increasing community education on the negative health and social effects of FGM as well as its illegality, and a focus on initiatives that have been identified as promoting FGM abandonment, such as encouraging girls to remain in school and supporting teachers and churches who actively oppose FGM. Yet it is precisely this dedication on the part of NGOs to continue funding anti-FGM activities that on some level fuels the adherence to "tradition."

Genital cutting practices need to be looked at in the larger sociopolitical, economic, and temporal context, as does the constitution of "tradition" (Hobsbawm and Ranger 1983). If we regard genital cutting as a primordial tradition, we risk not seeing the ways in which it is responsive to the demands and conditions of today. In the economic and political crises of the 1990s, prosperity declined sharply as a consequence of complex interacting influences, and the institutions and practices that had shaped Kenyan political life for at least a generation became unhinged. A panoply of national and international NGOs then filled the vacuum, which led to a rapid transformation of politics and patronage. People began to look for ways to earn a living by working with NGOs as an alternative to getting on the government payroll. Liberalization and globalization offered new channels for people to meet economic needs when deregulation challenged the viability of local culture and territory. Many Kuria saw economic opportunities in the arrival of organizations that came with their own agendas, language, and perspectives, and seized the chance to build a connection to funding sources.

At this point, the "tradition" of genital cutting became an avenue for economic development. Kuria, as a minority population in a district and province out of favor with the central government, had long been associated with backward, traditionalist elements. Obtaining a separate district and administrative infrastructure brought new resources into the area, and created a need to build a stronger ethnic identity to contest for influence. The economic uncertainty of the time precluded any significant improvement in the conditions of the district as a whole, but did begin to introduce new inequalities between individuals and lineages, those inside and those outside the emerging structure.

The global opposition to genital cutting spawned a number of organizations funded by powerful donors. Their modus operandi increasingly took the form of channeling resources through local-level organizations, the so-called community-based organizations (Nugent 2004). These organizations provided an economic pipeline into Kuria District at a time when there was little interest from the government or from other NGOs whose importance and power in distributing resources grew as the government weakened. Accordingly, the organizations opposed to genital cutting developed an extensive network in Kuria District and, as they were supported by funders, became very active in organizing initiatives to challenge the "tradition" of FGM. That they have not succeeded is partly a reflection of the ambiguous position of their "insider" staff of translators in Kuria society. If the translators were to be successful in eliminating FGM, they would terminate their position and lose some of the only resources channeled from NGOs into the district. As long as the CBOs and their staffs continue to work diligently, they will continue to hold onto the positions linking them to funding sources. Thus the translators use tradition in a modern way to gain access to an area of economic dynamism. Their existence depends on the persistence of the genital cutting tradition. For those translators, FGM persists not because people are stuck in the ways of the past, but because tradition is their path to taking advantage of the opportunities offered through the neoliberal system of contemporary society. Of all the elements of genital operations that have been studied over the years, the financial angle has only been examined in connection with the gains elders and circumcisers make as a result of initiation ceremonies. To date, no one has looked at the amount of money that is dedicated to the eradication efforts, or how it is channeled into the communities where the efforts unfold.

To determine which voice, among all the voices represented in this book, is the authentic one really misses the point. All of these voices raised in discussion of the practice of genital cutting are authentic. They take different positions, come from different places, and offer different alternatives, including the desire to maintain the custom being so hotly debated. Though I have included all the voices that I consider to be significant, this book centers on everyday conversations between people in the easternmost reaches of Kuria localities. They are working out the contradictions that currently run through their culture and responding to the social tensions created by two decades of pressure and change, change that often turns on the contrasting social positions of men and women, children and elders, leaders and followers. In that process, their social worlds are articulated and transformed (Regis 2003, xxi). For the rising generations of young people who in the course of their lives might not participate in or even witness the genital cutting ceremonies so familiar to their parents and grandparents, this book may serve as a chronicle of the social and cultural upheavals at the start of the third millennium.

Epilogue

The 2014 Season

The initiation season of 2014 burst into violence with an exchange of gunfire as police tried to arrest parents and initiates going for traditional genital cutting operations in Kuria East Constituency in rural Kenya. The assistant chief ordering arrests saw his office burned to the ground. The community was torn between the desire to maintain ethnic character and integrity by carrying out the rites of passage requisite in marking a transition to adulthood for its youth and the desires of various factions to challenge the tradition and move themselves and the clan toward modernity. As events unfolded, Samwel Ragita and Stephen Wambura phoned repeatedly and kept me abreast of the day-to-day developments of the raging conflict.

Subsequently, on the eve of the International Day of Zero Tolerance against FGM (February 6), the *Star*, a publication distributed by AllAfrica Global Media (allafrica.com), brought attention to a spike in the number of FGM cases in Kuria in December 2014. Despite the estimated prevalence of FGM among girls and women in Kenya having fallen from 32.2 percent in 2003 to 28.2 percent in 2008, Kuria was then still at 96 percent. It remained one of the regions with the highest prevalence, despite the passage of the Children Act of 2001, as well as the enactment of the Prohibition of Female Genital Mutilation Act of 2011. Despite being criminalized, FGM continues to be "deeply rooted in Kuria culture, and is widely practiced in Kuria East and Kuria West" (Bukania 2015).

Merida Omahe, the chairperson of an NGO and a CBO (both of which are among the organizations and churches spearheading the fight against FGM), describes their work as creating awareness and collaborating with health officers, the Children's Office in Kehancha, and the judiciary to prosecute those found culpable of perpetrating child rights abuses, which include FGM and forced early marriage. According to Merida, Kuria West subcounty saw as many as five hundred to eight hundred girls being cut every day. "The increase in numbBers was because girls who had undergone brites or gone to rescue centres in preceding years were purposely targeted" (Bukania 2015).

According to the article, cultural belief seems to defy all logic and law, while pressuring many girls to undergo FGM. Partly that is due to the uncut woman being called omosaagane, "a name that follows her like a bad smell until she dies." Partly that is due to the restrictions that uncircumcised females live under that always remind them of their lower status. Partly it is due to the ridicule they face. "Confronted with such hurdles, Kuria girls willingly submit themselves, in the process absolving the elders who as a rule, are not allowed to say no to willing initiates" (Bukania 2015).

The program officer for civil rights at ActionAid's Kuria office, Simon Wankuru, added that politicians, too, have failed to play their part in reducing FGM: "I think politicians do not speak up against FGM because elders are for it, and these older people are the ones who influence voting patterns." Omahe and Wankuru reflect on the apparent priority local politicians give to their own interests in securing votes, ignoring children's rights. Anti-FGM campaigners believe that it will be the children who will bring about lasting change. Organizations like ActionAid sponsor a range of programs that educate girls about their rights. "So far, we have distributed the anti-FGM Act, the Education Act and the Constitution to them" (Bukania 2015). At the same time, church organizations provide rescue centers for girls during circumcision season. There they hold seminars in which girls learn how to protect themselves from forced FGM.

In the words of the ActionAid program officer, "Changing culture cannot happen overnight, but we are making substantial progress. Our focus now is on education. If we use the role models and profile the success of those who refused the cut, one day…this generation of role models will be the decision makers. Then we will see the real change happening."

But the author concludes, "As the world marks the International Day of Zero Tolerance against FGM tomorrow, this goal seems a long way off for girls in Kuria."

Appendix

Bwirege Circumcision Sets

Esaaro	Date	Esaiga
Abangicharu		
Abamachare		
Abakirina		
Abamasai		
Abageteeba		
Abaromore		
Abanginaro		
Abakambuni		
Abatamesongo		Abatamesongo
Abakaramu		Abatamesongo
Abakeeha		Abatamesongo
Abamingisi	1928	Abamingisi
Abating'uri	1930	Abamingisi
Abangicharu	1934	Abamingisi
Abantonyo	1936	Abantonyo
Abangeresa	1938	Abantonyo
Abagitira		Abantonyo
Abakehocha	1940	
Abagetangosa	1944	Abagetangosa
Abagitira	1945	Abagetangosa
Abangine	1946	Abangine
Abamirika	1949	Abangine
Abanchong'ai	1950	Abangine
Abakirina	1951	Abakirina
Abagetanganya	1954	Abakirina

(Continued)

239

Esaaro	Date	Esaiga
Abamaasa	1955	Abakirina
Abagesambiso	1958	Abagesambiso
Abantome	1961	Abagesambiso
Abageteeba	1962	Abagesambiso
Abakehanga	1963	Abagesambiso
Abagibuna	1965	Abagesambiso
Abagimuri	1966	Abagimuri
Abagetaigwe	1969	Abagimuri
Abageteeba	1971	Abagimuri
Abanginobo	1974	Abanginobo
Abagetarasiani	1976	Abanginobo
Abageteeba	1979	Abanginobo
Abaromore	1983	Abaromore
Abaginaro	1986	Abaromore
Abagitira	1989	Abaromore
Abatamesongo	1992	Abatamesongo
Abagibura	1995	Abatamesongo
Abakambuni/Geteeba	1998	Abakambuni
Abakaramu	2001	Abakaramu
Abagitira	2004/05	Abakaramu
Abakehocha	2008	
Abagibura	2011	

Based on Prazak (1993, amended in 1995, expanded in 2003, and 2013).

Glossary

All Igikuria words presented have been checked against the only dictionary of the language, edited by Muniko, oMagige, and Ruel. I have conformed in my usage to their spelling, despite dialectal differences in pronunciation between ibiaro. It made no sense for me to create another form of writing.

aaruure ubunyinya – from the word irinyiinya ("outcast"), making a minor cut on the clitoris to satisfy the formal requirement of circumcision and prevent a girl from becoming an outcast, as opposed to the more extensive cut practiced traditionally

abagaaka – male elders; married men with circumcised and/or married children; men who have reached the ultimate stage of life; sing., omogaaka

abagaaka binchaama, abagaaka of the inchaama, or **abagaaka bikimiira** – elders of the secret conclave; the men who guard clan secrets and the cultural heritage of the people, and are responsible for the ritual well-being of the clan

abagotamotoe – persons who hold the head of an initiate at circumcision; also known as abagooti omotoe, "the holders of the head," ritual supporters; sing., omogotamotoe

abaiseke – young women, initiated but not yet married; sing., umuiseke

abakari – young married women with one or two children; sing., omokari

abakora nyangi – "performers of rituals"

abakungu – female elders; married women with circumcised and/or married children; sing., umukungu

abamura – initiated males, young men, "brothers, comrades, mates"; in the past, "warriors"; sing., umumura

abaramia – "ritual supporters"; child attendants to the protagonists of a ritual; sing., omooramia

abariisia – "herders"; uncircumcised boys; juniors; sing., umuriisia

abasaacha – young married men; sing., omosaacha

abasaagane – girls before initiation; junior females; sing., omosaagane

abasaamba – initiates during seclusion; sing., omosaamba

abasaari – circumcisers; sing., omosaari

abasubaati – married women; "sisters"; sing., umusubaati

abasubi – ritual elders who have performed the isubo ceremony; sing., umusubi

abaturiaani – the group of candidates who undergo circumcision before the rest; synonym amanaanai

abatuuri ba isaahi – settlers of the bush; literally, "people who forge into an area of bush"

amagiha – cooking stones (three make up the hearth); groups of people sharing descent from a common ancestor, with a closer kinship solidarity than those of an egesaku; lineage; sing., irigiha

amaibaako – praise poems about oneself or a group

amakora – generation classes; eight named generation classes, one of which everyone is born into; sing., irikora

amanaanai – the first eight persons whose circumcision opens an initiation season

amara – small intestines; liquid contained in small intestines

amaroa – beer

baraza – (from Swahili) "meeting, assembly, committee, council"; ebarasa in Igikuria

boma – (from Swahili) cattle enclosure; oboori in Igikuria

chang'aa – (from Swahili) locally distilled spirits; ichangaa in Igikuria

eeka – minimal lineage; an agnatically related group of males, usually sharing the same grandfather (in contemporary usage)

egesaku – "door, doorway"; people descended from the same ancestor, lineage, or clan (the most general term for a descent group); the descent grouping below a maximal lineage (ikiaro); plural, ibisaku

egeseemi – plant used in making strong walking sticks and tool handles, mostly found in arid places

egetaanke – brass wristlet worn by abasubi

egeteembe – a type of tree

eheero – one of three rooms in a traditional woman's house; the inner section or room whose door leads to the cattle corral, it is used for entertaining important visitors, beer parties, and formal occasions; goats are kept here at night

ehete – red seed used as medicine against excessive bleeding

ekebaga – the place of circumcision

ekebakuri – bowl, small plate

ekegaancha – beer pot; beer drinking group; container for drinking straws

ekegara – brass hoop earrings worn by abasubi

ekegoogo – bow-zither; traditional one-string instrument played with a bow

ekehe – basket woven from finger millet stalks used for serving ubukima; plural, ibihe

ekehonio – a feast meant to console or comfort an initiate, usually sponsored by the mother's brother; plural, ibihonio

ekeraandi – a gourd, a gourd container; a musical instrument akin to a rattle

ekewaasi – wildebeest-tail flywhisk

ekewaasi kieng'ombe – cow-tail flywhisk

emesaanga – bead necklaces

eng'ombe yi inyangi – ritually slaughtered cow

ensoa – a small grinding stone; from *ogosea*, "to grind"

esaaraara – a type of plant (*Justicia flava*); its soft leaves are often used for personal hygiene

esaaro – "initiation"; circumcision, circumcision ceremony; a period when circumcision takes place; those circumcised at the same time, a named age-set; plural, ichisaaro

esagarami – a fillet muscle; a recognized portion in the division of a cow or goat

esaiga – named age-set, age-group, a person's contemporaries; age-set formed by several (usually three) circumcision groups being combined

etaago – crushed red stones; red ochre pigment

etoti – inner organs of an animal

harambee – (from Swahili) "come together; let's pull together"

hoteli – (from Swahili) "restaurant"; ehoteeli in Igikuria

ibiaro – territorial clans; political communities; provinces (Ruel 1959); territories and groups of people; territories shared by members of one maximal lineage; in postcolonial society, territories and people of specific administrative locations; sing., ikiaro

ibihe – baskets woven from finger millet stalks used for serving ubukima; sing., ekehe

ibihonio – feasts meant to console or comfort an initiate, usually sponsored by the mother's brother; sing., ekehonio

ibiraandi – gourds, gourd containers, musical instruments akin to rattles

ibisaku – "doors, doorways"; people descended from the same ancestors, lineages, or clans (the most general term for descent groups); descent groupings below a maximal lineage (ikiaro); sing., egesaku

ibituumbe – stools, chairs, seats; sing., igituumbe

ichinsangiri – fillet; meat cut reserved for old men

ichisaaro – "initiations"; circumcisions, circumcision ceremonies; periods when circumcisions take place; those circumcised at the same time, named age-sets; sing., esaaro

igikuru – small gourd

igisiiriiti – a skin garment worn by abaiseke; an outfit made by her father while she is in seclusion and worn upon coming out of it; a large apron worn in the back; outfit worn by a mother on the occasion of the circumcision of her daughter, decorated with crushed red rock and many beads

igituang'a – piece of hide worn on the wrist or finger following certain rituals; wristlet; more prestigious wristlet worn by abasubi

igituumbe – stool, chair, seat; plural, ibituumbe

iguutwa – meat from the top vertebra, just below the head

ikiaro – territorial clan; political community; province (Ruel 1959); a territory and a group of people; a territory shared by members of the same maximal lineage; in postcolonial society, the territory and the people of an administrative location; plural, ibiaro

ikihita – gateway into the cattle enclosure; the ritual entrance to a homestead; line of descent stemming from a homestead head; a portion of meat

ikirundu – plant used in making toothbrushes (*Sida sp.*)

ikuno – type of tree

imitiambu – Kuria traditional dance performed by men wearing clog-like, hollow boxes on the feet (platforms), ostrich feather headgear, and skins of various wild animals, and women in traditional beaded belts and earrings

inchaama – secret council, a conclave

inyamunsi – plant with small narrow whitish leaves

inyumba – a house; the family formed by a woman and her children

iriburu – the house in which initiates live for the period of their seclusion; granary; a spot in the eheero room of a woman's house where an initiate sleeps on a skin spread on the ground

irigiha – cooking stone (one of three making up the hearth); a group of people sharing descent from a common ancestor, with a closer kinship solidarity than those of an egesaku, lineage; plural, amagiha

iriiko – a three-stone hearth, fireplace, or fire; a fig

irikora – a generation class; one of eight named generation classes into which everyone is traditionally born; plural, amakora

irinyiinya – "rejected one"

irirongoe – "a loudhailer"; an animal horn used like a bullhorn to alert or call in warning

irirungu – sleeping section of a house; the third room in a woman's house, which contains the bed, personal possessions, and foods for ready use (e.g. flour); has no opening to the outside of the house

iritiingo – musical instrument; boom box

iritongo – the country at large; the general public; a meeting to decide a public issue

isiibi – the coming-out dance for initiates

isiiga – a bachelor's hut

isubo – the ceremony of ritual elderhood

isungu – baton-like stick carried by circumcised boys to the isiibi dance; also called ikuno

kanga – a colorful, printed, store-bought cloth worn as a wrap by women; enkaanga in Igikuria

kuno – a blunt type of arrow

maamai – mother's brother; "uncle"

Majimboism – federalism; a political philosophy of decentralization; amachimbo in Igikuria

matatu – (from Swahili) converted pickup truck or other vehicle used for carrying passengers; ematatu in Igikuria

mooito – "in ours" or "of ours"

moone – "in mine" or "of mine"

mugiro – "it is taboo"

mzee – (from Swahili) "elder, old man"; a respected old man; omogaaka in Igikuria

mzungu – white person; umuchuungu in Igikuria

oboori – cattle corral

oboroe – finger millet

oboronge – "straightness, directness"; a particular direction

obosaagane – "girlhood"

obosaamba – period of seclusion for initiates; the songs being sung by initiates and candidates for initiation

obosara – fermented grain drink

ogokemba – "to watch, keep an eye on, look out for"; a young woman looks out for a husband

ogokomboora – to give food as a ritual act; the first meal an initiate eats after returning from the circumcision, cooked by the omogotamotoe, served in the eheero

ogosera – "to deride, slight, show contempt for"

ogosonsoora – to make ritually propitious, "to cleanse"

ogotaara – "to walk about, wander, stroll"

okogachoka – "to reach the top of a hill, to climb"

okogenderana – "to act against," to perform interclan witchcraft

okohonia – to comfort or console

okorea obosaamba – to partake in the experience of ritual celebrations and activities surrounding initiation; from okorea, "to eat, to consume, to appropriate"

okoroka – to come out of seclusion; "to vomit"

omogaaka – male elder; a married man with circumcised and/or married children; elders; men who have reached the ultimate stage of life; plural, abagaaka

omogai – "a ridge or a hillock"; neighborhood

omogotamotoe – person who holds the head of an initiate at circumcision; also known as omogooti omotoe, "the holder of the head," ritual supporter; plural, abagotamotoe

omokamona – "child's wife"; daughter-in-law

omokari – young married woman with one or two children; plural, abakari

omonto omokoro – old person, a mature person

omooramia – "ritual supporter"; child attendant to the protagonist of a ritual; plural, abaramia

omorekari – bride, a newly married woman without children

omosaacha – young married man; plural, abasaacha

omosaagane – girl before initiation, a junior female; plural, abasaagane

omosaamba – initiate during seclusion; plural, abasaamba

omosaari – circumciser; plural, abasaari

omosoocho – croton/spurge tree (Family *Euphorbiacae*)

omotembe – coral tree (*Erythrine indica*)

ono akong'a – "person matured"

orogena – grinding stone, the base stone

orohongo – winnowing tray; a flat basket woven from finger millet stalks used to separate grains from chaff

orootooti – fontanel (on top of the infant's head)

orosohani – a ritual occasion of smearing clay onto the initiates to cleanse their bodies, performed before the returning of the bead necklaces to their owners

posho – (from Swahili) "ration"; cereal; ebocho in Igikuria

rungu – (from Swahili) "club"; knobkerrie; iruungu in Igikuria

shamba – (from Swahili) "garden, place of cultivation"; irisaamba in Igikuria

shuka – (from Swahili) "bed sheet"; isuuka in Igikuria

sungusungu – vigilante group responsible for stopping cattle theft

taata – "father"; father's brother

tasoha inyumba – "welcome to the house/family; come in"

ubuhu – chyme; stomach contents

ubukima – staple food prepared from maize or from a combination of finger millet, sorghum, and cassava flour, boiled in water

ubusubi – elderhood

uguisaabia – to wash or bathe someone

UKIMWI – (from Swahili) stands for "Ukosefu wa Kinga Mwilini", lack of immunity in the body, AIDS; ubukimwi in Igikuria

ukubiuka – "having a descendant"

ukuhuuraania – "to run with pleasure, run in praise"; rejoice (especially during initiation); to invite to a celebration

ukuriina – "to climb, to climb up, to raise, to reach"

umuene umugi – homestead owner

umugi – "homestead"; father-centered family

umuguru – "bachelor"

umuimiirri – "one who stands by you"; a male initiate's assistant; the best man or bridesmaid at a wedding; the godfather or godmother at a christening

umuiseke – young woman, initiated but not yet married; plural, abaiseke

umukungu – female elder; a married woman with circumcised and/ or married children; plural, abakungu

umumura – initiated male, young man, "brother, comrade, mate"; in the past, "warrior"; plural, abamura

umuriisia – "herder"; uncircumcised boy; junior; plural, abariisia

umusubaati – married woman; "sister"; plural, abasubaati

umusubi – ritual elder who has performed the isubo ceremony; plural, abasubi

umuturiani – the first person of a circumcision set to have been circumcised; the leader of the circumcision set; a position of honor and respect

waane – "mine"

wazee – (from Kiswahili) "old men"; abagaaka; elders

wazee wa kimiira – (from Kiswahili) elders of the secret conclave or abagaaka binchaama

weito – "ours"

Notes

Introduction

1. I bear in mind the admonition of Edward Said that "No one has ever devised a method for detaching the scholar from the circumstances of life, from the fact of his involvement (conscious or unconscious) with a class, a set of beliefs, a social position, or from the mere activity of being a member of a society. These continue to bear on what he does professionally, even though naturally enough his research and its fruits do attempt to reach a level of relative freedom from the inhibitions and the restrictions of brute, everyday reality" (1978, 10).

I take heart from what follows: "There is such a thing as knowledge that is less, rather than more, partial than the individual ... who produces it" (10).

2. The importance of this point is made elegantly by Livingston. Though she is describing the cancer epidemic in Botswana, the larger point is pertinent in this context as well: "That translation is linguistic is not surprising. But translation is also critical in the ontological sense... Over time, translation brings new entities into being...These new entities are not neutral—they have a politics that is endowed through translation" (2012, 72).

3. The prefixes in Bantu languages carry meaning. Thus, *Bu*- designates place, making Bukuria "the place of Kuria." *Aba*- designates people (Abakuria), *omo*- or *mu*- a person (Mukuria), and *igi*- the language (Igikuria). "Bwirege" refers to the territory, "Abairege" to the people who inhabit it. I use the root "Kuria" throughout the book. In English, I simply use the term "Kuria" a to refer to all possible permutations. As is anthropological convention, I do not form the adjectival form Kurian. In recent years, some Kuria youths have begun to use the term Kurian to refer to their own identity, drawing a comparison with people coming from America being

designated as American. Hence people from Kuria are Kurian. But such usage remains rare, and I have avoided it in this book.

4. For comparison, the cohort of 391 Standard 8 pupils in 2007 was just 14 percent of an estimated 2,760 potential Standard 8 pupils (youth ages fifteen through nineteen, using the 1999 Kenyan census). The small number of pupils who make it through the eight years of primary school is a gauge of how few young people have access to horizons larger than the local community. In 2003, there were 330 youths in Standard 8, compared to 196 in 1993 and 132 in 1988. In 1998, Bwirege East and West Locations were consolidated into the Ntimaru Educational Zone. Standard 8 is equivalent to Grade 8 in North American schools.

5. *Mzungu* is the term applied to white people, foreigners, and outsiders.

6. Nyangi is a name given to me months after my arrival, to reference the fact that I entered the community during the season of celebrations (weddings).

7. He is also the grandson of a female circumciser.

8. In the past, initiations were carried out in August at the end of the long growing season, when a surplus would be available to host such extensive celebrations. The move to December accommodates the timing of the school year and gives initiates time to recover from the operations.

9. An example of this interest is an article by Shannon Brownlee and Jennifer Seter (1994) describing the case of Lydia Oluloro, a Nigerian woman in Portland, Oregon, making a plea to suspend her pending deportation in order to protect her daughters from being circumcised if returned to Nigeria. Referred to as the first case of its kind in the United States, it opened the door for this kind of argument in many deportation cases. See also Coffman (2007).

10. This abhorrence is labeled the "ew factor" by Claire Robertson (2002).

11. African Studies Association meetings in San Francisco, CA, November 2006. The session in which this outburst took place was titled "Managing Bodies in Today's Kenya: Subjected and Regulatory Bodies in Politics, Conservation and Health," organized by the author with Jennifer Coffman of James Madison University.

12. But because genital cutting can take place at any point in a person's life, no one can be fully removed from the risk of genital cutting if they live or find themselves within a practicing community during initiation season (see, e.g., Bukania 2015).

13. *Anthropology News* published an article by Edward Green (2000) pointing out the need for data on male circumcision to inform policy choices being made in the face of the spread of HIV in Africa.

14. Booth (2004) shows that this attitude underpins the belief system of Western-sponsored interventions against the spread of HIV.

15. Jomo Kenyatta was trained as a cultural anthropologist under Bronislaw Malinowski and wrote the now-classic monograph *Facing Mt. Kenya* (1965) about Gikuyu people. As a member of the ethnic group himself, he defended cultural practices that British colonists had targeted for elimination. He later served as the first postindependence president of Kenya.

16. Though not called missionaries, many of the NGOs concerned with genital cutting are religious organizations.

17. According to the 1999 census, the population of Kuria District was 151,887. Of this, the area that became Ntimaru Division had a population of 23,095. This is the area and population this book is primarily about. The 2009 census showed Kuria District to have 256,086 people, of whom 53,450 lived in Ntimaru Division.

18. The territory Kuria people occupy was first a part of South Kavirondo District, then of South Nyanza District, followed by Migori District, followed by Kuria District, then Kuria West and Kuria East districts, and currently Migori County.

19. English-speaking Kuria say this. I believe this is a mistranslation of the Igikuria word *ogosera*, which means "to deride, to slight, to show contempt for."

20. Though widely articulated, this is a bit of misinformation. President Moi comes from Tugen society, and this ethnic group performs genital cutting on both males and females (see, e.g., Barasa 2012).

21. Victor Turner (1969) identifies communitas as being achieved during the liminal period, the time when society is a largely unstructured and relatively undifferentiated community of equal individuals who submit together to the general authority of the elders (96).

Chapter 1: Trouble with Witchcraft

1. All names of individuals and places smaller than an administrative location have been changed.

2. A *matatu* is a commercially operated vehicle that carries passengers and goods.

3. Luo people do not circumcise, and during circumcision seasons, they are sometimes threatened with involuntary circumcision by the inhabitants of areas where genital cutting is practiced.

4. Nyabasi and Bukira are two of the four administrative locations within which Kuria live in Kenya. The other two are Bugumbe and Bwirege.

5. The poles were for telephone service, not for electricity, as I had assumed. An enterprising Umuirege had set up a phone business at the market. Electricity did not reach Bwirege until 2012.

6. During this time, Kuria were moving north to escape the harsh rule of German administrators.

7. Literally, the phrase *abaturi ba isaahi* means "people who forge into an area of bush." Maasai are both worthy opponents and competitors for cattle and pasture.

8. Kuria West and Kuria East constituencies of Migori County make up the area formerly known as Kuria District.

9. Majimbo, or majimboism, is a Swahili term meaning regionalism and is commonly used in Kenya to refer to the idea of political devolution of power to the country's regions. It is often used to justify tribal claims to resources and land, and to stir inter-ethnic violence.

10. My predicament closely mirrors one superbly described by Ashforth (2000), who writes,

> As far as I am concerned, there are no invisible forces or beings that shape the lives and destinies of the living, although I sometimes feel a sort of envy, a feeling of tone deafness, when witnessing others communicate with beings beyond my ken. I am free, too, of the fear that the invisible realms of which we humans are a part might not be an ethical order in which truth and justice prevail. And I've no need to wonder why God tolerates Evil in the world. I am thus spared the problem of identifying whether the invisible forces that are busily shaping our destinies are agents of Good or forces of Evil, and I never have to wrestle with the problem of interacting with such beings and entities in meaningful ways so as to bend their actions towards the best. I have no Sabbath to keep, and when I look to the heavens, I see only the sky. (249–50)

11. In 1998, approximately 61 Kenyan shillings (KShs.) equaled $1 US.

12. Contagious magic refers to ritual practices based on the idea that things that were once in contact continue to affect each other even when they are separated. Thus the belief that if one can secure a few strands of hair or nail clippings from an individual and work a spell over these things, the spell will affect that person. By extension, if one can acquire pieces of the body of an individual from Bwirege, putting a spell on those pieces would affect Abairege.

13. During the 1990s, national media were filled with stories of witchcraft, of Satanic churches and devil worship, of kidnappings, dismemberments, and the marketing of body parts for nefarious purposes. A discussion of this can be found in Smith (2008, 36–37).

14. Eating in public and eating alone are both transgressions of normal behavior in Kuria society. Thus, someone consuming meat alone in an outdoor spot could easily be taken for a witch (see, e.g., Sanders 1999, 122; Green 2003, 125).

15. Approximately $245 and $131, respectively.

16. This is especially true of females, whose membership in both their natal and conjugal lineage was always mediated through a male—father and husband/son, respectively.

17. The selection of a chief or a sub-chief is often informed by the competing interests of descent groups.

18. Ruel's translation of *ikiaro* as "province" is evidence that he saw its primary identity as territorially defined; thus, he does not describe it as a descent-based unit.

19. That is a preoccupation of analysts, not actors. It is really through the situations where incongruent terminology becomes contested that the importance of the system of classification is brought to the forefront.

20. The Abakehenche and Abarisenye are the two main Abairege descent segments. Their relative status is putatively due to Abakehenche descent from a first wife, Abarisenye being descended from the second wife. The exact nomenclature for these segments is ambiguous. In the 1950s, they were recorded as the ibisaku (sing., egesaku). In people's everyday usage, that terminology now applies to subdivisions of those groups, as one would expect in an existing segmentary lineage structure. Yet the terminology and the rights and responsibilities of the groups are negotiated, and the initiation season is one of the loci where negotiation takes place. A reference from colonial records indicates a rivalry between the Abakehenche and Abarisenye already (or previously) in August 1931 (Kenya National Archives, PC/NZA/2/1/3).

21. When initiations did start, Abaseese had their boys circumcised first. Usually, Abaseese, who are an isolated group from which most people do not marry, are not supposed to come first in anything, particularly not in initiation ceremonies, because they are the most junior of the groups.

22. A distinction is made between raiding and rustling. The former, aimed at gaining cattle for bridewealth, is condoned, whereas the latter, aimed at personal enrichment, is condemned.

23. Kuria vigilante justice has been written about by Heald (2000) and Fleisher (2000), but was not exclusive to this area. See Smith (2008) for similar experiences in Taita areas in southeastern Kenya.

24. Change of status is marked in the names that apply to the initiates after they come out of seclusion. Following initiation, females are called *abaiseke*, males are *abamura*.

Chapter 2: Boys Lead

1. Bwirege's southern administrative boundary is the international border with Tanzania. The genital cutting sites are not at the border, but in places deemed safe for this delicate procedure to take place.

2. The gender- and age-based hierarchy is expressed both in ritual contexts and everyday life by the marking of senior and male as active, leader, and of the right hand, versus junior and female as passive, follower, and of the left hand.

3. Since as a female I was barred from the boys' genital cuttings, there was no way to verify this information through observation.

4. This is the literal translation of the poem:
Our warriors, come out and / Take me for genital cutting. Why / Am I praising you and you are / Hiding from me as if I bite? / Take me to where Maswega / Is hiding so that he can take off / The part that prevents me from walking / Among the warriors. Whenever they / see me, they chase me away, as / If I am an orphan. / What I have likened you to is / The bomb. It blasted in Kenya and Tanzania / and when Moi saw the / Outcome, he believed. Together with / Mkapa, they wrote a card (condolence) / For what they saw, they kept / Asking themselves how they have / Built story houses, all of which / Have gone to waste.

And the following:
Our warriors, what are you like? / You're like Zaccheus (Swahili Zakayo). / He is the one they respect. / He is the one who designs missiles

that are / Feared by Arabs. In Nairobi and / Dar es Salaam they caused / Damage. And Moi and Mkapa / Fear and respect them.

5. For the neighboring Abanyabasi, a set ekebaga or circumcision ground exists, one where all boys and another where all girls of the clan are operated on.

6. A linguistic distinction is made to mark the relationship of various members of a coresident group to the homestead. The homestead head is the only one who can claim a homestead as his; everyone else says they live in it or belong to it. The homestead head speaks of his home or family as *waane* ("mine"), and all junior members speak of it as *weito* ("ours"). A wife speaks of her own house within the homestead as *moone* ("in mine"), and her children refer to it as *mooito* ("in ours").

7. The *ekegoogo* is a bow zither, *iritiingo* a kind of harp, and *ibiraandi* gourds filled with stones that sound like rattles.

8. If the circumciser takes two minutes per girl, she would be working for over thirteen hours that day, taking not a single break. Clearly, this number sounds quite excessive, though it was given by many independent sources.

9. Any medical practitioner in this area—usually a clinical nurse—is titled doctor. There are no medically trained doctors in the district.

10. People circumcised during each season form a named group. Usually three such groups are grouped together, given the name of one of those three, a unit known as *esaiga*. Such a group will be regarded as a corporate entity, and often forms the basic membership of development groups and so on.

11. Interview with Stephen Wambura recorded by the author on Tape No. 02-13, Sides A and B, on January 27, 2002. Though I asked Stephen Wambura to speak about his personal experience, he slipped between what he experienced during his own circumcision and what he sees as the common or normative experience. In this, as well as all other interviews, I have struggled to reach a comfortable ground, staying as close as possible to what was being said and to maintain readability, to paraphrase interviews in such a way as to accomplish both goals.

12. For example, in the year of the attack on the Twin Towers, Osama bin Laden featured in many of the poems. For the candidates of the 1998–9 initiation season, shortly after the bombing of the American embassies in Nairobi and Dar es Salaam, bombs and other explosives featured largely. The use of Osama bin Laden and other people who have attacked the United States is not an anti-American invocation, but a

positive comparison between a specific relative and the ability to do major things, something along the lines of a David and Goliath tale.

13. Magical potions.

14. Boys and their entourage generally run to the circumciser, so the length of time that trip takes is usually much shorter than the return trip home, when the candidate has a bleeding wound. The walk itself is punctuated by frequent stops as people come up to dance and praise the initiates. So the feeling that the return is faster references the relief the initiate is experiencing for not having disgraced himself by crying.

15. When a woman gives birth to a girl, she is allowed four days of rest. Similarly, a female initiate is expected to sleep on a skin on the ground for four days. Five is the number associated with males.

Chapter 3: Girls Follow

1. Women live in houses, but men, as well as circumcised youths, live in huts. The difference lies in the subdivision of the structures into rooms. An *inyumba* (house) is divided into three rooms; an *isiiga* (hut) is undivided.

2. The notes were printed in block letters in Kiswahili:
"KWA——UNAOMBWA KUHUDHURIA TOKARA YA MTOTO WANGU MNAMO TAREHE 18-12-9. FIKA BILA KUKOSE. NI WAKO _____."

3. This omnipresent plant is also known as the wait-a-minute bush because the very sharp curved thorns are tenacious and difficult to extricate from skin or clothing.

4. While a boy's circumcision in an open setting in 1998 cost KShs. 250, a girl's cutting cost KShs. 151 (with 130 going to the omosaari and 21 to the abagaaaka binchaama), and a clinic circumcision cost KShs. 300. KShs. 61 was equivalent to $1 US in 1998.

5. "Thrown away" or "discarded" are the terms used by English-speaking Abakuria to describe the disposal of the body of an uncircumcised child and the lack of ritual accompanying it. I was told the body may be left in a bushy or forested area, to be eaten by wild animals, or buried in the homestead but not within the cattle enclosure where men belonging to the eeka are customarily buried. Women were customarily buried under the floor of their houses, signifying their ambiguous status vis-à-vis the lineage. Contrary to what I was told, I attended several funerals for children. Though buried in coffins, they were buried outside

the fence that connects homestead houses. This might be evidence of the influence of Christianity.

6. Bledsoe's (2002) *Contingent Lives* develops this point in her study of contraceptive adoption in the Gambia. She highlights how the local circumstances contingent on unpredictable events that shape people's decisions can take numerous forms, not just two approaches to making a choice about contraceptive adoption. Distinctive applicable concepts, such as "fertility" and "aging," are among many historically constructed means that people use to represent and invoke their social and cultural order for personal and collective ends, and to give meaning and context to the decision whether to adopt contraception or not. Since we are social beings, these contingencies include the doings of others, and the management of our lives is all the more a moral accomplishment (xii–xiii).

7. This scenario is often problematic, particularly in the case that the first wife has sons who can rightfully count on the bridewealth cattle of their sisters for their own marriages. In such a case, when the husband diverts bridewealth that could have gone to a first wife's son and instead uses it for a second wife of his own, the house of the second wife is seen as dependent on that of the first, a disparity well beyond the usually expressed preferential treatment of seniority.

8. The dating of early circumcision sets and classes is only approximate.

9. Interviews with Pacifica Mokona were carried out over the course of fifteen years. Initiated in the early 1930s, she witnessed not only her own ceremony but also those of her children, grandchildren, and great-grandchildren. I estimated her age at the time of our last interviews on genital cutting (in 2003) to be about eighty-nine years. She had never gone to school, and in the late 1990s and 2000s looked after the youngest children of her grandson, a secondary school headmaster and my former research assistant. This account is based on Tape No. 88-13 recorded on October 13, November 10, and November 25, 1988; Tape No. 88-20 recorded on November 22, 1988; Tape No. 98-12 recorded on November 11 and December 21, 1998; Tape No. 98-13 recorded on December 28 and December 30, 1998; Tape No. 98-18 recorded on January 12, 1999; Tape No. 03-01 recorded on March 21 and April 1, 2003; Tape No. 03-02 recorded on April 15 and April 28, 2003; and Tape No. 03-15 recorded on July 30, 2003.

10. A survey of sexual health that I carried out in 1994 showed that the modal age for the onset of menstruation in my research communities was sixteen years of age. If indeed the age of menarche is decreasing,

Pacifica Mokona might well have been seventeen or eighteen at the time of her initiation, an approximate age she claims.

11. Two explanations are usually given. The first is that boys have to stand while being operated on, rather than sit, as the girls do. The second is that much more cutting takes place as the penis is literally circumcised, whereas female genital cutting entails only one cut.

12. Thus, in the songs and poems transcribed in this book, a line followed by [x2] means that it was performed twice.

13. "It" in this song refers to girlhood (obosaagane). The song is welcoming the boys, saying that the girlhood of the initiate in the homestead, who is singing the song, had "reached/climbed/risen" (*ukuriina*) to maturity, to the point where it is stretched beyond retraction (*okogachoka*). The singer enacts this point by evoking a parallel process, touching the top of her head to symbolize the closure of the fontanel (*orootooti*), the boneless area on an infant's head.

14. Mukwaya and Mosabi are ancestors of the lineage that Pacifica Mokona married into.

15. The interview with Klara Robi was conducted by me on January 11, 1999, and stored on Tape No. 98-17.

16. Klara attended secondary school in a Luo community some hours away from her home. The Luo do not circumcise girls or boys.

17. In Kuria culture, these age-status categories are much more reliable indicators of age than chronological years, which are often inexact. I found the discrepancy between reported age and elapsed time to be a constant irritant in my research. People revise their actual age in many circumstances to take advantage of opportunities. This inclination starts early in life, for example, because the government requires that children six years of age be in school; therefore parents give their child's age as six whenever they start them in school, regardless of the actual age. Or if police are recruiting young men under the age of twenty-five, the applicant will give his age as twenty-four, regardless of whether he is twenty-nine or thirty-five, as was the case in some instances about which I know directly. When most people do not have a birth certificate, there is no way for authorities to verify the ages given by applicants. Even today, most children are born at home, and birth certificates are seldom issued or required.

18. Linguistically, the verbs used to describe the marriage process clearly designate the differential roles according to gender. Boys "marry" while girls "are married." The agency clearly reflects communal constructions of gender.

Chapter 4: Something Different

1. Some field notes from this event have been previously published as "Witnessing a Rite of Passage," in *Bennington*, Fall 2000, 30–33.

2. The gossip on this was always accompanied by the justification for continuing the practice, that as long as the sons in those congregations continued to marry girls who had been operated on, what boys would marry their uncut sisters? At best, they could be married by outsiders/non-Kuria.

3. The finger millet, which often has to be purchased since fewer people grow it now that maize has become the staple cereal, is soaked for three days. When it has sprouted, the water is poured off and the grain dried. Then it is ground. For making obosara, the flour is added to heated water. People concerned with the hygiene of the drink worry that the water might not actually have boiled.

4. This was equivalent to roughly US$10, a large sum. The exchange rate in 1998 was approximately KShs. 61 to the US dollar, and the GDP per capita was $474 per annum.

5. The label FGM has, in the past decade or so, been supplanted by FGM/C or FGC. In all cases C designates cutting, so FGC stands for female genital cutting.

6. Currently the last of the comprehensive position statements by United Nations branches to create an environment that enables and supports abandonment of genital cutting through transformation of social norms and conventions is informed by a number of academics who offered extensive support, advice, substantive comments, and suggestions that were incorporated into the final version of the report. These academics also served as peer reviewers (UNICEF 2010, iii). I find the production of knowledge by NGOs problematic, as I do the role academics play in promoting and legitimizing NGO agendas. Following the critique leveled by Karim (2011), NGOs produce an enormous amount of development literature, monographs, and reports whose purpose is to authenticate the work of NGOs and their donors for a global audience. In her words, "Development knowledge is not innocent. The operation of knowledge in this sphere is primarily toward objective ends—to solve a problem, to raise funds, to develop a new program, and so on. This knowledge has political implications because it legitimizes certain types of interventions as necessary for 'improvements' in the economic and social fields, while at the same time, it tends to obscure other ways of organizing resources and people" (201).

Though writing specifically about NGOs concerned with microfinance, Karim's point, I believe, can be extended to other organizations dedicated to creating development through gender-based initiatives. "Given their enormous resources, clients, and global connections... NGOs create an order of power-knowledge about poor people's lives that becomes hegemonic in development-dominated spaces, which silences dissenting voices and thereby produces their 'truth'" (2011, 201). She anticipates that NGO-sponsored research will also face scholarly scrutiny in the years to come, a hope that seems unlikely to bear fruit when the scholarly community is itself participating in the production of NGO-sponsored research.

A recent article accentuates my concern. Taking on the concept of the "girl effect" (the idea that investment in the skills and labor of young women is the key to stimulating economic growth and reduction of poverty in the Global South) that has become a key development strategy of the World Bank and other aid agencies in partnership with corporate giants, Hickel (2014) argues that empowerment discourse and the "capability" approach on which the girl effect is based has become popular because it taps into ideals of individual freedoms that are central to the Western liberal tradition. However, in doing so, the empowerment project shifts attention away from more substantive drivers of poverty as it casts blame for underdevelopment on local forms of personhood and kinship (1355). As women and girls are made to bear the responsibility for bootstrapping themselves out of poverty caused by external institutions, they are to do so by abandoning local ideas of personhood and kinship, and blamed for underdevelopment and their weak position within society (1356). The individual and society are understood as fundamentally at odds, and traditional kinship poses a problem for the liberal conception of freedom because it represents an arrangement wherein persons are embedded in relations of dependence that appear to override their authentic desires and hamper their prospects for self-mastery (1359). Without a question, current discourse on genital cutting by NGOs and the government agencies they fund is embedded in this rhetoric of empowerment of girls, and the breaking down of traditional authority structures and ideologies of contemporary practicing societies. It is important to remember that in the neoliberal world, few institutions exist that provide safety nets for the vulnerable and the weak; now, as in the past, the family plays this role (Harden 1990, 96). Dismantling kinship relations is a risky strategy at best.

7. Though many people maintained this, others specified that only boys of the same irikora were circumcised by the same knife.

8. The growing use of health practitioners in Kenya for female genital cutting was recognized and reported on in the *Lancet* (Siringi 2002).

9. Sister is the title given to all nurses. In my opinion poll, all standard eight girls wanted to be sisters or madams (i.e., nurses or teachers).

10. Clergyman Murimi's interview was carried out by me on January 10, 2002, and is recorded on Tape No. 02-01, Side B.

11. The daily newspapers publish many stories on changes taking place in genital cutting practices in other areas of Kenya (see, e.g., Waruru 1999; Siringi 2002; Daily Nation 2003a, 2003b).

12. Her interviews were recorded by me on Tape No. 03-12 and Tape No. 03-14 (July 15, 2003; July 18, 2003; July 23, 2003).

13. KShs. 20 was approximately $0.27 in 2003.

14. Based on interviews recorded by me on Tape No. 03-19 (October 24, 2003) and Tape No. 03-20 (December 4, 2003).

15. The interview with Matiinde Rosa was conducted outside of Kenya, and by living abroad she had been exposed to criticism of the practice to a much more intense extent than simply challenges to the practice in the media and public discussion in Kenya. Abroad, the practice is seen as abhorrent, and that leaves women who have undergone genital cutting in a very difficult position. This is typified by Kate Kendel, from Sierra Leone and Denmark, in her film *The Secret Pain*.

Chapter 5: Consoling, Feasting, and Coming Out

1. The exact number of youths initiated during a season is difficult to estimate. In 1999, there were 40,473 youths between the ages of ten and nineteen in Kuria District. Based on the age/sex pyramid for Kuria District, there were approximately 6,100 youths ages ten through nineteen in Ntimaru Division. Because the age at circumcision is not set, I estimate one-third to one-half of youths aged ten to nineteen (2,047 to 3, 076) could have undergone circumcision during the 1998–99 initiation season. Males account for 50.8 percent of the age-group and females are 49.2 percent. There is no way to estimate the size of the influx of candidates from Tanzania, though most likely, the preponderance of those were female.

2. On this, as well as any other occasion where gift-giving is a part of the objective, a sponsor ensures that his or her gift is significant by recruiting followers or supporters to join in, to attend alongside the sponsor, and to also support the sponsor's gift by adding to it.

3. The soup or sauce that results from boiling the meat is presented to the initiates in the basket reserved for the abasaamba from the specific homestead where the ekehonio takes place.

4. "How big are you" is an approximate translation of *wang'ana ke,* which might, in the context of praise poetry or obosamba, also be translated as "How mighty are you?"

5. Mwanza is the largest major city close to Kuria country in Tanzania. The North refers to the elites from Europe.

6. In this stanza the singer expounds upon the idea that when grandmother was a young woman, the warriors who saw her would pick up their weapons and go raid Maasai settlements for cattle to bring as bridewealth to her parents. This would have been considered particularly brave, given the fierce reputation of Maasai warriors.

7. Nyantare and Getaboraare are both rocky promontories.

8. A vast wilderness whose specific referent is not remembered.

9. *Kiburuuha* is a brown bull, *kemahaara* is any color bull with white spots, and *kiriimbi* are names given to cows depending on coloring and spot pattern.

10. Ababirriira and abanting'uri refer to age-sets of the distant past, probably of more than a hundred years ago.

11. A Kuria town in Tanzania.

12. It's the one that covers the whole community.

13. This illicitly brewed alcohol is nicknamed "kill me quick."

14. Nyarogooso is a gold mine in Tanzania (Nyamongo clan territory).

15. Shillings.

16. Exposed in the sun to dry.

17. His age-mates, who will become policemen and go to Dar es Salaam.

18. The father of these children was circumcised in 1961, in the second set of Abagesambiso.

19. Nyakemori was chief of Bwirege from 1928 to 1939, when he was suspended for failing to report the crimes of his people to the colonial administration. His chieftainship was abolished and amalgamated with Nyabassi and Bukiria under Chief Daniel Murungi (Kenya National Archives, DC/KSI/1/4).

20. According to Ruel (1959), "In the past circumcision and clitoridectomy were performed after puberty: about 17–20 for boys, somewhat younger for girls" (119). In the 1950s, the operation was performed at puberty or as soon as possible afterwards. Kenyatta (1965) also claims 18–20 to have been the usual age of circumcising boys in the past for the Gikuyu, but by the 1930s the age had fallen to between 12 and 16 years of age (104).

21. Pamela Otaigo is the mother of recently circumcised Mary Robi, the wife of Pacifica's grandson. Mary Robi is Pacifica's great-granddaughter.

22. A very similar phenomenon is described for the Gikuyu by Whiting et al. (2004). "All mature males and females identified themselves by the year in which they were initiated and recognized a life-long bond with those initiated that year, considering themselves to be 'brothers' and 'sisters.' This identification was recognized in all Gikuyuland" (60). Further, "Among themselves, the members of an age-set demanded and encouraged cooperation, solidarity, and mutual help as a result of which an age-group exhibited a strong sense of comradeship and fraternal egalitarianism" (Muriuki 1974, cited in Whiting et al. 2004).

23. Names of sets are reused. When the last member of a set passes away, the name becomes eligible for reuse for the upcoming sets.

Chapter 6: Talk, Talk, Talk

1. While citations presented here are mostly from the *Daily Nation*, the paper most commonly found in Kuria District, such stories were routine material in other newspapers of the time as well. The citations were chosen to illustrate the range of media focus and provide a backdrop to events in Kenya.

2. This article also associates the World Health Organization with the use of the term "female genital mutilation" (FGM) in Kenya.

3. In 1998, the Parliament of Tanzania amended the Penal Code to specifically prohibit FGM. Section 169A(1) of the Sexual Offences Special Provisions Act provides that anyone having custody, charge, or care of a girl under eighteen years of age who causes her to undergo FGM commits the offence of cruelty to children.

4. The interview was carried out by me on January 12, 2002, and is recorded on Tape No. 02-02, Sides A and B. She had been named in 1988.

5. This was what was prescribed in the Children Act No. 8 of 2001 that came into force on March 1, 2002, in Kenya.

6. The interview was carried out by me on July 30, 2003, and is recorded on Tape No. 03-14, Side B.

7. In 2003, one US dollar was worth approximately Kshs. 75. A kilogram of meat cost Kshs. 120, and a liter of fresh milk Kshs. 40. All circumcisers, traditional as well as clinical, charge fees for the service.

8. Less than a year after the interview, Joshua Maskio was killed by cattle raiders at his home in Rift Valley.

9. Interviews were carried out by me on July 15, 2003, and recorded on Tape No. 03-12, Side A; on July 18, 2003, and recorded on Tape No. 03-12, Side B; and on July 23, 2003, and recorded on Tape No. 03-14, Side A.

10. The largest ear plug in the Kenya National Museum in Nairobi comes from Bukuria. It weighs 8 pounds. Ear plugs of increasing size were used by boys and girls to stretch the hole cut into their earlobe to the extent that for the most patient, the stretched earlobes reached their pectoral muscles. For elders, the lobes were emphasized by putting small brass earrings onto them. For other elders, who wished to appear modern, the challenge was to roll up the stretched-out lobes and wind them around the outer ear.

11. The interview was recorded by me on January 19, 2002, on Tape No. 02-09, Sides A and B.

12. The interview was recorded by me on January 24, 2002, on Tape No. 02-12, Side A.

13. Though Janet Robi had the top female score in Ntimaru Division, her combined score of 358 points was not enough to take her out of Kuria District for secondary school studies. And though she worked hard and got reasonable results in the local secondary school, she did not gain entry to university. In 2007, she was living with relatives in Nairobi, taking a bridging course in mathematics in the hope of raising her scores high enough to be called to university. Though she did not get outside of Bukuria for secondary school, nor called to university when she completed Form IV, Janet went to college in Nairobi and completed a course in accounting in August 2013. In Kenya, "college" is a word used to describe any privately owned school teaching a professional skill. She continues to live in Nairobi.

14. Nugent traces the process by which NGOs gained the trust of donor agencies, and examines the importance of humanitarian efforts being couched in the language of local "ownership" of programs and initiatives funded from abroad in the context of structural adjustment programs that led to NGO attempts to express themselves through the voices of African partners (2004, 326–67).

15. For a description of the same phenomenon in the context of theater for development, see Mwangi (2005). He raises concerns about the exploitation of local problems by scholars, artists, and NGOs to line their pockets through the performance of dramas. He argues that practitioners are driven by personal gains, and discusses how most of those who have gone into the effort have done so because it was an avenue for employment

and they "intimated that there was too much money from donors literally chasing for projects dealing with the so-called 'burning issues'—HIV/ AIDS, female genital mutilation . . . and gender sensitization among others." This conclusion parallels my own with regard to the introduction of alternative rites in Kuria District—that the practice is "just a method of passing across the NGOs' and donor messages to communities."

16. Interview was recorded by me on July 31, 2003, on Tape No. 03-17, Side B.

17. In Kiswahili, the word *maendeleo* means both "development" and "progress," and some Kuria informants give that double meaning to the word "development" in English, imbuing development with a positive valuation of progress, making the process unquestionably positive and desirable. The development/progress argument follows that if a girl does not undergo genital cutting she will remain in school, will finish primary and secondary education, and get a job. Or she will be married, but by marrying later she will have a more egalitarian relationship with her husband and fewer children, whom she will raise to become more conscious of possibilities of advancement within the society. The likelihood of such scenarios unfolding is confronted by the reality that there are virtually no employment opportunities in the rural areas, as the plethora of educated unemployed men shows. The problem in the scenarios is a lack of opportunities more so than genital cutting.

18. In an interesting moment of cross-cultural (mis)communication, I wondered whether he was embarrassed to be talking about this subject with a woman, though he sought me out to speak about it. Talk about sexual matters is quite rare in the community between people like us of adjoining generations. But also, he clearly was not expecting me to question why the practice ought to be stopped, and assumed that as a Westerner, I would applaud any plan to eliminate FGM.

19. According to him, there were 292 schools in the district, so the scope of the planned sensitization was immense.

20. Women's upper arms used to be encircled by metal coils.

21. Interview was carried out by me on July 30, 2003, and is recorded on Tape No. 03-17, Side A.

22. The groups she mentioned included Save the Girl, Girl Child, Pambazuka, and Crossroads.

23. The stilted language indicates to me that these are goals that have been articulated by someone else, and KDF has adopted them.

24. Interview was carried out by me on January 20, 2002, recorded on Tape No. 02-10, Side B and Tape No. 02-11, Sides A and B.

25. Bartenders are generally male, and the women who work in bars carry drinks to tables but also generally offer sex for money. To work in a bar for a female is synonymous with working in the sex industry. And because they have no power and no protection, they are extremely vulnerable to sexually transmitted diseases, including HIV/AIDS, and to violence.

26. The transaction for sexual services in certain circumstances includes an exchange for domestic services such as home-cooked meals, laundry services, and companionship, as described in the work of Luise White (1990).

Chapter 7: Where Do We Go from Here?

1. For a good summary of the shift from seeing female genital operations as a health issue to a human rights issue, see Shell-Duncan (2008).

2. In December 2004 major donors (including the Population Council, UNICEF, and several other NGOs) held a conference in Nairobi to assess efforts to stop FGM. The consensus at the conference was that programs for FGM eradication must be sustainable, collaborative, and multifaceted if they are to achieve any significant change in attitude and practice, and must be tailored to meet the needs of each specific community. The 2004 conference concluded that FGM would continue virtually unabated without the willingness of national governments in the international community to provide massive resources, time, and commitment (Richardson 2005). Amnesty International had reached the same conclusion seven years earlier in 1997, when the organization opined that the eradication of FGM would require a creative and thoughtful approach to a multifaceted human rights problem rooted in cultural traditions and systemic discrimination against women and girls. "[Eliminating FGM] demands the rethinking of AI's traditional techniques and a reorientation of its lobbying and awareness-raising efforts toward key sectors of society in addition to its focus on governments" (Amnesty International 1997).

3. Alternative rites of passage (ARP) have been performed in five districts in Kenya since 1996 under the auspices of Maendeleo ya Wanawake, with assistance from the Program for Appropriate Technology in Health (PATH). Reflecting on the experiences of three districts—Tharaka, Narok, and Gucha—the authors conclude that sensitization activities preceding and accompanying the alternative rite stood out as key in promoting behavior change toward adoption of the alternative rite (Chege,

Askew, and Liku 2001). Also important were the anti-FGM stances taken by some churches, and the existing beliefs of some individuals that FGM should be discontinued. Other variables to be considered for successful implementation elsewhere include a good understanding of the role of public (as opposed to familial) ceremonies in that culture, and an evaluation of what format the ritual should take to lead to the abandonment of female genital cutting (i). Significantly, the authors conclude that they could not determine the extent to which the programs and activities of the sponsoring organizations directly influenced decisions by girls and their families to discontinue the practice of genital cutting (42), since the alternative rites program is only the most recent intervention in an evolving series of activities that developed during the 1990s. The specificities of "traditional" practices in different locales were paramount in determining the outcomes of all levels of interventions.

4. In December 2004, major donors (including the Population Council, UNICEF, and several other NGOs) held a conference in Nairobi to assess efforts. They also identified problems with the National Plan of Action (Kenya Ministry of Health 1999) and the Children Act of 2001: first, these measures were not understood in local communities; second, politicians from practicing regions tended to speak very cautiously on the issue for fear they would not be returned to parliament if they openly condemned the practice; third, government had provided too little support for the enforcement of these laws; and fourth, the threat of imprisonment for those caught performing the procedure had driven the practice underground in some communities. While laws banning FGM were seen as necessary, top-down legal policies alone had been ineffective in changing people's attitudes. The conference participants agreed that a grassroots, community-level approach would be best, and those grassroots approaches were precisely what had been lacking (Richardson 2005).

5. The medicalization of female genital cutting was a widespread response to the raised alarm about the health risks involved in genital cutting (Siringi 2002). Some of the implications were debated by academics, trying to weigh whether this innovation was reducing harm or promoting a dangerous practice (Shell-Duncan 2001).

6. Personal communication, D. M. C., January 13, 2005; and personal communication, P. M., January 6, 2005. Population numbers must be viewed with caution, as they are based on estimates rather than a thorough, comprehensive system of recording vital statistics.

7. Personal communication, D. M. C., April 8, 2005.

8. Personal communication, D. M. C., January 13, 2005.

9. Personal communication, D. M. C., April 8, 2005.

10. Personal communication, D. M. C., January 13, 2005; and personal communication, J. M. M., December 22, 2004.

11. Personal communication, D. M. C., September 23, 2005.

12. Having undergone alternative rites in a secondary school compound in 2004, she again spent weeks during the initiation season in Bwirege in 2008 in a church rescue center in another ikiaro, receiving training on topics such as reproductive health, spiritual nourishment, communication skills, drug abuse, child rights, HIV/AIDS, peer pressure and adolescence, income-generating activities, and cocurricular activities. In 2008 she represented Kuria girls in an anti-FGM forum in Nairobi, an event televised by a local TV station. In November 2012 she underwent paralegal training sponsored by Foundations for Women in Kenya, and the same year joined People for Rural Change Trust as a paralegal and a youth leader in charge of girls' rights (personal communication, J. R. C., September 30, 2014).

13. Video clip, Worldfocus, March 9, 2009, Arlington, VA, distributed by American Public Broadcasting. Originally produced as "Walk to Womanhood" by Camerapix/Nairobi, by A24 Media.

14. Transcript was produced by M. Prazak, and quotes are included here by permission of A24 Media.

15. All the members are male, and their number is unknown in the community. Since their identity is secret, I have not knowingly interviewed a member of the inchaama. If, in the course of participation, I spoke with a member, I did not know it. The "official" positions of the inchaama are spread by word of mouth, or found in a note nailed to a tree in the marketplace.

16. Two such groups are Volunteers Young Organizations for Poverty Education in the Community (VYOPEC) sponsored by USAID Kenya and World Vision, and Education Center for Advancement of Women (ECAW) sponsored by Gender-Based Violence Prevention Network, NORAD, and American Jewish World Service.

17. With each round of the opinion poll, immediately after tabulating the results I would share the findings with teachers, headmasters, and the educational bureaucrats.

18. Though giving youths rights ought to do this, it is not altogether clear how well empowering the young works in a society that is based on gerontocratic principles, and where both employment and resources are scarce. But youths do embrace the legislation that grants them rights on some level and are eager for contexts they can invoke them in. However,

demanding respect for their right to not undergo genital cutting might lead to their parents' suffering consequences such as arrest, imprisonment, and fines, all of which would cause youths to lose the support of the parents who provide for them. Further, such a challenge does not fit with the notions of filiality to which the youth have been socialized since their earliest childhood.

19. Personal communication, D. M. C., January 13, 2005. This "Kasinga effect" is also discussed in Coffman (2007).

20. As the usual channels of recruitment for work dried up in the 1990s, tarmacking (i.e., traveling throughout the country in search of paid employment) became the major strategy of high school and university graduates to secure opportunities for employment. This strategy was more difficult for young women, due to familial reluctance to release them from family oversight and supervision.

21. Personal communication, D. M. C., January 20, 2012.

22. This rescue center was also mentioned in the previously cited letter from Dennitah Ghati (ECAW) to the provincial administration (*Nairobi Star* 2011).

23. Some of the difficulties inherent in the collection of such data are discussed in chapter 4, endnote 6.

Bibiliography

All web pages in references were accurate and accessible as of May 2, 2016.

Abusharaf, Rogaia M. 1998. "Unmasking Tradition." *Sciences* 38 (2): 22–27.

Adelman, Madelaine. 2008. "The 'Culture' of the Global Anti–gender Violence Social Movement." *American Anthropologist* 110 (4): 511–22.

Ahlberg, B. M., V. N. Kimani, L. W. Kirumbi, M. W. Kaara, and I. Krantz. 1997. "The Mwomboko Research Project: The Practice of Male Circumcision in Central Kenya and Its Implications for the Transmission and Prevention of STD/HIV." *African Sociological Review* 1:66–81.

Ahmadu, Fuambai. 2000. "Rites and Wrongs: An Insider/Outsider Reflects on Power and Excision." In Shell-Duncan and Hernlund 2000, 283–312.

Amnesty International. 1997. "Why and How Amnesty International Took Up the Issue of Female Genital Mutilation." September 30, 1997. https://www.amnesty.org/en/documents/act77/011/1997/en/.

An-Na'im, Abdullahi, ed. 2002. *Cultural Transformation and Human Rights in Africa*. London: Zed Books.

Ashforth, Adam. 2000. *Madumo: A Man Bewitched*. Chicago: University of Chicago.

Atieno, Redemptor. 2003. "Helping Girls Escape from Circumcision and Marriage." *Daily Nation* (Nairobi), August 6.

———. 2004. "Forget about FGM, Let's Educate Girls." *Daily Nation* (Nairobi), June 9. http://www.nation.co.ke/Features/Living/1218/13712/2x6aryz/index.html.

Bailey, R. C., R. Muga, R. Poulussen, and H. Abicht. 2002. "The Acceptability of Male Circumcision to Reduce HIV Infections in Nyanza Province, Kenya." *AIDS CARE* 14 (1): 27–40.

Baker, E. C. 1927. "Age-Grades in Musoma District, Tanganyika Territory." *Man* 27 (151): 221–24.

Barasa, Enos M. 2012. "Factors Influencing Persistence of Female Genital Mutilation among the Tugen in Baringo County." PhD diss., Kabarak University.

Baxter, P. T. W., and Uri Almagor. 1978. "Observations about Generations." In *Sex and Age as Principles of Social Differentiation*, edited by J. S. LaFontaine, 159–81. London: Academic Press.

BBC News. 2006. "Kenya Shock at Mutilation Death." June 23. http://news.bbc.co.uk/2/hi/5109094.stm.

Bernhardsdotter, Ann-Britt. 2001. "The Power of Being: A Study of Poverty, Fertility and Sexuality among the Kuria in Kenya and Tanzania." PhD diss., Uppsala University.

Bischofberger, Otto. 1972. *The Generation Classes of the Zanaki (Tanzania)*. Fribourg, CH: The University Press.

Bledsoe, Caroline H. 2002. *Contingent Lives: Fertility, Time and Aging in West Africa*. Chicago: University of Chicago Press.

Boddy, Janice. 1982. "Womb as Oasis: The Symbolic Context of Pharaonic Circumcision in Rural Northern Sudan." *American Ethnologist* 9:682–98.

———. 1989. *Wombs and Alien Spirits: Women, Men and the Zar Cult in Northern Sudan*. Madison: University of Wisconsin Press.

Booth, Karen M. 2004. *Local Women, Global Science: Fighting AIDS in Kenya*. Indianapolis: Indiana University Press.

Boseley, Sarah. 2011. "FGM: Kenya Acts against Unkindest Cut." *Guardian*, September 8. http://www.theguardian.com/society/sarah-boseley-global-health?page=2.

Brown, Peter G. 1998. "Rite of Shame." *Sciences* 38 (2): 4.

Brownlee, Shannon, and Jennifer Seter. 1994. "In the Name of Ritual." *U.S. News and World Report*, Health Section, February 7, 56–58.

Bruni, Frank. 2004. "Doctor in Italy Tries to Ease Pain of an African Tradition." *New York Times*, World Section, February 1. http://www.nytimes.com/2004/02/01/world/doctor-in-italy-tries-to-ease-pain-of-an-african-tradition.html.

Bryceson, Deborah F. 2002. "Multiplex Livelihoods in Rural Africa: Recasting the Terms and Conditions of Gainful Employment." *Journal of Modern African Studies* 40 (1): 1–28.

Bukania, Christine. 2015. "Kenya: FGM Is Alive and Well in Kuria." *Star,* February 5. Accessed April 22, 2015. http://www.the-star. co.ke/news/fgm-alive-and-well-kuria.

Caldwell, John C., I. O. Oroubuloye, and Pat Caldwell. 1997. "Male and Female Circumcision in Africa from a Regional to Specific Nigerian Examination." *Social Science and Medicine* 44 (8): 1181–93.

———. 2000. "Female Genital Mutilation: Conditions of Decline." *Population Research and Policy Review* 19:233–54.

CBS, MOH, and ORCM (Central Bureau of Statistics, Ministry of Health, and ORC Macro). 2004. *Kenya Demographic and Health Survey 2003.* Calverton, MD: CBS, MOH, and ORCM.

Chacha, Gabriel N. 1963. *Historia ya Abakuria na Sheria Zao.* Dar es Salaam, TA: East African Literature Bureau.

Chege, Jane Njeri, Ian Askew, and Jennifer Liku. 2001. *An Assessment of the Alternative Rites Approach for Encouraging Abandonment of Female Genital Mutilation in Kenya.* Frontiers in Reproductive Health. New York: Population Council. http://www.popcouncil.org/uploads/ pdfs/poster/frontiers/FR_FinalReports/Kenya_FGC.pdf.

CCIH (Christian Connections for International Health). 2004. "Alternative Rituals Raise Hope for Eradication of Female Genital Mutilation." PR Newswire, October 20. Accessed November 12, 2005. http://www.ccih.org/forum/9810-06.htm.

Ciekawy, Diane. 1998. "Witchcraft in Statecraft: Five Technologies of Power in Colonial and Postcolonial Coastal Kenya." *African Studies Review* 41 (3): 119–41.

Coffman, Jennifer. 2007. "Producing FGM in U.S. Courts: Political Asylum in the Post-Kasinga Era." *Africa Today* 53 (4): 59–84.

Cory, Hans. 1947. "Land Tenure in Bukuria." *Tanganyika Notes and Records* 23:70–79.

Daily Nation (Nairobi). 1995a. "Couple on Probation after Daughter's 'Cut'." April 25.

———. 1995b. "Ban Female 'Cut,' Govt Urged." December 1.

———. 1995c. "4 Die After 'Cut'." December 16.

———. 2003a. "Parents Defy Female Cut Ban." December 5.

———. 2003b. "Two Girls Flee Home to Escape the 'Cut'." December 23.

———. 2004. "Circumcision Story Leaves Group in Tears." September 17. http://www.nation.co.ke/News/-/1056/23748/-/pg-5gwaz/-/index.html.

———. 2005a. "Protect Us from FGM, Girls Appeal." December 20.

————. 2005b. "Educate Daughters, Community Urged." December 28.

Darby, Robert, and J. Steven Svoboda. 2007. "A Rose by Any Other Name? Rethinking the Similarities and Differences between Male and Female Genital Cutting." *Medical Anthropology Quarterly* 21 (3): 301–23.

Davidson, Basil. 1969. *The African Genius: An Introduction to African Social and Cultural History.* Boston: Little Brown and Company.

Davies, Owen. 1998. "Newspapers and the Popular Belief in Witchcraft and Magic in the Modern Period." *Journal of British Studies* 37 (April): 139–65.

Dorkenoo, Efua. 1994. *Cutting the Rose: Female Genital Mutilation, the Practice and Its Prevention.* London: Minority Rights Publications.

Douglas, Mary. 1999. "Sorcery Accusations Unleashed: The Lele Revisited, 1987." *Africa* 69 (2): 177–93.

Droz, Yvan. 2000. "Circoncision Feminine et masculine en pays Kikuyu: rite d'institution, division sociale et droits de l'homme." *Cahiers d'Etudes Africaines* XL 2 (158): 215–40.

Dugger, Celia W. 2013. "Genital Cutting Found in Decline in Many Nations." *New York Times*, July 23, Late Edition, A1–6.

Evans-Pritchard, E. E. 1937. *Witchcraft, Oracles, and Magic among the Azande.* Oxford, UK: Clarendon Press.

Evelia, Humphreys, Maryam Sheikh Abdi, and Ian Askew. 2008. "Technical Cooperation with the MOH/GTZ Anti-FGM/C Project in Kenya." USAID, Population Council and Frontiers in Reproductive Health, August. http://pdf.usaid.gov/pdf_docs/PNADN573.pdf.

Ferguson, James. 2006. *Global Shadows: Africa in the Neoliberal World Order.* Durham, NC: Duke University Press.

Fisiy, Cyprian, and Peter Geschiere. 1996. "Witchcraft, Violence, and Identity: Different Trajectories in Postcolonial Cameroon." In *Postcolonial Identities in Africa*, edited by Richard Werbner and Terence Ranger, 193–221. Atlantic Highlands, NJ: Zed Books.

Fleisher, Michael. 2000. "Sungusungu: State-Sponsored Village Vigilante Groups among the Kuria of Tanzania." *Africa* 70 (2): 209–28.

Galaty, John G. 1998. "The Maasai Ornithorium: Tropic Flights of Avian Imagination in Africa." *Ethnology* 37 (3): 227–38.

Gatheru, R. Mugo. 1964. *Child of Two Worlds.* London: Routledge & Kegan Paul.

Geertz, Clifford. 1973. *The Interpretation of Cultures.* New York: Basic Books, Inc.

Giladi, Avner. 1997. "Normative Islam versus Local Tradition: Some Observations on Female Circumcision with Special Reference to Egypt." *Arabica* 44 (2): 254–67.

Gordon, Daniel. 1991. "Female Circumcision and Genital Operations in Egypt and the Sudan: A Dilemma for Medical Anthropology." *Medical Anthropology Quarterly* 5 (1): 3–14.

Green, Edward. 2000. "The Circumcision and AIDS Debate." *Anthropology News* 41 (1): 22–23.

Green, Maia. 1997. "Witchcraft Suppression Practices and Movements: Public Policies and the Logic of Purification." *Society for Comparative Study of Society and History* 39 (3): 319–45.

———. 2003. *Priests, Witches and Power: Popular Christianity after Mission in Southern Tanzania.* Cambridge: Cambridge University Press.

Gruenbaum, Ellen. 2001. *The Female Circumcision Controversy: An Anthropological Perspective.* Philadelphia: University of Pennsylvania Press.

Gwako, Edwins Laban Moogi. 1995. "Continuity and Change in the Practice of Clitoridectomy in Kenya: A Case Study of the Abagusii." *Journal of Modern African Studies* 33 (2): 333–37.

Harden, Blaine. 1990. *Africa: Dispatches from a Fragile Continent.* Boston: Houghton Mifflin Company.

Hayes, Rose Oldfield. 1975. "Female Genital Mutilations, Fertility Control, Women's Roles, and the Patrilineage in Modern Sudan: A Functional Analysis." *American Ethnologist* 2:617–33.

Heald, Suzette. 2000. "Tolerating the Intolerable: Cattle Raiding among the Kuria of Kenya." In *Meaning of Violence: A Cross Cultural Perspective*, edited by Goran Aijmer and Jon Abbink, 101–21. Oxford, UK: Berg.

Hernlund, Ylva, and Bettina Shell-Duncan, eds. 2007. *Transcultural Bodies: Female Genital Cutting in Global Context.* New Brunswick, NJ: Rutgers University Press.

Hickel, Jason. 2014. "The 'Girl Effect': Liberalism, Empowerment and the Contradictions of Development." *Third World Quarterly* 35 (8): 1355–73.

Hobsbawm, Eric, and Terence Ranger, eds. 1983. *The Invention of Tradition.* Cambridge: Cambridge University Press.

Hosken, Fran P. 1981. "Female Genital Mutilations and Human Rights." *Feminist Issues* 1 (2): 3–23.

House-Midamba, Bessie. 1996. "Gender, Democratization, and Associational Life in Kenya." *Africa Today* 43 (3): 289–306.

Ikamari, L. D. E. 2002. "Persistence of Female Circumcision in Nyambene District, Kenya." *Health Line* 6 (3): 39–50.

Imathiu, Imanene. 1990. "Female Circumcision Irks DC." *Daily Nation* (Nairobi), December 13.

Immerman, Ronald S., and Wade C. Mackey. 1997. "A Biocultural Analysis of Circumcision." *Social Biology* 44 (3–4): 265–75.

IFHHRO (International Federation of Health and Human Rights Organizations). 2011. "Kenya Bans Female Genital Mutilation." September 20. http://ifhhro.org/news-a-events/302-kenya-bans-female-genital-mutilation.

James, Stanlie, and Claire Robertson. 2002. *Genital Cutting and Transnational Sisterhood: Disputing U.S. Polemics.* Urbana: University of Illinois Press.

Jan, Sister Marian. n.d. "The Circumcision Rite for Catholic Wakuria Girls." University of Dar-es-Salaam: Cory Collection.

Kago, Tony. 2004. "Man Sought over Bungled Forced Cut." *Daily Nation* (Nairobi), September 20. http://www.nation.co.ke/News/-/1056/24206/-/pg4vm0z/-/index.html.

Kanogo, Tabitha. 2005. *African Womanhood in Colonial Kenya 1900-50.* Nairobi, KE: East African Educational Publishers.

Karim, Lamia. 2011. *Microfinance and Its Discontents: Women in Debt in Bangladesh.* Minneapolis: University of Minnesota Press.

Kenya Ministry of Health. 1999. *National Plan of Action for the Elimination of Female Genital Mutilation in Kenya: 1999-2019.* Nairobi, KE: Government Printer.

Kenya National Archives. DC/KSI/1. "Annual Report 1907-1908."

———. DC/KSI/1/4, Annual Reports – South Kavirondo. "Annual Report – 1939" Sheet 16.

———. DC/KSI/3/3. "South Kavirondo District."

———. PC/NZA/2/1/3. "Safari Diary for August 1931."

Kenya National Bureau of Statistics. 2001. *The 1999 Population and Housing Census: Counting Our People for Development.* Nairobi, KE: Government Printer.

———. 2010. *The 2009 Kenya Population and Housing Census: Counting Our People for the Implementation of Vision 2030.* Nairobi, KE: Government Printer.

Kenyatta, Jomo. 1965. *Facing Mt. Kenya: The Tribal Life of the Gikuyu.* New York: Vintage Books.

Kigotho, Kirubi wa. 1996. "A Case for Female Circumcision." *Daily Nation* (Nairobi), Letters to the Editor, January 31.

Kirwen, M. C. 1979. "Kuria Customs for the Care of Widows: The Importance of Initiation Groups." Chap. 3 in *African Widows: An Empirical Study of the Problems of Adapting Western, Christian Teachings on Marriage to the Leviratic Custom for the Care of Widows in Four Rural African Societies.* Maryknoll, NY: Orbis Books.

Kjerland, Kirsten Alsaker. 1995. "Cattle Breed: Shillings Don't: The Belated Incorporation of the abaKuria into Modern Kenya." PhD diss., University of Bergen.

Klopp, Jacqueline M. 2001. "'Ethnic Clashes' and Winning Elections: The Case of Kenya's Electoral Despotism." *Canadian Journal of African Studies* 35 (3): 473–517.

Knudsen, Christiana Oware. 1994. *The Falling Dawadawa Tree: Female Circumcision in Developing Ghana.* Højbjerg, DK: Intervention Press.

Knudson, Mette, Simon Plum, and Kate Kendel. 2006. *The Secret Pain,* documentary video. Directed by Mette Knudson. Lyngby, DK: Angel Production A/S.

Kouba, Leonard J., and Judith Muasher. 1985. "Female Circumcision in Africa: An Overview." *African Studies Review* 28 (1): 95–110.

Kratz, Corinne A. 1993. "'We've Always Done It Like This...Except for a Few Details': 'Tradition' and 'Innovation' in Okiek Ceremonies." *Comparative Studies in Society and History* 35 (1): 30–65.

———. 1994. *Affecting Performance: Meaning, Movement, and Experience in Okiek Women's Initiation.* Washington, DC: Smithsonian Institution Press.

———. 1999. "Contexts, Controversies, Dilemmas: Teaching Circumcision." In *Great Ideas for Teaching about Africa,* edited by Misty L. Bastian and Jane L. Parpart, 103–18. Boulder, CO: Lynne Rienner Publishers.

Kreamer, Christine Mullen. 1995. "Transformation and Power in Moba (Northern Togo) Initiation Rites." *Africa* 65 (1): 58–78.

Lawuyi, O. B. 1998. "Acts of Persecution in the Name of Tradition in Contemporary South Africa." *Dialectical Anthropology* 23:83–95.

Leonard, Lori. 1996. "Female Circumcision in Southern Chad: Origins, Meaning, and Current Practice." *Social Science and Medicine* 43 (2): 255–63.

Lightfoot-Klein, Hanny. 1989. *Prisoners of Ritual: An Odyssey into Female Genital Circumcision in Africa.* New York: Harrington Park Press.

Livingston, Julie. 2012. *Improvising Medicine: An African Oncology Ward in an Emerging Cancer Epidemic.* Durham, NC: Duke University Press.

Lyons, Harriet. 1981. "Anthropologists, Moralities, and Relativities: The Problem of Genital Mutilations." *Canadian Review of Sociology and Anthropology* 18 (4): 499–518.

Mackie, Gerry. 1996. "Ending Footbinding and Infibulation: A Convention Account." *American Sociological Review* 61:999–1017.

———. 2000. "Female Genital Cutting: The Beginning of the End." In Shell-Duncan and Henlund 2000, 253–81.

Matoke, Tom. 1995. "'Surgeon' Knife Kills Two Boys." *Daily Nation* (Nairobi), December 3.

Mbiti, John S. 1969. *African Religions and Philosophy.* Nairobi, KE: East African Educational Publishers.

McGarrahan, Peggy. 1991. "The Violence in Female Circumcision." *Medical Anthropology Quarterly* 5 (3): 269–70.

Mehta, Deepak. 1996. "Circumcision, Body and Community." *Contributions to Indian Sociology* 30 (2): 215–43.

Merry, Sally Engle. 2006a. *Human Rights and Gender Violence: Translating International Law into Local Justice.* Chicago: University of Chicago Press.

———. 2006b. "Transnational Human Rights and Local Activism: Mapping the Middle." *American Anthropologist* 108 (1): 38–51.

Muchuku, Johannes. 1996. "Female Circumcision: Other Side of the Story." *Daily Nation* (Nairobi), October 26.

Mugo, Beth. 2005. "FGM is Barbaric and Retrogressive." *Daily Nation* (Nairobi), Op-ed Section, July 25. http://www.nation.co.ke/oped/-/1192/72578/-/wetmauz/-/index.html.

Muniko, S. M., B. Muita oMagige, and M. J. Ruel. 1996. *Kuria-English Dictionary.* London: International African Institute.

Murray, Jocelyn. 1974. "The Kikuyu Female Circumcision Controversy, with Special Reference to the Church Missionary Society's 'Sphere of Influence'." PhD diss., University of California.

———. 1976. "The Church Missionary Society and the 'Female Circumcision' Issue in Kenya, 1929-1932." *Journal of Religion in Africa* 8 (2): 92–104.

Mwakisha, Jemimah. 1999. "Alternatives that Are Working." *Daily Nation* (Nairobi), April 14, 29.

Mwangi, Evan. 2005. "Theatre for Development and Communities in Crisis." *Daily Nation* (Nairobi), July 10. Accessed November 16, 2005. http://www.nation.co.ke/Features/lifestyle/-/1214/69760/-/6o8uso/-/index.html.

Mwangi, Kimani wa. 1990. "Govt Bans Women's Circumcision – Ogot." *Daily Nation* (Nairobi), June 6.

Mwaura, Peter. 2004. "Seek Other Means of Curbing Female Cut." *Daily Nation* (Nairobi), March 13.

Nairobi Star. 2011. "Kenya: Kuria Urged to Step Up Fight against Female Cut." December 5. http://www.makeeverywomancount. org/index.php?view=article&catid=37%3Aviolence-against-women&id=2223%3Akenya-kuria-urged-to-step-up-fight-against-female-cut&tmpl=component&print=1&layout=-default&page=&option=com_content&Itemid=63.

Naitore, Jane, and Lawi Joel. 1994. "No Early End to Female Circumcision in Samburu." *Daily Nation* (Nairobi), December 27.

NCPD, CBS, and MI (National Council for Population and Development, Central Bureau of Statistics, Office of the Vice President and Ministry of Planning and National Development of Kenya, and Macro International Inc). 1999. *Kenya Demographic and Health Survey 1998.* Calverton, MD: NCPD, CBS, and MI.

Natsoulas, Theodore. 1998. "The Politicization of the Ban on Female Circumcision and the Rise of the Independent School Movement in Kenya: The KCA, the Missions and Government, 1929-1932." *Journal of Asian and African Studies* 33 (2): 137–58.

Njue, Carolyne, and Ian Askew. 2004. "Medicalization of Female Genital Cutting among the Abagusii in Nyanza Province, Kenya." New York: Population Council. http://www.popcouncil.org/uploads/pdfs/frontiers/FR_FinalReports/Kenya_FGC_Med.pdf.

Njuguna, Michael. 1990. "Mob Forces Four to Face the Knife." *Daily Nation* (Nairobi), September 17.

Ntarangwi, Mwenda. 2005. "'I Have Changed My Mind Now': Students' Responses to Female Circumcision in Africa." Paper presented at American Anthropological Meetings, Washington, DC, November 30–December 4.

Nthiga, Silas. 1994. "Bid to End Female 'Cut'." *Daily Nation* (Nairobi), November 17.

Nugent, Paul. 2004. "Invasion of the Acronyms: SAPs, AIDS and NGO Takeover." In *Africa since Independence,* 326–67. New York: Palgrave Macmillan.

Obermeyer, Carla Makhlouf, and Robert F. Reynolds. 1999. "On Cutting Women's Genitals: Female Genital Surgeries, Reproductive Health and Sexuality: A Review of the Evidence." *Reproductive Health Matters* 7 (13): 112–44.

Oboler, Regina Smith. 2001. "Law and Persuasion in the Elimination of Female Genital Modification." *Human Organization* 60 (4): 311–18.

Okwubanego, John Tochukwu. 1999. "Female Circumcision and the Girl Child in Africa and the Middle East: The Eyes of the World Are Blind to the Conquered." *International Lawyer* 33 (1): 159–87.

Olamijulo, Samuel, Kabba T. Joiner, and Gabriel A. Oyedeji. 1983. "Female Child Circumcision in Ilesha, Nigeria: The Present and the Future." *Clinical Pediatrics* 22 (8): 580–81.

Oloo, Habil, Monica Wanjiru, and Katy Newell-Jones. 2011. "Female Genital Mutilation Practices in Kenya: A Role of Alternative Rites of Passage. A Case Study of Kisii and Kuria Districts." Feed the Minds, March. http://www.popcouncil.org/uploads/pdfs/2011RH_FGMPracticeKenya.pdf.

Ombulor, Joe. 2004. "Early Marriages Cut Short the Lives of Young Girls." *Daily Nation* (Nairobi), November 27. Accessed November 16, 2005, from www.nationmedia.com.

Otieno, Elisha. 2004. "Villagers Beat Mother Opposed to Female Cut." *Daily Nation* (Nairobi), December 31.

Otieno, Jeff. 2004. "New Tactics Needed to Fight the Cut." *Daily Nation* (Nairobi), October19. Accessed November 16, 2005, from www.nationmedia.com.

Parker, Melissa. 1995. "Rethinking Female Circumcision." *Africa* 65 (4): 506–24.

Prazak, Miroslava. 1993. "Cultural Expressions of Socioeconomic Differentiation among the Kuria of Kenya." PhD diss., Yale University.

———. 1999. "'We're on the Run': Ideas of Progress among Adolescents in Rural Kenya." *Journal of African Cultural Studies* 12 (1): 93–110.

———. 2000. "Seeds of Continuity, Lines of Change: Families and Work in Rural Kenya." *Anthropology of Work Review* 21 (4): 21–30.

———. 2007. "Introducing Alternative Rites of Passage." *Africa Today* 53 (4): 19–40.

————. 2012. "Studying Life Strategies of Orphans in Rural Kenya." *Africa Today* 58 (4): 45–66.

Prazak, Miroslava, and Heather Booth. 1995. "Measurement and Meaning: Community-Based Research on Child Mortality in Rural Kenya." Working Papers in Demography No. 59, Research School of Social Sciences, Australian National University, Canberra, AU.

Rahman, Anika, and Nahid Toubia, eds. 2000. *Female Genital Mutilation: A Guide to Laws and Policies Worldwide.* London: Zed Books.

Ranger, Terence. 1983. "The Invention of Tradition in Colonial Africa." In Hobsbawm and Ranger, 1983, 211–62.

Richardson, Gemma. 2005. "Ending Female Genital Mutilation? Rights, Medicalization, and the State of Ongoing Struggles to Eliminate the FGM in Kenya." *Dominion,* February 11. http://dominionpaper.ca/accounts/2005/02/11/ending_fem.html.

Riesman, Paul. 1986. "The Person and the Life Cycle in African Social Life and Thought." *African Studies Review* 29 (2): 71–137.

Robertson, Claire. 1996. "Grassroots in Kenya: Women, Genital Mutilation, and Collective Action, 1920–1990." *Signs* 21 (3): 615–42.

————. 2002. "Getting Beyond the Ew! Factor: Rethinking U.S. Approaches to African Female Genital Cutting." In James and Robertson, 2002, 54–86.

Ruel, Malcolm J. 1959. "The Social Organization of the Kuria: A Fieldwork Report." Unpublished manuscript.

————. 1962. "Kuria Generation Classes." *Africa* 32 (1): 14–37.

————. 1965. "Religion and Society among the Kuria of East Africa." *Africa* 35 (3): 295–306.

Said, Edward W. 1978. *Orientalism.* New York: Pantheon Books.

Sanders, Todd. 1999. "Modernity, Wealth, and Witchcraft in Tanzania." *Research in Economic Anthropology* 20:117–31.

Sekoh, Jacinta. 1996. "Female Cut: Is the Rite Dying a Natural Death?" *Sunday Nation,* Lifestyle 6–7, September 1.

Shell-Duncan, Bettina. 2001. "The Medicalization of Female 'Circumcision': Harm Reduction or Promotion of a Dangerous Practice?" *Social Science & Medicine* 52:1013–28.

————. 2008. "From Health to Human Rights: Female Genital Cutting and the Politics of Intervention." *American Anthropologist* 110 (2): 225–36.

Shell-Duncan, Bettina, and Ylva Hernlund, eds. 2000. *Female "Circumcision" in Africa: Culture, Controversy, and Change.* Boulder, CO: Lynne Rienner Publishers.

Shell-Duncan, Bettina, Katherine Wander, Ylva Hernlund, and Amadou Moreau. 2011. "Dynamics of Change in the Practice of Female Genital Cutting in Senegambia: Testing Predictions of Social Convention Theory." *Social Science & Medicine* 73:1275–83.

———. 2013. "Legislating Change? Responses to Criminalizing Female Genital Cutting in Senegal." *Law & Society Review* 47 (4): 803–35.

Shweder, Richard A. 2013. "The Goose and the Gander: The Genital Wars." *Global Discourse: An Interdisciplinary Journal of Current Affairs and Applied Contemporary Thought* 3 (2): 348–66.

Sipakati, Safari. 1988. "When It's Time for Boys to Graduate into 'Manhood'." *Daily Nation* (Nairobi), August 5.

Siringi, Samuel. 2002. "Kenyan Health Professionals Participate in Female Circumcision." *Lancet* 360:2057.

Soori, Nnko, Boerma J. Ties, Washija Robert, and Urassa Mark. 1997. "The Popularization of Male Circumcision in Africa: Changing Practices among the Sukuma of Tanzania." *African Anthropology* 4 (1): 68–79.

Smith, James Howard. 2008. *Bewitching Development: Witchcraft and the Reinvention of Development in Neoliberal Kenya*. Chicago: University of Chicago Press.

Stambach, Amy. 2000. *Lessons from Mount Kilimanjaro: Schooling, Community, and Gender in East Africa*. New York: Routledge and Kegan Paul.

Stewart, Pamela, and Andrew Strathern. 2004. *Witchcraft, Sorcery, Rumors, and Gossip*. Cambridge: Cambridge University Press.

Strayer, Robert W. 1978. "The CMS and Female Circumcision," coauthored with Jocelyn Murray. In *The Making of Mission Communities in East Africa: Anglicans and Africans in Colonial Kenya, 1875–1935*, 136–55. London: Heinemann.

Standard (Nairobi). 2003. "Five NGOs Form Anti-FGM Front." February 8.

Thomas, Lynn M. 1996. "'Ngaitana (I Will Circumcise Myself)': The Gender and Generational Politics of the 1956 Ban on Clitoridectomy in Meru, Kenya." *Gender & History* 8 (3): 338–63.

———. 1998. "Imperial Concerns and 'Women's Affairs': State Efforts to Regulate Clitoridectomy and Eradicate Abortion in Meru, Kenya, c.1910–1950." *Journal of African History* 39 (1): 121–46.

———. 2003. *Politics of the Womb: Women, Reproduction, and the State in Kenya*. Berkeley: University of California Press.

Bibliography / 285

Tobisson, Eva. 1986. *Family Dynamics among the Kuria: Agro-Pastoralists in Northern Tanzania.* Gotenborg, SE: Acta Universitatis Gothoburgensis.

Turner, Barry, ed. 2002. *The Stateman's Yearbook: The Politics, Cultures and Economies of the World.* New York: Palgrave.

Turner, Victor. 1967. *The Forest of Symbols: Aspects of Ndembu Ritual.* Ithaca: Cornell University Press.

———. 1969. *The Ritual Process: Structure and Anti-structure.* Ithaca: Cornell University Press.

UNICEF (United Nations Children's Fund). 2010. *Dynamics of Social Change: Toward the Abandonment of Female Genital Mutilation/Cutting in Five African Countries.* Florence: Innocenti Research Center.

United Nations. 1999. "Eradication of Female Genital Mutilation (FGM) in Kenya." *United Nations Chronicle* 36 (3): 74–76.

———. 2002. "Rights Activists Decry Mungiki Circumcision Threat." Office for the Coordination of Humanitarian Affairs, Integrated Regional Information Network, April 25.

———. 2006. "Razor's Edge—The Controversy of Female Genital Mutilation." Office for the Coordination of Humanitarian Affairs, Integrated Regional Information Network. IRIN Web Special. Accessed November 3, 2006, from http://www.irinnews.org/.

———. 2008. "Hiding from the Cruelest Cut." Office for the Coordination of Humanitarian Affairs, Integrated Regional Information Network. IRIN Web Special. Accessed December 17, 2008.

Van Gennep, Arnold. 1909. *The Rites of Passage.* Translated by Monika B. Vizedom and Garielle L. Caffee. London: Routledge and Kegan Paul.

Van Vuuren, Chris J., and Michael de Jongh. 1999. "Rituals of Manhood in South Africa: Circumcision at the Cutting Edge of Critical Intervention." *Suid Africkaanse Tydskrif vir Etnologie* 22 (4): 142–56.

Walley, Christine J. 1997. "Searching for 'Voices': Feminism, Anthropology, and the Global Debate over Female Genital Operations." *Cultural Anthropology* 12 (2): 405–38.

Wanyama, Bernard. 1990. "Circumcision: Govt Told to Take Action." *Daily Nation* (Nairobi), August 18.

Waruru, Maina. 1999. "Alternative 'Female Cut' Winning Acceptance." *Daily Nation* (Nairobi), April 1.

White, Luise. 1990. *The Comforts of Home: Prostitution in Colonial Nairobi.* Chicago: University of Chicago Press.

Whiting, Beatrice, John Whiting, John Herzog, and Carolyn Edwards, with Arnold Curtis. 2004. "The Historical Stage." In *Ngecha: A Kenyan Village in a Time of Rapid Social Change*, edited by Carolyn Pope Edwards and Beatrice Blyth Whiting, 53–90. Lincoln: University of Nebraska Press.

Williams, Lindy, and Teresa Sobieszczyk. 1997. "Attitudes Surrounding the Continuation of Female Circumcision in the Sudan: Passing the Tradition to the Next Generation." *Journal of Marriage and the Family* 59:966–81.

Winterbottom, Anna, Jonneke Koomen, and Gemma Burford. 2009. "Female Genital Cutting: Cultural Rights and Rites of Defiance in Northern Tanzania." *African Studies Review* 52 (1): 47–71.

WHO (World Health Organization). 2006. "New Study Shows Female Genital Mutilation Exposes Women and Babies to Significant Risk at Childbirth." *Lancet*, June 2. Accessed June 21, 2006. http://www.who.int/mediacentre/news/releases/2006/pr30/en/print.html.

———. 2008. "Eliminating Female Genital Mutilation: An Interagency Statement OHCHR, UNAIDS, UNDP, UNECA, UNESCO, UNFPA, UNHCR, UNICEF, UNIFEM, WHO." Geneva: WHO.

———. 2010. "Global Strategy to Stop Health-Care Providers from Performing Female Genital Mutilation." Geneva: WHO. http://www.who.int/reproductivehealth/publications/fgm/rhr_10_9/en/.

Worldfocus. Video clip, March 9, 2009. Arlington, VA: American Public Broadcasting. Originally produced as "Walk to Womanhood" by Camerapix/Nairobi, by A24 Media.

Yassin, Rukia. 2011. "Female Genital Mutilation Illegalized as Kenya Passes Law against 'the Cut'." Deutsche Geselleshaft für Internationale Zusammenarbeit (GIZ), October 24. http://www.gtzkenyahealth.com/blog3/?p=9308.

Zingaro, Linde. 2009. *Speaking Out: Storytelling for Social Change*. Walnut Creek, CA: Left Coast Press.

Index

Abachuma, 23
abagaaka; of the inchaama, 232; seclusion, ending of, 154
abagaaka binchaama, 76, 128, 145, 161, 165, 187, 188, 197, 216
Abagesambiso, 164; work party responsibilities, 167
Abagimuri, 71, 166; work party responsibilities, 166
Abagumbe, 53, 189
Abagusii, 125, 126; customs of, 126
Abahirichacha, 53
Abairege, 4, 7, 33, 34, 46, 50, 56, 66, 189, 201; circumcision and, 7; history of, 34; initiation frequency, 164; migration and, 51; okogenderana and, 47; totem of, 53; warfare with Maasai, 164
abaiseke, 108, 109, 154, 161, 163, 167, 222. *See* initiates, female; marriage and school, 154
Abakehenche, 53, 54, 55, 56, 60, 131, 168, 188
Abakira, 46, 189
Abamasa, 167; work party responsibilities, 167

Abamingisi, 93, 98; initiation, 98
abamura, 64, 71, 87, 108, 109, 163, 167. *See* initiates, male; duties of, 64
Abangoroime, 189
Abanyabasi, 36, 41, 46, 50, 57, 189; okogenderana and, 47
Abanyamongo, 53, 189
abaramia, 147
abariisia, 64, 107
Abarisenye, 53, 54, 55, 56, 60, 131, 161, 168, 188
Abasaae, 23
abasaagane, 107
abasaamba, 57, 66, 67, 74, 129, 136, 147, 153, 157, 161, 169; gender equality and, 145; healing of, 154; leaders, 147; liminality and, 144; school and, 142; stature of, 153; taboos, 147, 153
abasaari, 141, 167. *See* circumcisers
Abaseese, 56
abasubi, 111
Abatimbaru, 189
abaturiaani, 168
academics, 2, 209, 217
accommodators, 225
ActionAid, 198, 206, 238; Kenya, 194, 211

providers and, 8; health
effects, 177, 179; obstetrical,
178; psychological, 178;
sexual, 178; human rights
watch groups and, 8, 15;
immigration officers and, 8;
international law and, 209;
international observers,
177; international scene
and, 8; interventions, 19,
141, 157; empowering local
communities, 19, 25; ending,
177; financial and technical
support, 19; legislative,
20; prohibition, 156;
sensitization, 20; Kenyan
law, 19; laws, 55, 178;
against, 226; lineage and, 12;
marriage and, 122, 162, 200;
education and, 178; media
and, 10; media coverage,
177, 224; medicalized, 24,
123; medicine and, 93,
106; Meru African District
Council ban, 18; moral
opprobrium, 12–13; myths,
178, 199; nongovernmental
organizations (NGOs) and,
15, 21; opposition to, 16–20,
18, 18–19, 24, 128, 138;
colonial, 138; government,
18; international
development agencies, 18;
missionary, 138; professional
associations, 18; responses,
11; United Nations, 18;
women's organizations,
18; outcomes, 15, 18, 89;
outlawing in Tanzania,
141; parents and, 88;

Parliamentary debate
over, 177; perspectives;
academic, 122, 138;
activists, 122; debate over,
17; government, 122, 123;
insider, 127; media, 180;
NGOs, 122; non-Kuria, 138;
policymakers, 122; Western,
10; physical mutilation
and, 11; policymakers
and, 8, 16; poor academic
performance and, 220;
power relations and, 12;
practices, 15; pressure for,
117, 132; prevalence, 179,
208, 228, 237–238; rate,
27; procedure, 5, 89, 93;
promoting maturity, 221;
proponents of, 11, 18; public
views on, 141, 169, 201;
reasons for, 11, 122, 198;
relativistic tolerance of,
12–13; reproductive health
and, 19; resistance to, 193;
responses to; condemning,
25, 138; cultural relativism,
179; debates, 180;
defending, 179; feminism,
12; humanist political, 12;
impact of, 25; media, 177;
opposition, 123, 124, 179;
outsider, 138; support of,
18; willing/embracing,
117, 238; seclusion after,
23; sexual activity after,
11, 12, 102; limiting, 154;
sterilization and, 178;
subjective experience of,
27, 93, 101–107, 112, 213;
symbolic act, 12; traditional,

challenges of 1998, 168;
pressure, 117; school and,
142; traveling during, 55;
witnessing, 7; youths and,
30
initiation season, 237
institutional adaptation, 231
intact. *See* uncircumcised
condition
international; development
agencies, 207; justice, 20;
observers, 24–25, 193–195,
226; scene and female
genital cutting, 8
International Conference
on Population and
Development, 19
International Day of Zero
Tolerance against FGM,
237
International Monetary Fund,
183
interventions, 25, 209, 228,
233. *See also* female genital
cutting, interventions;
alternatives, 125, 130, 138,
139, 176, 179, 180, 187,
194, 197, 207, 211, 222,
228, 232; banning, 177, 182;
changing attitudes, beliefs,
behaviors, and practices,
24, 118, 122–123, 125, 138,
157, 169, 176, 181, 185,
190, 195, 198, 212, 226, 229,
233; education, 138, 180,
195, 198, 205, 208, 211, 216,
228, 229, 238; empowering
girls, 117, 191, 229, 233,
238; empowering local
communities, 25, 194, 232;

ending, 177, 199, 205, 208,
216, 219, 230, 232; financial
and technical support, 25,
196; galvanizing political
will, 177, 194, 209, 226;
harm reduction, 118;
imposing external values,
207, 229; increased technical
and advocacy capacity
of NGOs, 180, 183, 194,
209, 216, 218; laws versus
practice, 181; legal action,
237; medicalization, 68,
120, 138, 203; motives,
216; opposition, 117, 157;
outcomes, 208; outlawing,
237; outlawing/legal
action, 130, 141, 177, 181,
201, 208, 211, 213, 233;
outsider, 217; plans, 209;
preaching against, 189, 197;
prohibition, 156; rescue
camps, 228; sensitization,
25, 138, 139, 177, 179, 180,
196, 197, 198, 205, 206, 210,
218, 222, 227; strategies,
169; alternative rites, 169;
church input, 169; debates,
169; legislation, 169; NGOs
and, 169
interviews, 71
inyumba, 84
iritongo, 56
Isenye, 20
isiibi, 98, 164
isubo, 216

J

Jamhuri Day celebrations, 57
Jehovah's Witnesses, 196

jobholders, 159

joking. *See* cultural practices, joking

justice, 230; vigilantes, 56

K

kanga, 69, 147

KenClub and Kuria Girl Child Organization (KOGUO), 195

Kenya, 1, 7, 20, 130, 133, 138, 187, 195, 201, 213, 215, 217, 219, 237; abasaamba, 168; border, 201; Children Act of 2001 in, 18; circumcising communities in, 176; colonialism, 16; district commissioner, 56; economic change, 39; initiations in, 7; Kuria ibiaro in, 55; law, 19; media, 13, 39; coverage of circumcision (1980), 13; medicalization, 124; national identity, 34; National Plan of Action for the Elimination of Female Genital Mutilation in, 18, 19; parliament defeat of genital cutting in 1966, 18; political; change, 39; will in, 177; schools, 141; trend of female genital cutting, 237; view of Kuria, 34; witchcraft, 37

Kenya Alliance for the Advancement of Children, 211

Kenyatta, Jomo, 16, 145

Kikuyu, 145, 232

kin, 64, 74, 75, 94, 100, 119, 129, 141, 142, 145–146, 146, 167, 190, 224

kinship, 45; norms, 23

Kisii, 126, 133, 180, 181, 188, 190, 211, 228

knowledge brokers, 230; power of, 230

Kratz, Corinne, 26, 100

Kuria, 1, 6, 8, 20, 35, 90, 92, 126, 138, 181, 188, 189, 191, 195, 196, 199, 201, 206, 209, 211, 213, 214, 222, 227, 228, 229, 232, 233, 237, 238; Abairege clan, 33; academics, 7; adulthood in, 14; as backward, 233; boundaries, 20, 21; chiefs, 52; circumcision, 14; circumcision and, 8; clan, 34, 78; clergy, 190; clitoridectomy, 14; communities, 72, 89, 107, 229; cultural; norms, 109; order, 78; spaces, 144; strands, 6; uniqueness preservation, 58; customs of, 126; descendants and, 110; descent, 50, 78, 144; de-emphasis of system, 52; patrilineality in, 50; education and, 35; women, 197; youth, 219; elders, 22, 184; employment, 35; esaaro and, 15; families, 107; female genital cutting, 117; in missions, 123; generation classes, 44, 60; system of, 23; genital cutting; family concerns, 8; individual concerns, 8; opposition to, 138;

structural ties; descent and, 144;
segmentary opposition and,
144
students, 219
Sudan, 207; genital cutting and,
12; witchcraft, 37
sungusungu, 56

T

taboos, 91, 94, 96, 104, 105,
126, 142, 147, 189, 215,
216, 219, 238; abasaamba
and, 147, 153; parents and,
142; between parents and
children, 143
Tanzania, 20, 34, 37, 42, 49, 55,
60, 63, 66, 93, 130, 187, 201,
213, 222; abasaamba, 168;
bewitchment in, 43; borders,
201; circumcision laws,
141; Kuria ibiaro and, 55;
legislature of, 181; schools,
141; closings, 50
teachers, 4, 125, 143, 159, 177,
193, 194, 197, 205, 211, 216
territory, 78, 233
totem, 53, 55
tradespeople, 4
tradition, 237
traditions, 6, 8, 12, 24, 26, 27, 33,
58, 59, 68, 70, 84, 102, 118,
124, 127, 129, 131, 132, 134,
181, 188, 193, 195, 201, 206,
213, 214, 215, 216, 225, 233,
234; assumptions about, 100;
authority of, 190, 215; as
backward, 231; construction
of, 99–101; daily life and,
26; as ignorant, 231; as
irrational, 231; persistence

of, 234; preservation of, 176,
215, 221; witchcraft and, 37
transition, 182
translators, 217, 230, 231, 234

U

Uasin Gishu, 180
ubusubi. *See* rites of ritual
elderhood
umugi, 51, 110, 164, 182. *See
also* family; *See also* home; *See
also* homestead
umuimiirri, 73
umuiseke. *See* initiates, female
umukungu, 110
umumura. *See* initiates, male
umuriisia, 89
umuturiani, 99
uncircumcised boys, 64, 107
uncircumcised condition, 189,
192, 211
UNIFEM, 181
United Nations, 124
universalism, 207, 230; stance
of, 207
university students, 205

V

values, 77
vernacularization, 230
vigilante justice, 56
virilocal, 109
voices, 2, 5, 17, 20, 28, 29, 32,
138, 169, 176, 203, 212, 229,
234, 310
VYOPEC Kenya, 227

W

Walley, Christine, 12, 229